ACTA UNIVERSITATIS STOCKHOLMIENSIS
Studia Fennica Stockholmiensia
9

Language contact and structural change

An Old Finnish case study

Merlijn de Smit

Stockholm University

ISSN 0284-4273
ISBN 91-85445-53-3

Printed in Sweden by Intellecta, Stockholm 2006
Distributor: Almqvist & Wiksell International

To my grandmother, Marie Beets-de Jong, whose abiding interest in languages and history inspired me.

Contents

1. PRELIMINARIES ... 11
1.1. Swedish influence on Finnish morphosyntax: The research problem ... 11
1.2. The problem of contact-induced structural change ... 12
1.2.1. Dichotomies ... 12
1.2.1.1. Tadpoles and cuckoos ... 12
1.2.1.2. Internal and external ... 16
1.2.1.3. Causation and teleology ... 20
1.2.2. The results of structural change ... 23
1.2.2.1. Direct contact-induced structural change ... 23
1.2.3.2. Indirect contact-induced structural change ... 24
1.2.3. The motivations of contact-induced structural change ... 26
1.2.3.1. Interlingual identifications as a starting point ... 26
1.2.3.2. Long-term convergence and metatypy: interlingual isomorphism ... 27
1.2.3.3. Contact-induced change and iconicity: intralingual isomorphism ... 29
1.2.4. The mechanisms of contact-induced structural change ... 33
1.2.4.1. Analogy ... 33
1.2.4.2. Reanalysis, extension and borrowing ... 34
1.2.4.3. Overt and covert interference ... 36
1.2.4.4. Contact-induced structural change as bilingual reanalysis and extension ... 38
1.2.5. Conclusion, by way of Whitehead ... 41
1.2.5.1. Whitehead's philosophical system ... 41
1.2.5.2. Structure and process ... 46
1.2.5.3. Contradictions and contrasts ... 51
1.2.5.4. Advantages of a Whiteheadian framework ... 54

2. THE SOCIOHISTORICAL BACKGROUND OF FINNISH-SWEDISH LANGUAGE CONTACT ... 57
2.1. Brief sketch of the history of Finnish ... 57
2.2. Direct contact between Finnish and Swedish communities ... 58
2.2.1. Swedish-speaking communities in Finland ... 58
2.2.2. Finnish-speaking communities in Sweden ... 62
2.2.3. Swedish as a language of the Finnish élite ... 64
2.3. The history of Literary Finnish ... 66

2.3.1. Old Finnish: birth and consolidation ... 66
2.3.2. Old Modern Finnish: Reform ... 69
2.3.3. Conclusion ... 71

3. CORPUS AND RESEARCH OBJECT ... 73
3.1. The corpus ... 73
3.2. Alignment and case-marking in Modern and Old Finnish ... 78
3.2.1. Subject and object case-marking ... 78
3.2.2. Alignment ... 80

4. THE PASSIVE ... 85
4.1. The passive in modern Finnish ... 85
4.2. The passive in Old Finnish ... 87
4.3. Distribution of the passive in the corpus ... 92
4.4. Swedish source constructions ... 93
4.5. The object of the negated passive ... 97
4.6. Agreement ... 106
4.7. Periphrastic passives with *tulla* ... 109
4.8. Agent phrases ... 111
4.9. Overview ... 113

5. NECESSITIVE CONSTRUCTIONS ... 116
5.1. Introduction ... 116
5.2. Distribution of the necessitive verbs *pitää* and *tulla* ... 117
5.3. Subject-marking and transitivity ... 120
5.4. Subject-marking and lexical categories ... 122
5.5. Word order and subject case-marking ... 127
5.6. Explaining the redistribution of case-markers in M and L1 ... 129
5.7. Differences in subject-marking between *pitää* and *tulla* ... 133
5.8. Reanalysis of subject as object? Active and passive infinitives . 135
5.9. Evaluation: contact-induced change and internally driven change in case of *pitää* ... 147

6. RELATIVE PRONOUNS ... 152
6.1. Introduction ... 152
6.2. Relative pronouns as subject and object ... 157
6.3. Relative pronouns and other variables ... 160
6.4. Relative pronouns in the Swedish source text ... 166
6.5. The origins of relative *kuin* ... 172
6.6. Evaluation ... 179

7. LANGUAGE CONTACT AND STRUCTURAL CHANGE IN OLD FINNISH ... 181
7.1. Language contact and alignment change ... 181
7.2. Direct and indirect contact-induced structural change ... 184
7.3. Language contact and structural change ... 187

SUMMARY 194

ACKNOWLEDGEMENTS 200

REFERENCES 201
Corpus 201
Other references 202

APPENDIX A 213

APPENDIX B 217

APPENDIX C 221

APPENDIX D 224

Abbreviations

1, 2, 3	Personhood
ABL	Ablative
ACC	Accusative
ADESS	Adessive
AGENT	Agent Participle
ALL	Allative
COND	Conditional
ELAT	Elative
ESS	Essive
GEN	Genitive
ILL	Illative
IMPER	Imperative
INESS	Inessive
INF	Infinitive
IPF	Imperfect
NEG	Negative auxiliary
NOM	Nominative
PART	Partitive
PARTIC	Participle
PASS	Passive
PF	Perfect
PL	Plural
PLPF	Plusquamperfect
POST	Postposition
PR	Present
REL	Relative pronoun
SG	Singular
TRANS	Translative

1. PRELIMINARIES

1.1. Swedish influence on Finnish morphosyntax: The research problem

It is well-known that the Swedish language has exerted its influence upon all subsystems of Finnish – according to Häkkinen (1997: 45), Swedish loanwords in Finnish number in the thousands. Also, in the wake of loanwords, the phonemes *b*, *g*, *d* and *f* have been integrated into Finnish phonology – even if all of them, with the exception of *d*, are quite marginal. The voiced dental stop (having developed from a voiced dental spirant) is much more frequent due to its usage, probably as a result of Swedish influence, as a weak-grade equivalent of *t*. Aside from this, one could mention the retaining of initial consonant clusters in loanwords in particularly the West Finnish dialects (Ojansuu 1906: 25-26, Häkkinen 1997: 40). Finally, Swedish influence on the morphosyntax of both dialectal and literary Finnish has been observed – some examples will be presented later.

In these circumstances, it is rather surprising that Swedish influence upon Finnish as such is a rather underresearched area. Papers dealing with the subject as a whole may be counted with one hand (Cannelin 1926, Häkkinen 1997) and no monograph on the subject yet exists (though Nau 1995, dealing with particularly Swedish influence on Finnish from the perspective of contact linguistics comes close). On loanwords, one should mention Streng's (1915) and Maija Grönholm's (1988) monographs, the latter dealing with Swedish loanwords in the dialect of Turku, as well as Häkkinen's (2003) recent paper. On the subject of phonological influence, we have Ojansuu (1906). The first object, then, of this research, is to provide an addition to the scarce research literature on the subject by studying the morphosyntactic influence Swedish has exerted upon Finnish during the period of the Old Finnish literary language (1540-1809). Second, I intend to provide an addition to the research literature on structural contacts in general, a field still full of controversies, which I will treat in some detail in chapter 1.2.

I will deal with the relevant research literature in more detail in the context of the individual problems I will treat, but suffice to say for now, that there are a few areas which, despite the scarcity of research on the subject in general, nevertheless provide valuable source material. First of all, there is the body of literature that exists on the morphosyntax of Old Finnish, in which phenomena possibly originating from contact influence are often dealt with. One could mention Osmo Ikola's (1949, 1950), Pirkko Forsman-Svensson's (1990, 1992a, 1998, 2000) and Marja Itkonen-Kaila's (1991, 1992, 1997) research. Second, possible contact influence from Swedish has been taken into account in literature studying Finnish dialectal morphosyntax. (T. Itkonen 1964a, 1964b: 229-230, Savijärvi 1977, Laitinen 1992: 58). Third, there is a body of literature, particularly before the Second World War, which deals with putative sveticisms from a prescriptivist point of view (for example, Saarimaa 1942, Sadeniemi 1942a, 1942b). And finally, one should mention the growing research on Finnish varieties spoken in Sweden, both Tornedal Finnish or *Meänkieli* in the far north, as well as the language spoken by immigrants from the 1960s and the 1970s and their offspring (Wande 1982, Kangassalo, Nemvalts and Wande 2003). In dealing with the problem at hand, I will try to take all of these into account.

This introductory chapter will concern itself with the general problem of structural contact-induced change (1.2.), the sociohistorical background of Finnish-Swedish language contact and its results in both Finnish dialects and the Finnish written language (2), as well as the corpus of my study (3).

1.2. The problem of contact-induced structural change

1.2.1. Dichotomies

1.2.1.1. Tadpoles and cuckoos

Can Achilles ever overtake the tortoise, if the latter is given some headway? Surely, Achilles would first have to move across the path already taken by the tortoise, and by that time, no matter how quick the pace of Achilles, the tortoise will have moved on a bit. Zeno's paradox has been attacked for being mathematically wrong (Whitehead 1929: 95): the fact that the distance Achilles would travel in the spate of a single second might be sub-divided to infinity does not change anything about the fact that he travels it in a single second. This notwithstanding, as Whitehead (1929: 94) allows, Zeno's paradox points to an inherent problem with our concept of time and change: based on our commonsense view of the world, and of formal logic, which does not allow a thing to be non-identical with itself, we can conceptualize change only as a succession of states. Due to metabolism, the perpetual perishing and growing of cells, etc. I am a slightly different person than I was when I started writing the paragraph above. Then how do we account for identity propagating through time? Hegel's (1975 [1830], §88) solution was to depart from the insistence on things being identical with themselves, and allowing logic to play with contradictions: becoming is analyzed as the dialectic of being and not-being, a unity which is

> also inherent unrest - the unity, which is no mere reference-to-self and therefore without movement, but which, through the diversity of Being and Nothing that is in it, is at war with itself

and therefore can account for change. In case of planets:

> At this moment the planet stands in this spot; but implicitly it is the possibility of being in another spot; and that possibility of being otherwise the planet brings into existence by moving (Hegel 1975 [1830]: §81).

Whitehead's (1929: 96) solution was to scuttle the idea of time as a kind of universal background against which the change and permanence of entities plays itself out. Rather, the universe is conceptualized as "atoms of experience" which themselves gain their determinacy, their process of becoming, outside of time - the process of becoming itself includes gaining temporal extension. Identity, in this atomistic concept in the universe, is accounted for through the insertion of properties and characteristics of past actual occasions, "atoms of experience", in new ones.

The problem of identity through change has also played its role in linguistics, and not merely as a matter of metaphysical preference. As Johanna Laakso (1995: 70), critiquing a concept of genetic relationship which transcends genetic transmission, and includes contact relationships in a holistic fashion, wrote:

> Is a language – as historical linguists obviously claim – a fixed entity, the essence of which never changes? This does not mean that even fundamental things could not change, for reasons internal and external. According to an old saying: a spade is always a spade: sometimes you put in a new shaft, sometimes a new blade, but you still call it "your spade" (and in a structuralist view, it is the same spade all the time).

The problem here is, acutely, that the genetic identity of languages changing through time is an emergent phenomenon: it is rooted in their linear transmission from generation to generation, but there is not anything "in language itself" which can be taken as a marker for genetic identity. However, the search for such a marker has left its traces deeply in the research literature on language change, and to the detriment of contact linguistics: this will be the subject of the following chapter, which deals with the dichotomy between external and internal factors in linguistic change. In general linguistics, the search has not been so much for the smoking gun of genetic origins, but for innate linguistic structures, and this has lead to the banishment of structural change to the phase of language acquisition, and, concomitantly, the marginalization of contact-induced change.

Aitchison (1995) counterposes various conceptualizations of linguistic change, naming them "tadpoles" (change-as-metamorphosis, in which the propagation of identity becomes acutely problematic), "cuckoos" (change-as-substitution) and "multiple births" (change as generating a variety of alternatives, some or one of which will spread through the speech community. In generationalist models of linguistic change, change is substitution: namely, the child constructs a grammar on the basis of linguistic input by a process of abduction (Andersen 1973, 1974: 23), and this grammar may be more or less different from that of previous generations. All deep-going structural changes must be located here; changes occurring during the "lifetime" of an idiolect are superficial.

It is easy to see why generational models have been popular. By locating structural change in the transition between generations, the theoretical distinction between synchrony and diachrony, central to linguistic structuralism, found an analogy in a model of linguistic change, and, as Weinreich et al. (1968: 114) write:

> If chronological changes in language can be superimposed on the turnover of population, the need for a theory of change as such is canceled, since one can then simply think of the speakers of one dialect replacing those of another.

Furthermore, the analogies between evolutionary biology and linguistic change are tempting (see Yang 2002: 233-234, Briscoe 2002a: 1-3, see also other papers in the same volume). Changes to the phenotype are generally superficial – the weathering of the skin, scars, etc. – and they cannot be transmitted to offspring as such. It is the changes in the genotype, through random mutation, that are the engine of biological evolution. But it is not easy to reconcile the idea contact-induced structural change with such a model: rather, one would have to regard structural change in *langue* itself as internal or rather as something to which the distinction between external and internal does not apply – taking place during the language-acquisition process of small children (Briscoe 2002b: 256) – whereas *language contact* would have led to variation or ambiguity on the level of *parole* or relatively minor, cosmetic changes in the individual grammars of adults, which could later lead to (internal) reanalysis by new generations of language learners (Lightfoot 1988: 319). As Yang, who builds a model of competing grammars analogous to the model of variation and selection of evolutionary biology, writes (2002: 248):

> It is important to recognize that, while sociological and other external forces clearly affect the composition of linguistic evidence, grammar competition as language acquisition (the locus of language change) is internal to the individual learner's mind/brain.

And indeed, as Nau (1995: 11-12) points out, these models tend to marginalize contact-induced structural change as an area of research. However, 'generational' models of language change have been criticized in recent years, particularly by Aitchison (1995: 2, 2001: 209), who notes that:

> Overall, young children have little of importance to contribute to language change – perhaps not surprisingly. Babies do not form influential social groups. Changes begin within social groups, when group members unconsciously imitate those around them. Differences in the speech forms of parents and children probably begin at a time when the two generations identify with different social sets. (Aitchison 2001: 209).

Harris and Campbell (1995: 34-45) have levelled criticism at Lightfoot's proposals concerning a generationalist view on diachronic syntax, particularly criticizing the less-than-clear seperation between deep-going structural changes restricted to language acquisition and superficial, cosmetic changes.

In any event, language acquisition would have to include cases of language shift by adult speakers, to account for the structural effects the latter may have on the recipient language. Language shift has a crucial position in Thomason and Kaufman's (1988: 50) terminology, as distinct from *language maintenance.* In situations of language maintenance, the recipient language is the native language of the agents of transfer, and the material transferred is mainly lexical, with possibly indirect reverberations on the phonology and morphology of the recipient language and some structural interference when the pressure exterted by the source language is extremely intense, and the process of transfer is *borrowing* – note that borrowing is defined here in a considerably more narrow sense than I will use it. In situations of language shift, the recipient language is the language to which speakers shift, and in favour of which the source language is being abandoned. In this case, the material transferred would be mainly structural – the agents of the linguistic transfer would learn the recipient language imperfectly, leaving interference features from the dwindling source language in mainly phonology, syntax, but hardly the lexicon (Thomason and Kaufman 1988: 50, 212), and the process of transfer is *shift-induced interference*. In other words, in cases of borrowing, the transferred items tend to be iconic – those items which speakers can identify and more or less consciously manipulate, notably the lexicon. In cases of shift-induced interference, the items transferred are mainly symbolic – items outside the conscious identifiability and manipulability of the speaker, and hence more difficult to acquire, notably phonology and syntax. A pioneering study of shift-induced interference is Posti's (1953) *From Pre-Finnic to Late Proto-Finnic*, in which Posti argues that most of the phonological changes setting the developing Finnic proto-language apart from the common ancestor of

Finnic and Sámi preceding it were due to a Germanic substratum: early Proto-Finnic phonology was "filtered" through a Proto-Germanic framework as speakers of Germanic shifted to Finnic – the phonological innovations would later have shifted to "native" speakers of Finnic. In a recent examination of Posti's hypothesis, Kallio (2000: 96-97) finds that, as a whole, it holds water, even though individual details would need to be revised.

In Guy's terminology (1990: 48), the terms used are *borrowing* and *imposition*. Clearly, both situations are different sides of the same coin – a given contact situation may include both shift and maintenance, since the dwindling language would, for some time, continued to be spoken – and be subject to contact-induced change typical of maintenance situations – within the speech-community and among bilingual individual speakers shifting to another language (Filppula 1991: 26, Lauttamus 1991: 32-33). This would also surely be the case for Posti's hypothesis alluded to above: Proto-Germanic loanwords in the Finnic languages are numerous (Kallio 2000: 81). Also, contact-induced change through borrowing, in which the agents are speakers the recipient language, and change through imposition, in which the agents are native speakers of the source language, are not discrete entities: the distinction between them may become blurred when dealing with balanced bilinguals, who have learned both languages involved from a very early age (Guy 1990: 50).

This is just one of the areas in which research on contact-induced linguistic change provides a challenge for generationalist models of linguistic change. The more subtle difference between substitutionalist and "kaleidoscopic" views on temporal change in general will be a theme that returns later throughout this part. In any event, the "generationalist" view on structural change reflect an underlying dichotomy between "internal" and "external" factors in language change, which themselves has been singled out for criticism.

1.2.1.2. Internal and external

Contact-induced structural change – the influence languages may exert on each other's structural, here, morphological and syntactical domains – is an area where one very easily finds counterposed and contradictory statements. Thus, where some researchers regard syntax as one of the subsystems of language most impervious to contact-induced change:

> In general, the lexicon is most easily and radically affected, followed by the phonology, the morphology and finally the syntax. (McMahon 1994: 209)

Others have taken an opposite position, for example Birnbaum (1984: 34):

> It should be noted at the outset that the most commonly held view is that syntax is indeed highly permeable as compared to, at any rate, phonology and morphology.

Similarly, a number of researchers have argued that contact-induced structural change occurs mainly or exclusively as an indirect consequence of lexical borrowing (Sankoff 2002: 652, King 2000: 82-83), whereas others have regarded rule borrowing as eminently possible (Thomason, forthcoming) and indeed syntactic borrowing itself as an independent mechanism of change (Harris and Campbell 1995: 150). Finally, the borrowing of free grammatical morphemes like function words has been generally seen as rare (Romaine 1995: 64), whereas for example Stolz and Stolz (1996: 88-89) have pointed to the ubiquity of conjunctions and discourse markers borrowed from Spanish in the native languages of South America. One could add to this the numerous conjunctions borrowed from Russian into Eastern Finnic languages, such as Olonets Karelian: Pyöli (1996: 211) mentions the conjunctions *a* 'but', *da* 'and', *i* 'and' as well as *ˇsto* 'that'. As will be mentioned later, even the borrowing of bound morphemes has been attested.

There are probably a number of reasons one can mention for the controversy surrounding the domain of contact-induced structural change. The first, doubtlessly, is an effort to specify either absolute constraints on contact-induced change, or a hierarchy of relative permeability of linguistic subsystems as a direct function of those stratificational subsystems themselves. Such endeavours are of no small interest to genetic linguistics, since an impenetrable subsystem of language would constitute an important guide to genetic relationships (much like the extremely regular occurrences of mitochondrial DNA make mitochondria very important guides to human genetic relationships, or, as Palmer (1972: 371) mentions, the regular decay-rate of radiocarbon as a clock to date archaeological remains). However, as Thomason and Kaufman's (1988), and recently, in his attempt to construct a hierarchy of change, Field's (2002) work points out, one cannot specify such hierarchies of permeability independently of the specific languages involved in the contact situation, or the specific social structure of the contact situation. Without recourse to these, there appear no absolute constraints on what can be transferred from one language to another (Thomason and Kaufman 1988: 19).

Thus, one subsystem traditionally regarded as being extremely resistant to borrowing is inflectional morphology:

> The adoption of bound morphemes has been stated by many authors to be among the most resistant features of languages to contact-induced change. After reviewing the literature, I am more convinced than ever that this is true. Only a few cases come to light, and almost all involve morphemes that are, if not entirely free, not really bound either. (Sankoff 2002: 656).

Nonetheless, examples of transfer of even verbal inflectional morphology do exist, though they are rare. One example cited in the literature (Thomason and Kaufman 1988: 98, Thomason 2001: 77) is the borrowing of Bulgarian inflectional verb endings (*-m*, 1th p., *-ˇs*, 2th p.) by Meglenite Rumanian, which has them attached to the original Rumanian inflected forms (*aflu* 'I find' --> *aflum*, *afli* 'you find' --> *afliˇs*,). Another example of borrowed inflectional morphemes may be the instrumental *–l* found in East Sámi languages, probably borrowed from Karelian (Korhonen 1981: 233).

Also, diffusion of grammatical affixes among genetically unrelated languages seems to have occurred in Eastern Arnhem Land in Australia (Heath 1981: 335). Another more extreme example might be Ma'a, a language of East Africa which retains a Cushitic core vocabulary but which has borrowed virtually all its inflectional morphology from Mbugu, a neighbouring Bantu language. The problem in the latter case is that the historical circumstances underlying the genesis of Ma'a remain opaque: whereas the language can be seen as Cushitic, with massive structural borrowing from neighbouring Bantu (Thomason 2001: 82), Field (2002: 175) hypothesizes that speakers of a dwindling Cushitic language might have, while shifting to Bantu, more or less consciously imported their basic lexicon into the Bantu language as a marker of ethnic identity. In any event, it seems that while some features may be less likely to be transferred than others, no absolute constraints on borrowability exist (Lass 1997: 184-189).

An elaborate proposal for a relative hierarchy on borrowability has been made recently by Field (2002), who regards borrowability as conditioned partially by the typologies of the languages involved in the contact situation through the Principle of System Compatibility:

> Any form or form-meaning set is borrowable from a donor language if it conforms to the morphological possibilities of the recipient language with regards to morphological structure. (Field 2002: 41)

Thus, an agglutinative language upholding a strict one meaning – one form iconicity in its morphology would not borrow fusional affixes – unless a fusional affix is reanalyzed as compatible with the morphological typology of the recipient language (Field 2002: 44). This principle would interact with a number of other factors: notably the relative phonological and semantic saliency of a given form (Field 2002: 98) – phonologically elaborate morphemes, or morphemes bearing a one-to-one relationship with their referents – would be borrowed earlier than phonologically reduced or portmanteau morphemes, leading to the borrowing of lexical items being more frequent than the borrowing of affixes. It should be noted that, with this, Field raises the speakers of a language to a central position in determining borrowability: saliency is a perceptual factor. A similar point is made by Anttila (1989: 169), who remarks:

> (...) grammatical morphemes show the greatest resistance to borrowing, but it still occurs (the reason is, perhaps, the great frequency and abstractness of such units. They are unconscious and "too obvious" to draw attention).

This would reduce linguistic structure itself as a determinant of possible linguistic change to the possible observations and generalizations made by speakers as a determinant of linguistic change, thus tying it more closely with social factors, which as Thomason and Kaufman (1988: 19) remark are, in the absence of any absolute linguistic constraints on transfer, the overarching factors determining the linguistic outcomes of language contact.

The whole search for subsystems of language impervious to contact-induced change reflects the traditional dichotomy between external and internal mechanisms of change, which many researchers in the field of language contacts have expressed their distress over (Hartig 1983: 67, Nau 1995: 12, 30). The most obvious areas where the dichotomy breaks down are the possibility of crosslinguistic influence on relatively 'internal' mechanisms of change like syntactic reanalysis and extension (Harris and Campbell 1995: 51, 122) which leads to difficulties in assigning relative importance to internal and external factors, as Thomason and Kaufman (1988: 57-58) put it:

> It may well be, that, as some have argued, phonemic retroflexion in Indic arose in a series of phonetically plausible stages, but the original stimulus or trigger for that series of changes was surely the Dravidian substratum influence.

Add to this the fact that every linguistic innovation, regardless of its origin, spreads through a speech-community through contact between speakers, and through time by contact between generations:

> The spread of any feature is borrowing as long as it is happening. (Anttila 1989: 154).

The dichotomy between internal and external change, then, reflects a more or less hypostasized view of language – language as a more or less concrete object, with a more or less fixed internal structure, prone to changes from within its own system, and this reflected in a concept of grammar as internal to the brain of the speaker/listener, and more or less constantly there. As Anttila pointed out in the statement quoted above, linguistic changes are by definition contact-induced and thereby "external" if we conceptualize language as rooted in the usage of signs by speakers, rather than a more or less fixed grammar. This conception has been taken the farthest by Hopper (1987) in his notion of emergent grammar:

> (...) structure, or regularity, comes out of discourse and is shaped by discourse as much as it shapes discourse in an on-going process. Grammar is hence not to be understood as a pre-requisite for discourse, a prior possession attributable in identical form to both speaker and hearer. Its forms are not fixed templates but are negotiable in face-to-face interaction in ways that reflect the individual speakers' past experience of these forms, and their assessment of the present context, including especially their interlocutors, whose experiences and assessments may be quite different. Moreover, the term Emergent Grammar points to a grammar which is not abstractly formulated and abstractly represented, but always anchored in the specific concrete form of an utterance.

In this view, there is simply no place for any dichotomy between "internal" and "external" factors in linguistic change.

As mentioned, the dichotomy has also been corroded, albeit indirectly, by the work of, among others, Thomason and Kaufman (1988), and their emphasis of social factors as the main determinants of contact-induced linguistic change. Because in this conception, it is not linguistic structure in itself which provides constraints on the outcomes of contact-induced change: it is the speakers of the language and the social situation in which they communicate which ultimately determine the outcome of language contact. Regardless of whether one wants to go as far as Hopper in regarding grammar as emergent upon linguistic usage, it is clear that once we place the speaker and the usage of signs on the centre stage, we end up with a view on history in which an event is determined by the intentions of those speakers and the background in which he uses language, in a holistic fashion. In such a view, internal and external factors would necessarily co-occur, if they can even be distinguished.

1.2.1.3. Causation and teleology

As mentioned, Thomason and Kaufman (1988) have proposed an elaborate taxonomy of contact-induced change, taking the social situation, as reflected in either language maintenance or language shift, as the primary determinant of the outcomes of linguistic contact. However, as Thomason (2000: §3) stresses, this may be overriden by other social factors, in particular the attitudes of speakers towards their own language. Thus Montana Salish, a Salishan language, and Nez Perce, a Penutian language, both spoken in the northwestern United States, have, while under extreme pressure from English, undergone extremely little lexical interference and almost no structural interference from English. In a contact situation treated in detail by Aikhenvald (2003: 4-7), Tariana, a moribund Arawak language of the Vaupés area in the northwest Amazon region has undergone extensive structural influence from the neighbouring, genetically unrelated, East Tucanoan languages with virtually no transfer of lexical items or grammatical morphemes. The situation here seems to be one of language maintenance – the East Tucanoan Tucano language becoming the *lingua franca* of the Vaupés region, a region marked by institutionalized multilingualism based on language group exogamy, and it seems that strong cultural resistance towards lexical borrowing has resulted in this anomalous situation (Aikhenvald 2000: 1-2, 2003: 5).

If speakers of a language consciously cling to their language as a marker of ethnic identity in the face of pressure to shift to a dominant language, the lexicon on their language will be seen as the most salient feature of their language and be the subsystem of language most shielded against foreign influence, whereas structural interference might seep through a language more or less unnoticed (Thomason 2000: §2). This factor thus stresses the agentivity of speakers, who may more or less consciously manipulate certain subsystems of language – notably the most iconic and salient, lexicon and morphology – more easily than other, more symbolic ones, notably syntax. The same attachment of speakers to their own language, and particularly to the lexicon, also may have resulted in the anomalous contact-induced changes marking Ma'a – massive borrowing of morphology and structure with the lexicon remaining intact:

> Each of these communities, despite a fully bilingual population, has resisted the pressure to shift to the dominant language, showing a stubborn loyalty to the ethnic-heritage language and maintaining the most salient part of that language – the lexicon. The development of these languages underscores the point that we cannot predict with confidence what will happen to a language as a result of intense cultural pressure from a dominant group's language. (Thomason 2001: 82-83).

The primacy of social factors as a determinant of contact-induced change has been challenged by Treffers-Daller (1999), who, examining Dutch-French contacts in Brussels and Alsatian-French contacts in Strasbourg, concludes that despite sociolinguistic differences of the two contact situations, there are striking similarities between their linguistic results, and that, therefore,

> structural factors rather than sociolinguistic factors are the *primary* determinants of the linguistic outcome of language contact. (Treffers-Daller 1999: 20).

However, as Singh (1999) in his commentary on Treffers-Daller's paper (see also other papers in the same volume) stresses, the linguistic results themselves are predicted by Thomason's and Kaufman's social distinction between language maintenance and language shift – substratum influence in French, lexical influence in the Germanic languages (Singh 1999: 89). Of course, structure in a sense is a determinant in that it provides the speakers with the material upon which change can be carried out:

> Grammar, in other words, merely supplies the materials with which history (in the appropriate sense) plays the linguistic games it has defined the rules for. Those rules, of course, include some cooperation with grammar, but it is (sociolinguistic) history that holds all the trumps. (Singh 1999: 88).

Thus, neither the structure and typological make-up of languages participating in a contact situation, nor the social circumstances of the contact itself provides absolute constraints and strong predictions as to what can be transferred and what not. Relative hierarchies of borrowability, as well as the analysis of the social situation in which the contact takes place, may lead us to predictions as to what *probably* would be borrowed or what not, but these predictions can be overridden in particular by conscious human activity – especially conscious resistance to borrowing – as a factor.

This automatically would lead to a view in which language change is primarily a teleological process, rather than a causal one – one in which necessary and sufficient antecedent conditions for any given change to occur can be specified. Linguistic change would be the result of agency of the speakers of that language, who are endowed with free will: language change is not caused by either language structure, or the presence of language contact – either only provides the speakers of a given language with the material upon which they can consciously or unconsciously carry out change (Harris 1982: 13-14, Nau 1995: 6-7). This unpredictability – the fact that a given innovation *may* take place but never necessarily does take place – results automatically in linguistic variation on the synchronic plane: not only do different linguistic codes, languages, dialects and the like vary among each other, and speakers are quite capable of using more than one of these, but speakers of any given single language may have different styles, registers and varying realizations of a given single linguistic form at their disposal. Language change – the replacement of a given form at the expense of another within the community of speakers of that language – always involves the activity of speakers, both in causation of change and in the mechanisms by which change proceeds.

The intrinsic unpredictability of linguistic change, as historical processes are in general, leads to limitations in the extent to which historical linguistics can explain linguistic change. On one level, historical linguistics is, of course, explanatory by definition, since any synchronic configuration of events is a function of all its past stages – therefore any given linguistic state may be explained by referring to the way it developed from earlier states. But explaining *why* a given linguistic innovation takes place at a given place and a given time is more problematic. As Lass (1980: 3) points out, the deductive-nomological scheme of explanation, in which a given event is explained by referring to the general laws governing it, cannot be explained to language history – the product of the actions of people. Explaining language change by referring to the possible aims and benefits of people engaged in a communicative situation is necessarily particularistic, and *post-hoc* (Filppula 1991: 13, McMahon 1994: 44-46): within a given community, a consonant group may change from *mt* to *nt*, an innovation obviously motivated, and "explained" by striving after articulatory ease – but another speech community may not choose to implement the same innovation, given exactly the same circumstances (Langacker 1977: 98). Otherwise, of course, historical linguistics would not exist, since it is exactly the fact that innovations may cease to spread in a given speech-community, the fact that speakers may not implement a change, which allows historical linguists to "roll back" language history, and discern linguistic change where it has occurred. Paradoxically, the same factors which cause the weakness – at least as viewed from a positivist ideal of science – of our explanatory mechanisms, which Lass (1980: 80) laments, also make our discipline possible.

Thus, rather than specifying which linguistic innovations will necessarily occur given a certain specific social and historical situation, or whether any absolute constraints on contact-induced change can be specified, the historical linguist can, at best, isolate factors which may have plausibly played a role in a given linguistic innovation, among which language contact.

1.2.2. The results of structural change

1.2.2.1. Direct contact-induced structural change

In his study of syntactic borrowing from Spanish into Pipil, Campbell (1987: 253-254) distinguishes between 1) the direct borrowing of structures including their phonological counterparts, for example, the comparative particle *mas* borrowed from Spanish into Pipil, 2) shifts in native structures motivated by (accidental) phonetical similarity with a model structure, i.e. grammatical accommodation, 3) expansion in the function of structures to match model structures, 4) changes in the frequency (or "thrust") of native structures which conform well to model structures and 5) contact-induced boundary loss. Weinreich (1974: 30-31), in his famous study of language contact, distinguishes between three types of morphosyntactic transfer, namely "the use of A-morphemes in speaking (or writing) language B", i.e. the transfer of morphemes themselves, "the application of a grammatical relation of language A to B-morphemes in B-speech or the neglect of a relation of B which has no prototype in A.", and "through the identification of a specific B-morpheme with a specific A-morpheme, a change (extension, reduction) in the functions of the B-morpheme on the model of the grammar of language A." The transfer of grammatical relations or functions presupposes an identification made between a given morphological structure in one language and one in the other made by bilingual speakers (Weinreich 1974: 39-40), based on either formal or functional similarity, possibly also chance phonological similarity, a process known as grammatical accommodation (Aikhenvald 2003: 2, see also Campbell 1987: 263). Phonological similarity, either due to chance or due to a common origin in case of two closely related languages, has been studied as a factor conditioning the speed with which bilinguals translate words in two different languages – thus Schelletter (2002: 94) refers to experiments showing that bilinguals are able to translate or recognize words more quickly if they are phonologically (and semantically) similar to words in their other language.

1.2.3.2. Indirect contact-induced structural change

Importantly, in addition to direct transfer or remodelling of morphosyntactic patterns in the recipient language, contact-induced structural change may proceed as a secondary reverberation of lexical borrowing. Borrowed lexical items may bear both morphology – derivational affixes but also number or case marking – and phonological features, including, for example, stress patterns which are borrowed into the recipient language together with them. Both the morphology and phonology of borrowed lexical items may either be totally lost with the integration of the borrowing into the recipient language's structure, however, it may also retain morphological marking or phonological features, which may themselves remain confined to the borrowing or to a class of borrowings, or become productive in the recipient language (Weinreich 1974: 31). Thus, Nahuatl seems to have borrowed a numeral affix *-s* together with an influx of Spanish loanwords, however, the imported affix is largely confined to Spanish loanwords (Field 2002: 156), whereas Asia Minor Greek seems to have acquired partial vowel harmony – applied to both loanwords and indigenous lexical material – through a massive influx of Turkish loanwords (Thomason forthcoming: 6).

Sankoff (2002: 652) regards this secondary or indirect grammatical borrowing as the main pathway by which morphosyntax may be seen to be transferred from one language to another:

> (...) many students of language contact are convinced that grammatical or syntactic borrowing is impossible or close to it (...). These authors generally see grammatical change subsequent to contact as a consequence of lexical or pragmatical interinfluence, that may then lead to internal syntactic change.

The view expressed by Sankoff has been defended in great detail recently by King (2000), who argues that ostensible grammatical borrowing is always a secondary consequence of lexical influence. As a starting point, King takes a principled-and-parameters approach in which syntactic structure

> is thought to be largely determined by lexical information, more precisely, by the feature specifications associated with particular lexical items. (King 2000: 53)

This means that it would be impossible for syntactic structure to be transferred from one language to another without the concomitant transfer of lexical items who basically carry that syntactic structure. Thus King (2000: 82-83) writes:

> (...) many linguists conceive of lexical borrowing as the borrowing of "merely" words. Recall that the approach taken in the present study, following recent work in generative grammar, is that words are borrowed in a fairly abstract form, and the transfer of bundles of syntactic and semantic features along with phonological information is involved. Since our focus is on the borrowing process, many phenomena characterized in the literature as grammatical or structural borrowing are viewed here as lexical. This includes the classification of the borrowing of function words, of affixes (when they are borrowed in conjunction with their stems), and of syntactic rules (when borrowed function words cause reanalysis of syntactic features in the borrowing language).

An example King mentions is the appearance of preposition stranding in Prince Edward Island French: Prince Edward Island French has borrowed a number of prepositions from neighbouring English, and, unlike in Standard French, both borrowed as well as indigenous prepositions may appear in a stranded position. However, King argues, the syntactic mechanism of preposition stranding has not been borrowed from English, since preposition stranding in Prince Edward Island French is not subject to the same constraints as it is in English: a stranded position in English following an adverbial phrase or indirect object would be hardly grammatical (for example *W*hat did you speak yesterday to John about?*), but quite acceptable in Prince Edward Island French (*Quoi ce-que tu as parlé hier à Jean de?*), and thus, what has actually been transferred has been the possibility to appear stranded together with the English-origin prepositions, which has subsequently been extended to indigenous prepositions, not preposition-stranding as a syntactic rule in and of itself (King 2000: 145-147).

This view of syntactic borrowing as *always* being an indirect consequence of lexical interference is argued against by Thomason (forthcoming), who notes that particularly in situations of language-shift, structural interference may appear without any lexical or morphological borrowing. Among the examples Thomason lists are a number of shift-induced interference features in Shina, an Indic language with a strong Burushaski substratum: Shina has developed a rule in which interrogative and indefinite pronouns take plural verb agreement, as well as a singulative construction which have close analogues in Burushaski but seem not to have involved any transfer of lexicon or grammatical morphemes (Thomason 2003: 14). Also, the contact-induced changes in Tariana which have developed under Eastern Tucanoan influence, as described by Aikhenvald (2003) may also be regarded as an argument against the indirect nature of syntactic interference, since there seems to have been no transfer of lexical or grammatical morphemes among these languages (Aikhenvald 2003: 5). It seems to be rather clear that grammatical patterns can be transferred without concomitant transfer of lexicon or morphemes in, at least, cases of shift-induced interference. Part of the controversy undoubtedly lies in whether or not shift-induced interference can be regarded as borrowing, as many – for example Winford (2003: 63-64) – would not, and whether source-language activity with results typical for shift-induced interference and recipient-language activity with results typical for language maintenance can be distinguished in situations of stable bilingualism (Winford 2003: 79-80). Notably, the speakers of Tariana studied by Aikhenvald seemed to strongly resist borrowed vocabulary. Similar cases, in which "default" borrowing hierarchies are overruled by social and cultural factors, may not be that infrequent in linguistic history. Thus the 19th century period of language reform in Finland initially focused particularly on those items whose foreign extraction was most easily recognizable – namely, loanwords (Häkkinen 1994: 504). However, some doubtlessly foreign morphosyntactic patterns, such as the ablative agent of the Old Finnish passive, subsisted until the end of the 19th century (Häkkinen 1994: 478), and others may have survived for far longer, as it witnessed by the prescriptive literature of the pre-WWII period (see, for example, Saarimaa 1942, Sadeniemi 1942b), shielded by their comparatively lesser salience and, in some cases, quite dubious pedigree (see, for example, Lindén 1963 for the controversial origin of verb-initial negative clauses).

1.2.3. The motivations of contact-induced structural change

1.2.3.1. Interlingual identifications as a starting point

In his groundbreaking work *Languages in Contact* Weinreich stressed interlingual identifications made between lexical items, grammatical patterns or sounds of different languages by bilingual speakers – on the basis of a perceived (partial) similarity of meaning or function – as a prerequisite to language contact (Weinreich 1974 [1953]: 39-40). Crucially, such interlingual identifications negate the inherent difference between any two linguistic signs of two different linguistic systems, since, from a structuralist point of view, they will always be imbedded in different systems of distinctive features (Weinreich 1974 [1953]: 7, Selinker 1992: 43). Following Sebuktetin, Selinker (1992: 83-84) uses the term diaform for:

(...) forms which are identified consistently as same in translation and function from the source language to the target. The smalles dialinguistic unit is the 'diamorpheme', and the largest is the 'diasentence'.

1.2.3.2. Long-term convergence and metatypy: interlingual isomorphism

Malcolm Ross (1999) has proposed the principle of *metatypy*, which he defines as:

> the change in morphosyntactic type and grammatical organization which a language undergoes as a result of its' speakers bilingualism in another language.

remarking that the modified language is quite often a strong marker of ethnic identity, whereas the model language may be a local *lingua franca* (Ross 1999: 1). Examining the case of Takia, an Austronesian language on the northern coast and some adjacent islands of Papua New-Guinea, which has undergone extensive structural influence from Waskia, a neigbouring Papuan language, Ross (1999: 2) observes that the two languages have converged to such an extent that there exists interlingual isomorphism, translatability, between the two languages on the word level. On the basis of further cases, Ross remarks that interlingual translatability seems to proceed from the phrase level down to the world level, but only in one case – namely, that of the multilingual Indian village of Kupwar – seems to have reached total isomorphism on the level of morphosyntax (Ross 1999: 12).

The contact situation in Kupwar is described in detail by Gumperz and Wilson (1971) and has been cited in the literature extremely often (for example: Weinreich, Labov and Herzog 1968: 158, Anttila 1989: 172-173, McMahon 1994: 215, Thomason and Kaufman 1988: 86-88, Ross 1999: 12, King 2000: 45, 84, Aitchison 2001: 138-139, Thomason 2001: 45, Campbell 2002: 26). In Kupwar, people of various social castes speak Urdu, Kannada and, to an extent, Telugu, whereas Marathi has the status of a local, more or less neutral *lingua franca*. According to Gumperz and Wilson (1971: 154-155), centuries of stable multilingualism among the local population has led to a situation in which the three main languages involved (Urdu, Marathi and Kannada) are virtually totally intertranslatable by a simple morph-for-morph substitution:

> (...) the codes used in code-switching situations in Kupwar have a *single syntactic surface structure*

and that, moreover, they seem to be identical on the level of phonetics as well. Though this particular situation seems to have been made possible to a great extent because of the specific social situation in which the languages are spoken – Urdu and Kannada being important markers for caste and ethnic identity, ensuring their persistence, whereas Marathi is often used as a neutral language for intergroup communication (Gumperz and Wilson 1971: 153-154), similar situations may exist elsewhere as well, for example in New Guinea:

> Language contact in New Guinea is so pervasive that Arthur Capell once commented that while adjoining languages in the island's central highlands have their own seperate vocabularies, their grammatical features 'recur with almost monotonous regularity from language to language' (Thomason 2001: 17)

or in Fort Chipewyan in Alberta, with French, English, Cree and Chipewyan as the participating languages (Romaine 1995: 69). As Ross (1999: 12) points out, the Kupwar case may be a very extreme manifestation of a process underlying long-term contact-induced change in general, and observeable to various degrees in different languages.

It should be noted, though, that the existence of interlingual isomorphism in Kupwar or other more or less similar situations is not uncontroversial – thus King (2000: 45-46) criticizes the, in her view, slim evidence for the existence of such in Kupwar, and Heath (1981: 365) stresses that, despite exceptionally intensive contact, including borrowing of grammatical affixes, there seems to be no sign of a Kupwar-type situation of intertranslatability in sight among the genetically unrelated languages of Arnhem Land in Australia. Regardless of the validity of its most extreme example, one could regard metatypy as defined by Ross as a contact-induced linguistic macroprocess:

> grammatical calqueing is simply a dimension of metatypy and inseperable from it. (Ross 1999: 13)

and regard the easing of the cognitive burden brought about by the regular use of and switching between more than one language as its primary motivation. A similar explanation has been put forth by McMahon (1994: 213-214):

> The motivations for such developments may involve ease of learning and communicative efficiency. Convergence typically occurs in situations where communication between linguistic groups is essential, and all, or the majority of speakers must learn and use two (or more) languages (...) It will clearly be easier for the individual to learn the grammars, and therefore master the languages, if the grammars are similar. What seems to happen in extreme cases of convergence is a gradual approximation of the rules that generate the two languages over time, so that the structures generated correspondingly become more and more similar.

However, regarding also the controversy about the existence of such radical metatypy as in Kupwar, it is important to keep in mind Thomason's (2001: 125) warning, who is somewhat reserved on the possibility of total grammatical merger and hence intertranslatability:

> One feature that characterizes all well-established linguistic areas is a tendency, in a long-term Sprachbund, towards isomorphism, or convergence, in everything except the phonological shapes of morphemes. But it is important to stress that this does not justify an assumption that a natural outcome of a long-term Sprachbund is total merger of grammatical structures of the languages. In fact, there is no evidence whatsoever that such a thing has occurred in any linguistic area anywhere in the world, so that arguing for it as a realistic possibility seems rash.

1.2.3.3. Contact-induced change and iconicity: intralingual isomorphism

Language is a socially determined system of signs, which is used by speakers to communicate with one another, and hence, language change must, according to Anttila (1989: 181) be explained by reference to the communicative needs of its speakers, more specifically:

> The driving force is the mental striving to adopt language for communication with least effort, that is, the psychological motive and the necessity of fulfilling the functions of speech.

Langacker (1977: 103-110) distinguishes *signal simplicity*, the striving towards maximal economy in speech production, *perceptual optimality*, the striving to maximal clarity in the reception and interpretation of linguistic signals by for example using periphrastic constructions, *constructional simplicity*, the preference, for example, for unmarked categories instead of marked ones, and *transparancy*, the striving towards iconicity, i.e. the principle 'one meaning – one form' (Anttila 1977: 55, 1989: 100-101, 406-407). Striving for maximal smoothness in the production of speech is, of course, the basic motive behind many phonological changes like, for example, a change of a consonant group *mt* to *nt*. Striving towards maximal clarity in the perception of speech, i.e., striving towards iconicity – an isomorphic relationship between our language and the world we live in – and the principle of one meaning – one form, can be discerned behind many structural changes, most saliently in analogical changes like analogical levelling (Anttila 1989: 355, McMahon 1994: 86). McMahon mentions that that other mighty machinery of structural change besides analogy – grammaticalization – may also have a striving towards iconicity at its roots, mainly in providing the input to grammaticalization by ensuring that semantically associated elements are situated closely together in a sentence (McMahon 1994: 171-172).

Obviously, the results of these two main teleological processes, striving for ease in the production of speech and striving towards perceptual clarity, often cancel each other out, the former possibly leading to allomorphy which disrupts the principle of one meaning – one form (E. Itkonen 1978: 41) whereas, as Esa Itkonen (1978: 42) points out, analogical levelling – an attempted increase in iconicity, may lead to an actual decrease in iconicity by, for example, making a verbal paradigm an exception within the total class of verb systems.

Now in case of lexical borrowing, considerations of prestige are an important motivation, as well as the need to adapt the lexicon to the ever-changing demands posed by society (McMahon 1994: 201). In case of contact-induced change in general, Andersen (1974: 23) and Esa Itkonen (1978: 61) mention linguistic solidarity – the striving to adapt one's speech to that of one's fellows (and perhaps, to distinguish it from that of others as well) as an important motivator, however, according to Esa Itkonen (1978: 61), linguistic solidarity as a teleological factor is superimposed on that of iconicity:

> (...) contact innovation, ot adoption of a change, presents a *teleology sui generis*, based on the concept of linguistic solidarity and the rewards and sanctions that go with it. It is clear enough, however, that contact innovations are superimposed on the teleology explicated, in morphology, by the principle of isomorphism (...).

A similar point is made by Anttila (1989: 177):

> Even if borrowings often complicate the grammar, especially in phonology, it can still be seen that the total communicative situation becomes more iconic in that sense that more of the language moves to the greater efficiency of 'one meaning, one form'.

In case of lexical borrowing, the principle of one meaning – one form is at work of course in the adaptation of new loanwords to designate previously unknown referents or concepts. However, contact-induced structural change, too, may be seen as motivated by a striving towards iconicity.

Taking Romaine's point (1995: 8), that

> (...)linguists who study language contact often seek to describe changes at the level of linguistic systems in isolation and abstraction from speakers. Sometimes they tend to treat the outcome of bilingual interaction in static rather than dynamic terms, and lose sight of the fact that the bilingual is the ultimate locus of contact. Bilingualism exists within cognitive systems of individuals, as well as in families and communities.

I would like to distinguish between *language* as a) a system of shared behavioral norms shared between a group of speakers who constitute a speech-community and b) the individual competence of speakers, who may be mono-, bi- or multilingual, with a) being an emergent dimension of b):

A)

LANGUAGE A	LANGUAGE B

B) SPEAKERS: A A A A A A A A AB AB AB AB AB B B B B B B B B B
(monolinguals) (bilinguals) (monolinguals)

Interlingual identifications, and the subsequent establishment of diaforms, takes place on level b) – that of individual, bilingual competence, or, to be precise, individual *usage*. Regarding contact-induced structural change as a transfer of form and function within a diaform, established through the interlingual identification made by a bilingual, it is clear that we are dealing with here is a very dialectical process: the presence of a contradiction between the sameness of two linguistic forms (similarity in grammatical function, or even isomorphism between two syntactic patterns) and their difference (the form in language A might lack a function present in language B, and so forth) and the subsequent negation of their difference. A prototypical situation could look like this:

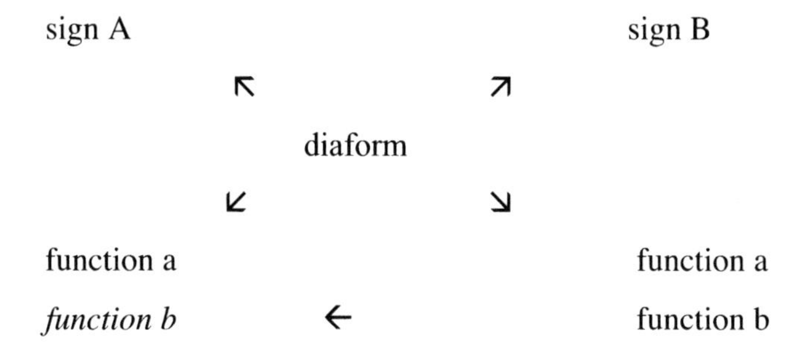

As Weinreich (1974 [1953]: 7) pointed out, from a strictly structuralist point of view, a phoneme in one language can never be “the same” as one in another language, as they are both embedded in different relational systems of distinctive features. Identification between them negates this inherent difference, and transfer negates the contradiction between sameness and difference in case of a diaform.

On the basis of an interlingual identification between signs A and B, which share a grammatical function a, function b, present in language B but not in A, is transferred to language A as well. It should be noted that, aside from the respective grammatical functions of the signs, their phonological surface forms can coalesce as well – in such a case, we would have an example of code-switching. And, of course, another possible consequence of interlingual identification is the loss of a function which does not happen to have a counterpart in the diffusing language (Weinreich 1974 [1953]: 30-31).

The basis for the establishment of diaforms can be similarity in function, isomorphism in structure, or a combination thereof, but, crucially, surface phonological isomorphism as well (Krausch 1926: 36-37, Palmer 1972: 240, Campbell 1987: 263, Aikhenvald 2003: 2). Cases where accidental phonologic similarity induced the establishment of diaforms and subsequent structural change have been discussed by Campbell (1987) in the case of Spanish influence on Pipil. Noting that the Pipil relational noun *-pal*, originally designating possession and occuring only with possessive prefixes, i.e. *nu-pal* 'mine', now occurs freely without possessive prefixes, as a preposition meaning 'in order to, so that', Campbell (1987: 263) argues that this change was modeled on the Spanish preposition *para*, and that a chance phonetic similarity between the Spanish preposition and the Pipil relational noun played an important role in actuating this change. As mentioned, Aikhenvald (2003: 2) names such structural changes induced by phonological similarity *grammatical accommodation*, defined as:

> (...) reinterpretation of a native morpheme on the model of the syntactic function of a phonetically similar morpheme in the diffusing language.

As mentioned, structural change as a consequence of interlingual identification can be regarded as a negation of the inherent difference between forms on the basis of a perceived similarity. From that, however, it is only a short step to connect processes like these with general, "internal" processes of change which, in a teleological fashion, work towards establishment of iconicity, a relationship of one meaning-one form:

diaform: [sign A – sign B] → diaform [sign A – sign B]
↓ ↘ ↓

shared function a non-shared function b shared functions a and b

What this means is that, on the level of language as the individual competence of speakers, monolingual and bilingual, the same teleological, dialectical processes underlie both contact-induced changes and "internal" changes, namely, a striving towards iconicity, the only difference being that, in the case of "internal" change, this striving takes place within a single, unitary system of signs, whereas in the case of contact-induced change, it takes place within a partially dual, partially merged system of signs:

> Bilingualism is just another kind of synchronic variation for the speaker with code switching occurring in certain situations. This variation goes through the whole language, both grammar and vocabulary. From the psychological (if not the social) point of view, this is an enormous burden, hostile to the efficient principle 'one meaning, one form'. When social forces permit, simplification results in the two complete codes ending up as only one. (Anttila 1989: 170).

It seems clear that the two motivations for contact-induced structural change mentioned here are merely two sides of the same coin: moving towards a greater iconicity between meaning and structure within the partially merged system of individual bilingual competence – with it's seperate phonological surface forms and morphosyntactic rules, but it's shared semantic, conceptual basis, automatically leads to greater intranslatability between the two languages at the avail of the bilingual. A macroprocess that may arise out of this is metatypy – which, in its most radical forms as in Kupwar and perhaps other places as well can be seen as the crystallization of individual compound bilingualism at the level of language as a system of shared behavioral norms.

1.2.4. The mechanisms of contact-induced structural change

1.2.4.1. Analogy

The previous section described structural change as the transfer of forms within a diaform, an interlingually identified "compound" of two signs. This change is essentially analogical, i.e. it establishes isomorphical relationships between parts of a system. Analogy can be, as Esa Itkonen (2005: 12) states, both be regarded as a state and as a process. As a state, analogy is the main centripetal force keeping language systems together: the structure of phonological systems, with, for instance, isomorphic series of unvoiced and voiced stops, as well that of grammar, where paradigms of nouns and verbs are isomorphic to each other, is essentially analogical (E. Itkonen 2005: 12). Analogy as a process establishes analogy as a state, and hence, the type of contact-induced change mentioned above would be a particular kind of analogy.

Analogy is ubiquitous in knowledge, as well as in the world at large – the flippers and fluke of a dolphin, the wings of a bird, and the legs of a human being may be seen as analogous:

> The person who discovered the analogy between bird and fish was practicing zoology, not cognitive science. Similarly, those who discovered the wave-character of light were practicing physics, not cognitive science. Of course, they were making use of their cognitive capacities (as every human being is

> at any moment), but this is a different matter. It is impossible to deny that in these and similar cases the analogy is in the 'things themselves', and not only in the human mind. (E. Itkonen 2005: 20).

The same point is made by Cabot Haley (1988: 47-51), who regards Keats' metaphor of stars as "trembling diamonds" and the sense of wave-motion or oscillation provided it, as a great poetic metaphor because it *discovers* a feature of the reality around us:

> While the poets' metaphorical perception is highly imaginative, the perceived similarity is not imaginary. It is real. (Haley 1988: 47).

Analogy, finally, is an essential property of the universe in Whitehead's cosmology (Whitehead 1929: 450).

Following Esa Itkonen (2005: 112) and Harris and Campbell (1995: 112) I would reserve the term "analogy" in the following for an underlying principle structuring language and a metacondition of change, rather than as a mechanism of change proper, such as reanalysis and extension: analogy can often stimulate the latter. However, the two need not be tightly distinct. In an emergent view of grammar as proposed by Hopper (1987), analogy could re-appear as a process, and exert its centripetal force on linguistic structure in the constant re-creation of linguistic structure in actual usage.

1.2.4.2. Reanalysis, extension and borrowing

Harris and Campbell (1995), in their typology of mechanisms of syntactic change, define syntactic borrowing as

> (...) a change in which a foreign syntactic pattern (either a duplication of the foreign pattern or at least a formally quite similar pattern) is incorporated into the borrowing language through the influence of a donor pattern found in a contact language. (Harris and Campbell 1995: 122)

and regard it as an independent mechanism of change, distinct from both reanalysis and extension (Harris and Campbell 1995: 150), reanalysis being a reinterpretation of grammatical rules – for example, a slight shift in the relationships between a surface pattern and a given grammatical function – without any modification of surface structure, and extension being a modification of surface structure without any change in the underlying grammatical patterns – analogical levelling being a prime example of the latter. This basic trichotomy of reanalysis, extension and borrowing, with an underlying division between internally-motivated and externally-motivated changes (Harris and Campbell 1995: 52), appears in Hennig Andersen's (1974) typology of change as well. Andersen (1974: 19-23) distinguishes between (externally motivated) 1) adaptive innovations, motivated by the communicative context in which language is used and therefore including borrowings as well as lexical neologisms and the like, and 2) (internally motivated) evolutive innovations, which include 2.1) abductive innovations – the reinterpretation of grammatical rules – and 2.2) deductive innovations, the actualization of those reinterpreted grammatical rules in the surface grammar (Andersen 1974: 23).

Reanalysis and extension are thus *logical* processes, and can be identified with such operations as abduction (Anttila 1977: 18, E. Itkonen 2002, 2005: 31). Esa Itkonen draws a comparison between the hypothetico-deductive method in science and processes of reanalysis and extension in language, regarding them both as manifestations of the same underlying analogical process (E. Itkonen 2005: 110-111). Whereas abduction in science proceeds by proposing a hypothesis to deal with the encountered facts, much like a detective makes up a hypothesis to account for the murdered lord, the bloody knife in the butler's drawer, etc., and then recasting the process in terms of deduction of the facts from the theory adopted, reanalysis proceeds by assigning a new underlying structure to linguistic input. However, as Esa Itkonen points out, both processes are by themselves circular: the new theoretical interpretation of encountered facts will only prove fruitful if it makes testable, and confirmed, predictions: likewise, the new structure arrived at by reanalysis remains "invisible", and the linguistic output ambiguous, unless extended into non-ambiguous environments, or:

> extension as an analogue of deducing new predictions is not about new events to be observed, but about new actions to be performed by the speaker him-/herself. Moreover, the analogue of deducing (new) true predictions consists in performing (new) actions that will be accepted by the linguistic community. New predictions are discovered to be true but new actions are accepted to be correct. Some amount of reflection is needed to grasp this distinction fully. (E. Itkonen 2002: 430).

The independence of borrowing as a mechanism of syntactic change has been challenged in a recent paper by Alexandra Aikhenvald (2003), who discusses structural change in Tariana, a moribund Arawak language from the Vaupés area in Brazil, under the influence of neigbouring, genetically unrelated East Tucanoan languages, and argues that grammatical borrowing cannot be seen as a unitary phenomenon but one which necessarily occurs together with internal mechanisms of change like reanalysis and grammaticalization (Aikhenvald 2003: 3). Among her examples, Aikhenvald mentions the development of a topical nonsubject case marker in Tariana according to an East-Tucanoan model, however, the case marker itself, -*naku, -nuku*, has developed from an earlier locative case marker, and internal mechanisms like reanalysis and reinterpretation must be involved in its change of function, even if the role of an East Tucanoan model pattern seems obvious, similarly, Tariana seems to have lost the Arawak system of locative cases, extending the function of one particular allative marker to a general locative case ending, again bringing it closer in line with Eastern-Tucanoan (Aikhenvald 2003: 7-10) – as Aikhenvald (2003: 10) points out:

> (...) Tariana has 'imported' the abstract feature system of East-Tucanoan cases – with one, catch-all, locative – losing most of the original locative distinctions and extending the sphere of the original suffix. This reinterpretation involves reanalysis of a feature system together with a reanalysis of the system of realization for these features.

Language contact, in Aikhenvald's words,

> is a condition – or an externally motivated situation – under which the above three mechanisms (reanalysis, extension and grammaticalization – *MdS*) can apply in an orderly and systematic way. (Aikhenvald 2003: 3).

Regarding the analyses of contact-induced changes in Tariana, Aikhenvald (2003: 27) remarks that

> to just lump them under an umbrella label of 'borrowing' or 'calqueing' is an oversimplification which obscures the different possible historical scenarios for each case.

1.2.4.3. Overt and covert interference

Before dealing with syntactic borrowing and contact-induced reanalysis and extension, it is important to distinguish it from another type, or better, another category, of contact-induced structural change, which has been labeled *covert interference* by King (2000: 89), following Mougeon and Beniak, *convergence* by Chaudenson et al (1993: 68) and Romaine (1995: 73-75) – in order to distinguish this from convergence as a macroprocess, I will use the former term. Covert interference can be defined as the tendency for a linguistic sign or pattern which happens to be part of a diaform to be used more frequently than a functionally similar pattern which is not associated through interlingual identification with a pattern of another language. Often, the pattern associated as a diaform with a foreign-language pattern is more or less isomorphic with that foreign-language pattern, an isomorphism which is the basis of the interlingual identification itself. On the long run, the interlingually identified pattern would become the unmarked choice for speakers, with the functionally similar pattern becoming gradually marginalized. This process of change, which Aitchison (1995: 3) regards as a major factor in determining the outcome of any competition between two synonymous patterns, should be distinguished from contact-induced structural change proper as being restricted to the level of language use or *parole* (Birnbaum 1984: 41).

However, covert interference may be a factor in bringing about a change in structure, particularly through loss of features not favoured by isomorphism between a construction in the recipient language and one in the model (source) language, but also through grammaticalization of a form favoured by isomorphism with a foreign model and hence increasing in frequency.

Campbell (1987: 271-272) defines the outcome of such a change in language structure brought about by covert interference as follows:

> Several aspects of Pipil grammar, while probably not unknown before Spanish contact, seem to have changed "in spirit" to conform to Spanish norms. That is, in some cases, originally more marginal native constructions have been enhanced, become more salient, due to the more central role played in Spanish grammar of constructions with corresponding functions.

As an example, Campbell (1987: 272) mentions the use of articles in Pipil, which had a more restricted and more demonstrative-like function before identification between them and the Spanish article brought about their increase in frequency. Other instances of covert interference are dealt with widely in the literature, for example, by Nadkarni (1975: 678) who discusses the competition of a borrowed and hence rather isomorphic (and probably, interlingually identified) relative-clause structure in Konkani, an Indic language, with a marginalized indigenous variant (the borrowed or indigenous origin of any of the two competing structures in processes of covert interference is, of course, irrelevant to the application of the process), and by Thomason, who discusses a tendency among her Montana Salish informants to use highly marked sentence structures isomorphic with English in speaking with her, rather then the unmarked type, which is structurally extremely dissimilar to the English translation equivalents. Thomason (forthcoming: 10) notes that

> If such translation equivalents should become the norm in Salish, the language would have changed dramatically, both morphologically and syntactically, in the relative frequencies of the two sentence-types, and the change would certainly be contact-induced.

however,

> (...) calling the changes rule borrowing would still be problematic, because both sets of morphosyntactic rules already exist in Montana Salish. (...) A claim of rule borrowing in such cases seems more promising if we focus on discourse-level rules rather than on sentence-level rules, since the current distribution of the patterns in Salish is governed by discourse rules.

Clearly, covert interference in bilingual discourse is both fed by contact-induced structural change in diaforms which make interlingually identified patterns more isomorphic, and at the same time produces the materials for such contact-induced structural change by continuously favouring the use of structurally isomorphic forms, including those who underwent contact-induced structural change, which may then be established more firmly as diaforms within a bilingual speech-community. As the twin engines of long-term convergence, the two go hand in hand.

One might counterpose covert interference to its hypothetical counterpart – the marginalization or absence of a structure, despite its clear possibility, because of the lack of an isomorphic equivalent in model languages. Thus Häkkinen (1994: 471) points out that the Finnish agent participle – a nominal verb form used as an attribute and therefore a semantic equivalent to the attributive usage of past passive participles in the Germanic languages – was marginal in older literary Finnish, as opposed to more isomorphic structures.

1.2.4.4. Contact-induced structural change as bilingual reanalysis and extension

As mentioned above, internal structural change and contact-induced structural change do not only mirror each other in their motivations and causes, since both can be seen as strivings towards iconicity between meaning and form – in case of contact-induced structural change, iconicity between meaning and interlingually associated forms within the competence of a bilingual speaker. However, following Anttila (1989: 170) I would argue that the two also mirror each other in the processes by which they take place. The suggestion is that in cases of contact-induced structural change, as in the transfer of functions from morphemes in language A to those of language B as mentioned above, we are dealing with essentially the same processes of reanalysis and extension: a reanalysis, and respectively, extension *sui generis*. Or, as Anttila (1989: 170) puts it:

> (...) such a rule borrowing in syntax is not an abstract occurrence – it is based on bilingualism and a *correspondence* between the two languages. Like loan translation, it is *analogy* between two languages.

The basis of reanalysis is the identification between two, erstwhile distinct, morphemes or allomorphs made by speakers – in the case of contact-induced structural change, we are dealing with morphemes belonging to the grammatical systems of distinct languages, but *it is only on the more abstract level of language as a system of shared behavioral norms that we can speak of distinct languages*, not on the level of individual speaker competence, where the semantic substructures of the two languages are partially merged through interlingual identification. My argument is that the establishment of diamorphs constitutes a reanalysis – the assignment of two surface phonological forms to one semantic meaning or grammatical function – and that subsequent contact-induced changes in the meaning or function of either part of those diamorphs constitutes an extension based on such a reanalysis. One might even extend this to code-switching, as a case of extension *sui generis*, with borrowing as an internal process of reanalysis subsequent to code-switching.

One could visualize this as such:

Table 1:1. *Contact-induced structural changeas bilingual reanalysis and extension.*

Process:	One language involved:	Two languages involved:
Reanalysis	Identification of two morphemes based on allomorphy or surface ambiguity.	Identification of two morphemes based on isomorphy of structure, phonology etc.
Extension	Negation of allomorphy: analogical levelling.	Transfer of meaning, function or form.

Quoting, again, Anttila (1989: 104):

> Extension is similar to borrowing in that a form is lifted from one environment in another, though, in borrowing, the source environment is in a different language, dialect, or even idiolect, whereas, in extension, it is within the same grammar in another grammatical environment or in another part of the vocabulary (lexicon). This parallelism with borrowing has even led to calling extension *borrowing from within* (the same grammar)

Grammatical borrowing, conversely, can be regarded as *extension from without*.

As mentioned, surface phonological similarity between morphemes of different languages has been raised in the literature as a basis towards the establishment of diaforms. This process if anything is very strongly reminiscent of similar internal mechanisms of change, notably the so-called hermit crab processes mentioned by Heath (1998), which involve the replacement of morphemes which are in danger of losing their distinctiveness through phonological wear and tear by phonologically (but not necessarily semantically) similar lexical items within the same language. In this case, we have a reanalysis carried out on the basis of surface phonological similarity, with the affixation of the erstwhile lexical items as an extension of that reanalysis. The difference between internal processes of change involving chance surface phonological similarity – one could mention folk etymology, etc., here as well – and that between contact-induced processes of change in which surface phonological similarity plays a role in the interlingual identification of two items is only that in the latter case two languages are involved – but from the vantage point of individual, partially compound bilingual competence, it is, I believe, questionable whether it is really sensible to speak here of different languages and hence external change.

Thus I would suggest that, on the level of individual speaker competence, grammatical borrowing is not a unitary and discrete mechanism of change: it is a particular instance of the same mechanisms of linguistic change which apply to internal processes of change as well, it just happens that in this instance, there are two partially – but not entirely – distinct codes involved. I would also suggest that *transfer* – among which, grammatical borrowing, is a concept applicable only on the level of languages as shared behavioral norms. Transfer, after all, is a transitive concept: it must by necessity involve two discrete entities. On the level of individual speaker competence, languages may partially merge, their underlying semantic representational systems coalesce, and they are not entirely discrete entities. On the more abstract level of shared behavioral norms, the *loci* of which are partially coalesced in the form of bilingual speakers, they are, and internal change can be distinguished from external change. Thus it would be possible to define transfer as an emergent consequence of the successive reanalyses and extensions of those reanalyses made by bilingual speakers.

A model in which contact-induced structural change and internal structural change are seen as identical in the basis underlying their actuation, the mechanisms by which they are carried out and the teleological factors guiding their actuation could be summarized as follows:

Table 1:2. *Basical identity of external and internal mechanisms of change.*

	Monolingual	Bilingual
Situation	Absence of language contact as a factor: a single system of signs.	Partially compound system of signs: discrete phonological surface forms in two languages based on a partially merged semantic substructure.
Stimulus for change	Negation of iconicity between meaning and form: surface ambiguity or allomorphy.	Negation of iconicity between meaning and form involving compound signs.

Mechanisms of change	Reanalysis and extension.	Reanalysis in the establishment of diaforms, extension in the transfer of features between both parts of a diaform.
Motivation of change	Iconicity between form and meaning.	Iconicity between form and meaning.

This implies that, to an extent, I agree with Aikhenvald's objection to Harris and Campbell's (1995) trichotomy: language contact is a background condition of reanalysis and extension, and syntactic borrowing is not a mechanism of change in its own right. To treat the three of them as parallel mechanisms of change would be a category mistake. It should be noted, though, that Harris and Campbell (1995: 51) emphatically state that:

> Language contact is often a catalyst to change through reanalysis or extension, while borrowing, of course, can come about only through language contact.

However, it nevertheless seems to me that positing syntactic borrowing as an independent mechanism of change is the result of superimposing the distinction internal/external on a typology of syntactic change. But it is best to scuttle this dichotomy: innovations themselves do not arise either internally or externally: in language structure, they are the outcomes of logical processes performed by a speaker, and those processes may well operate on a bilingual diaform. Their spread is not internal nor external either: all linguistic innovations spread through contact between speakers. I feel therefore that regarding syntactic borrowing as bilingual reanalysis and extension does more justice to the basic logical nature of those processes. In other words, "syntactic borrowing" seems to me to be a similar concept as "England invaded France". To describe the results of a historical process succinctly, it is very usual. However, in studying the mechanisms by which England invaded France, a process including the individual and collective actions of thousands of individuals, it is clearly in the wrong place.

1.2.5. Conclusion, by way of Whitehead

1.2.5.1. Whitehead's philosophical system

To recapitulate, the main suggestions made in the previous sections would be that:

1) There is no place for a dichotomy between internal and external in a typology of the mechanisms of linguistic structural change. The basic mechanisms are logical, cognitive processes: reanalysis and extension, both analogous to abduction. Analogy is a condition which permeates linguistic structure and motivates both "internal" and "external" processes of change.
2) A reason for this is that languages should not be hypostasized as entities which can do things, such as influence each other or borrow stuff from each other. Linguistic change is rooted in the actions of speakers, and the difference between languages fades in the interlingual identifications made by speakers.
3) From this it also follows that structural change should be regarded as a teleological process, rather than a causal one in the sense of the physical sciences. Establishment of the principle "one meaning – one form" can be regarded as a primary motivator for both contact-induced and other structural innovations.
4) Finally, this would lead us to a view of linguistic change in which the "causes" of a given innovation do not exclude each other. The "cause" of any given innovation is the whole situation in which a given speaker interprets, misinterprets or remodels a linguistic structure, and in which other speakers adopt a new structure. It is never possible to exhaustively describe causes of change: one can, at most, isolate factors which may have plausibly contributed to a given innovation. Language contact being one of those factors.

As I feel that an explicit philosophical base is preferable over a merely implied one, it seems to me that these and other considerations will gain coherence if embedded in a process-philosophical or "Whiteheadian" framework, following Fortescue's (2001) application[1] of Alfred North Whitehead's philosophical system towards language. For an elaborate introduction to Whitehead, the reader is referred to Fortescue (2001) – below, I will briefly mention the main categories of Whitehead's metaphysic[2]. I will not return to Whitehead until the conclusions of this research, so the impatient reader might want to skip the following excursion.

---

[1] Though indebted to Fortescue (2001), the following interpretation of Whitehead to historical linguistics may differ in various parts from Fortescue's. Fortescue's introduction to Whiteheadian linguistics contains a general, sweeping view on all aspects of general linguistics. In the following much less elaborate and precise application, I will focus mainly on the 'historical' part of historical linguistics, i.e. those dealing with motivation and teleology of change.

2 Whitehead's philosophy has gained traction mainly within theology, Protestant and to a lesser extent Judaic. Theological introductions to Whitehead are not hard to find. Whitehead 1933 includes an introduction to his philosophy which is more accessible, though much less elaborate, than Whitehead 1929. In the following, I will, for simplicity's sake, mainly not use Whitehead's precise, but complex terminology. Thus I will mostly use 'event' or 'linguistic event' for 'actual occasion', 'becoming' for 'concrescence', and 'pattern' for 'eternal object'. The only term which I will consistently use is 'prehension', as the most obvious alternative, 'relation', lacks the important subjective and dynamic connotations of 'prehension'.

Part of what makes Whitehead's metaphysic hard to understand is that it turns the common-sense view of durable substances (tables, chairs, elephants, people) moving through space and time on its head. The most basic building-block of the universe with Whitehead is the actual entity or *actual occasion* (Whitehead 1929: 29), basically, an "event" endowed with some modicum of experience. These "units of experience" make up all of mind and matter in the universe: there is no reality outside of them:

> There is no going on behind actual entities to find anything more real: God is an actual entity, and so is the merest puff of existence in far-off empty space. But, though there are gradations of importance, and diversities of functions, yet in the principles which actuality exemplifies, all are on the same level. The final facts are, all alike, actual entities; and these actual entities are drops of experience, complex and interdependent. (Whitehead 1929: 24-25).

This means that both strict materialism and Cartesian dualism between mind and matter are rejected: actual occasions are *dipolar,* having a material, physical and a subjective, mental side (Whitehead 1929: 151): some kind of mentality is thus regarded as a fundamental property of the universe, rather than an emergent or epiphenomenal property of matter. The resulting idea has been described as "panexperientialism", rather than "panpsychism".

In case of actual occasions such as elementary particles, this mentality is of course extremely minimal. Actual occasions may, however, be organized in a "nexus" or more or less structured *societies* which may be more or less durable as they are propagated down time (Whitehead 1929: 46-47). Some societies, such as rocks, tables or chairs, exhibit no mentality above the level of events which make them up. Others, such as people and other animate beings, of course do.

Actual occasions relate to each other through *prehensions*, alternatively termed feelings (Whitehead 1929: 24-26; 1933: 226-227): these prehensions include everything from raw, physical causality to perception by animate beings, and conceptual thought. Causality is regarded as a kind of perception (Whitehead 1929: 334). There are, however, no prehensions possible between any two contemporary events: each event can relate only to events objectified in its own past (Whitehead 1929: 91). This past can be extremely recent, but it is the past nonetheless: the tree I may perceive through my window represents an extremely recent past, the stars in the sky a quite distant one. Thus an event can be described as riding the crest of its own little wave in time: however, it can only perceive what lies in its own wake. This said, for Whitehead (1933: 251), the future, too, is immanent in the present in the sense that:

> What is objective in the present is the necessity of a future of actual occasions, and the necessity that these future occasions conform to the conditions inherent in the essence of the present occasion.

This idea is quite compatible with Collingwood's (1993 [1946]: 365-366) statement that the past is ideal and has no real existence: the past exists only in as far as it is immanent in the present (by causation, memory, etc.).

The specific characteristics of an event are described as coming into being in a process of *concrescence* – becoming concrete (Whitehead 1929: 213, 299-300, 1933: 303). This becoming does *not* take place in physical time – during its becoming, the event gains its spatiotemporal extension (Whitehead 1929: 401). During becoming, the event gains determination by relating to or "prehending" events in its own past which have become "objectified". Objectification, however, always involves loss (Whitehead 1929: 482): as there is no reality beyond actual events, past ones lose their subjective pole and only become 'objects' that may live on, dismembered and eviscerated as the subjectivity that lent them coherence is gone, in future events. Or not. In this sense, the past is immanent in the present. In addition to this, Whitehead (1929: 29) distinguishes *eternal objects,* "forms of definiteness" which signify qualia or patterns which may be actualized repeatedly in events. Qualia and patterns, however, have no real existence outside of their actualization in events: outside of them, they exist merely as possibilities. This recalls the Peircean distinction between possibility and actuality as described by Haley (1988: 5).

Prehensions, or feelings, can be causal or conceptual – corresponding to the dipolar physical/mental nature of an event – Whitehead (1929: 339) stresses that conceptual prehensions do not imply consciousness, rather, they apply to the actualization of qualia, patterns and structure in events. Prehensions are also positive or negative: *negative prehensions* exclude an eternal object from actualization in an event (Whitehead 1929: 31-32, 54). As Fortescue (2001: 16) remarks:

> In the case of a negatively prehended eternal object, although it does not form part of the objective data, its exclusion nevertheless contributes its own subjective form (however remote or trivial) to the complex of feelings to be resolved. One can envisage all perception (including that of words and their intended referents) and all action consequent to perception (decisions to act that unfold through time) as complex, contrast-enhancing patterns of interacting negative and positive prehensions. Especially the former play a key role in modulating the flow of human thought, at both its physical and mental poles.

The role of negative and positive prehensions in establishing contrasts during their determination of an event is a theme that will return later.

Conceptual valuations and *conceptual reversions* are conceptual prehensions relating to qualia and patterns inherent in some past event: conceptual valuations derive structure, qualia, patterns from an event or a nexus or society of those: perceiving an apple as "red" would then be an act of conceptual valuation (Whitehead 1929: 349-352). Conceptual reversion prehends contrasts between qualia and patterns on the basis of a common ground of identity (Whitehead 1929: 352-353). *Transmutation* applies to the prehension or abstracting of qualia and patterns from a diversity of events, and thus perceiving the pattern or qualia as determining characteristics of a society of events. Transmutation allows us to prehend, say, a society of events forming a table as a *table*, an enduring object, and analogy plays a primary part in transmutation: "There's a table, and hey, there's another table!" (Whitehead 1929: 36, Fortescue 2001: 14)[3]. Other types of prehensions include *propositional prehensions* and these include *imaginative perceptions*, which predicates qualia and patterns not derived from the logical subject in question: "this red apple might have been green" (Whitehead 1929: 362-373). Whitehead distinguishes propositional prehensions from *judgments* in that a proposition, a link between a logical subject and an eternal object as predicate, can be true or false without reference to the judging subject, where a judgment concerns the coherence of the objectified past events that are actualized into an event, i.e., it is part of the becoming of a judging subject and relative to him (Whitehead 1929: 271). Thus, "elephants are grey" would be a proposition, whereas "this particular elephant is grey" a judgment. Intuitive judgments reflect a proposition on the objectified data defining an event, or, in other words, it integrates physical perceptions with logical propositions (Whitehead 1929: 383, Fortescue 2001: endnote 15) – but differs from it in the key role played by imagination (Whitehead 1929: 386-387). Judgments, in addition to be affirmative or negative, can be suspended:

> In the suspense-form the predicate is neither identical, nor incompatible, with the pattern. It is diverse from, and compatible with, the pattern in the nexus as objectified: the nexus, in its own 'formal' existence, may, or may not, in fact exemplify both the pattern and the predicate." (Whitehead 1929: 282-283)

or:

> It is the feeling of the contrast between what the logical subjects evidently *are*, and what the same subjects in addition *may be*.

Finally, *hybrid prehensions* are prehensions of prehensions: namely, of conceptual prehensions belonging to another subject (Whitehead 1929: 149) and they are thereby the stuff of the hermeneutic.

3 The notion of 'analogy' here may be considerably wider than that of Esa Itkonen (2005: 63): "There is, in principle, an analogy between one bird and one fish, but not between two birds, because in the latter case the similarity is material, not structural. (As expected, there has to be a grey area between material and structural, as e. g. in comparing a sparrow and an ostrich.) Thus, phenomena related by similarity associations fall outside of analogy."

Once an event has fulfilled its process of becoming, once it has become fully determinate – it perishes, though may partially survive as an object to be prehended by succeeding events. Events, therefore, are not subject to change (Whitehead 1929: 81), Whitehead's answer to Zeno is an atomism of events raining down in time: temporal change is the consequence of a succession of events, rather than inherent in the event itself (Whitehead 1929: 48-49).

It is notable that Whitehead's system, as a whole, is cast in aesthetic, sensitivist terms, and that both physical causation and logic are included in the category of prehensions or feelings. For Whitehead, a primary property of the universe is *creativity*, the creation of novelty: creativity is the way in which the many objectified events of the past find unity in the becoming of an actual event, and in which the actual event is novel from the multiplicity it unifies (Whitehead 1929: 28, Fortescue 2001: 5). Events, in their mental pole, ultimately strive for depth of experience, and this is conditioned upon the maximalization of contrasts abstracted from the objective data of an event by conceptual reversion (Whitehead 1929: 392-393).

1.2.5.2. Structure and process

It should be noted that Whitehead was developing a metaphysics, a rather sweeping cosmological system, and wrote little about language as such, at one point remarking that spoken language "is merely a series of squeaks" (Whitehead 1929: 374). Nonetheless Fortescue (2001: 2) regards it as one of the main advantages of Whitehead's system in that it bridges the rationalist view on the world (in its category of eternal objects) and the empiricist view (in its insistence on regarding experience as primary):

> This apparently unbreachable chasm persists to this day (in one of its many guises) in the antagonism between the functionalist or generative (or nativist) approaches to linguistics.

This divide has been alluded to in the previous section – particularly as a tendency to regard contact-induced structural change as marginal and to localize deep-going structural change in language acquisition (a view which Fortescue (2001: 194) accepts – more on this later).

The bridging of the two consists in Whitehead's (1929: 31) conception of patterns as lying in the realm of possibility alone – unless they are actualized in an event (Fortescue 2001: 5, 204): linguistic structures would thus be eternal objects, only actualized through the mediation of speakers, with memory, subjective aims, etc. Whitehead's conception of the dipolar, physical and mental, nature of an event may, when imposed on (historical) linguistics where an event would be a moment of linguistic cognition (Fortescue 2001: 9) involving both the sign and the speaker/listener using or interpreting a sign, account for both structure and (purposeful) usage, in

Coseriu's terms (1974 [1958]: 37-39), *érgon*, finished structure, and *énergeia*, activity – the former of which results from the latter (Coseriu 1974 [1958]: 41, Anttila 1989: 111), and would be, in a Whiteheadian view, an eternal object ingressing in the latter. In Coseriu's words:

> Auch in dieser Sicht muss natürlich klar sein, dass die Sprache allein im und durch das Sprechen existiert: in der "Geschichte, die geschieht" (*res gestae, Geschichte*), gibt es nur individuelle Sprechakte, die Sprachmodi benutzen und frühere Muster wiedergeben; dagegen verwandelt sich die Sprache f`r die "Geschichte, die das, was geschieht, systematisiert und untersucht" (*historia rerum, Historie*) in ein einmaliges "sich entwickelndes" Objekt. (Coseriu 1974 [1958]: 41)

Whitehead's concept of symbolic reference is extremely broad, basically regarding symbolism as the integration of the perceptual modes associated with, respectively, the physical and mental pole of the event – causal efficacy and perceptual immediacy (Whitehead 1929: 236). If we perceive a grey stone:

> what is directly perceived, certainly and without shadow of doubt, is a grey region of the presented locus. Any further interpretation, instinctive or by intellectual judgment, must be put down to symbolic reference. (Whitehead 1929: 242).

The principles are the same in symbolism in a more restricted sense: two species of percepta are integrated on the basis of a common ground. Fortescue (2001: 59) associates Whitehead's notion of symbolism with his idea of the repeatability of qualia and patterns, eternal objects:

> forms of definiteness that mediate the symbolic transfer concerned; they ensure that the same symbol type is recognized as having the same or analogous meaning (by social convention), for both sender and receiver.

Thus linguistic structures may be associated with Whiteheadian eternal objects – Fortescue (2001: 59) identifies eternal objects with Peircean iconic diagrams.

In Peircean semiotics, a sign can be an icon, index or symbol. Icons relate to their referents through similarity, indices through contiguity (smoke is a sign or *index* of fire), symbols through convention. Fortescue (2001: 60) casts this trichotomy on Whiteheadian terms: grasping a sign as an icon requires grasping a similarity to a previously experienced pattern by such prehensions as conceptual valuation and imaginative prehension; grasping a sign as an index requires grasping a metonymical relationship which, for Fortescue, corresponds to a Whiteheadian intuitive judgment; finally, the relationship between symbol and referent is basically metaphorical. The regular patterns among symbols allows them to be prehended more or less directly as structures:

> their stepwise origin in indexical-iconic perceptual reality is now "short-circuited" as it were. (Fortescue 2001: 60, see also 64).

In dealing with language, the event or actual occasion corresponds, for Fortescue (2001: 34) in a cognitivist interpretation, to:

> roughly the span of immediate conscious focus, more specifically that of a unitary perception plus interpretive integration (of an utterance) resulting in a unitary reaction

elsewhere (Fortescue 2001: 9):

> one moment in a speaker-hearer's 'life-line' that is actively engaged in negotiating meaning and expression (either to itself or to another): multiple felt motivating factors are selectively integrated into the on-going concrescent process via prehensions of various sorts (according to the relevant subjective aim).

It should be noted here, again., that the linguistic event is not the sign or the utterance in itself, but the speaker-listener experiencing a sign – this subjective experience identifiable with the mental pole of the event: the outer form of the linguistic sign is thus an object in the event as a whole.

As mentioned, one way to comprehend the Whiteheadian "eternal object" in language would be to regard the linguistic patterns and structures as actualized in language usage – actual occasions – as eternal objects, as Fortescue does: eternal objects are interpreted in a cognitive fashion as "concepts and percepts stored in the mind/brain" (Fortescue 2001: 6) and, in specifically linguistic fashion, "forms of definiteness" ensuring that "the same symbol type is recognized as having the same or analogous meaning (by social convention)" (Fortescue 59, also 63). This seems to mesh well with the Whitehead's statement that "any entity whose conceptual recognition does not involve a necessary reference to any definite actual entities of the temporal world is called an 'eternal object'" and that eternal objects are repeatable, whereas actual occasions never are (Whitehead 1929: 30). Fortescue distinguishes rituals, rules and social conventions as "institutional objects" from other eternal objects (Fortescue 2001: 13) and elsewhere regards language itself as a complex eternal object (Fortescue 2001: 206).

The problem is here that where eternal objects are repeatable, they are not subject to change: there can be no novel eternal objects (Whitehead 1929: 30). Now, to a big extent this depends on the rigidly substitutionalist, rather than kaleidoscopic, view of change that Whitehead's atomism is committed to. Events are not subject to change: they become, and perish, and may be succeeded by other events in which different qualia and patterns are actualized:

> 'Change' is the description of eternal objects in the evolving universe of actual things. (Whitehead 1929: 81).

As qualia and patterns/eternal objects exist merely as potentials until actualized in an event, one might envision an indefinitely large pool of possible linguistic patterns, and language change as the substitution of one by the other.

Nonetheless, one might feel that, at first sight, a conception in which structures are subject to *constant* re-creation, change, and dissemination through contact between speakers, as well as the "contradictory" structural nature of diaforms and ambiguous structures which are subject to reanalysis, fits ill with the identification of linguistic pattern and eternal object. For Fortescue, however, this is not a problem, as Fortescue is beholden to a generationalist view of structural change in which

> incremental changes may accrete within a language community throughout the lifetime of any given speaker (e.g. as regards lexicon and the 'markedness' of particular processes and structures), but any change of system – in particular ones involving reinterpretation – must involve the transmission process, and there we are dealing with the abstraction by new learners of patterns (eternal objects) potential in the adult speech behaviour they are exposed to, within the constraints set by their cognitive structure. (Fortescue 2001: 194).

An alternative might start from Everett W. Hall's (1963 [1930]) criticism of Whiteheadian eternal objects: Hall argues that objectified past events, though their "immortality" in the present, may well serve to lend the permanency and continuity to a self-propagating society or nexus of events, which Whitehead would deem the task of eternal objects:

> Whitehead might object that repetition itself implies that the same eternal object is ingredient in several occasions. But it seems to me that the objectification or objective immortality of actual occasions could very well be taken as performing this function; that is, an objectified occasion of a certain degree of relevance can define that common characteristic or similarity of many occasions in virtue of which they are spoken of as being "repetitions" or forming "one line of inheritance". (Hall 1963 [1930]: 106).

The view on linguistic structure which would follow from such a conception would seem to me to be close to the radical view of emergent grammar proposed by Hopper (1987, Bybee and Hopper 2001) – one significantly more radical than the one Fortescue (2001: footnote 1) holds. In this view, lexicon and grammar cannot be kept clearly distinct as the "units of storage" stored in memory are not so much linguistic patterns as "chunks" of actual discourse: words, and frequently occurring groups of words (Hopper and Bybee 2001: 8). Grammar emerges from discourse but has no real existence apart from discourse: rather, it would be an abstraction based on the repetition, and continual reinforcement, of frequently used chunks of language:

> It has been noted before that to a very considerable extent everyday language is built up out of combinations of such prefabricated parts. Language is, in other words, to be viewed as a kind of pastiche, pasted together in an improvised way out of ready-made elements. (Hopper 1987)

The experience of prior usage and exposure to discourse would be the main criterion by which grammaticality is judged (Hopper and Bybee 2001: 19). In this view, the objectified remnants of past linguistic event would be the primary determinants of structure, rather than eternal objects: structure would continually "crystallize" by the repeating and reinforcing regularities inherent in discourse, but never quite gain any independent reality. This notion fits well with the view of language as inherently diachronic and subject to constant re-creation put forth by Coseriu (1974 [1958]: 244-247), and, in terms of language contact, with the idea of code-switching and borrowing as opposing ends of a continuüm by Filppula (1991: 8-9) and Lauttamus (1991: 43).

This view would be, at first sight, more consonant with the view on contact-induced structural change outlined before, as language would be regarded as something constantly "re-created" and thereby *constantly* subject to cognitive processes such as reanalysis and extension. However, one might object that Hopper's view on emergent grammar goes too far in deferring structure, and it is not entirely clear to me to what extent past events, rather than the 'eternal objects' actualized in them, may lend repeatable patterns to actual events. It should also be noted that Fortescue's cognitive interpretation of Whitehead does not fall into the other, Nativist, extreme: indeed, eternal objects are identifiable with concepts and perceptual types stored in memory (Fortescue 2001: 12). Fortescue stresses that eternal objects have no actual existence aside from their ingression in actual occasions (of language use, not restricted, of course, to communication with another person), stating that:

> (...) these eternal objects are **only** effective (and real) for the individual speaking/hearing subject through their ingression in that individual's memory, which is anchored in past experience and its mode of causal efficacy. (Fortescue 2001: 204).

As it is, two events are involved in a communicative situation: one involving the experiencing subject producing linguistic signs, the other, subsequent (not contemporary!) one, comprehending those signs, which find their actualization as an object into the actual event itself. Whitehead (1929: 37) regards the maximalization of "subjective intensity" (of experience) as part of the teleology of events – but this subjective intensity can be directed to the future as well as the present:

> The greater part of morality hinges on the determination of relevance in the future. The relevant future consists of those elements in the anticipated future which are felt with effective intensity by the present subject by reason of the real potentiality for them to be derived from itself. (Whitehead 1929: 37).

This meshes well with the maximalization of communicative clarity and articulatory ease as teleological factors in linguistic change, including contact-induced change. The outcome of the striving for "subjective intensity", for Whitehead, is "balanced complexity" in the form of contrasts between qualia and patterns (Whitehead 1929: 393).

In other words, in a Whiteheadian framework, an event might be seen as the integration of a mass of colours and sounds into a unified experience, which may include a "series of squeaks" which the event regards as significant enough to turn, by the extraction of relevant qualia and patterns through conceptual valuation and reversion, and the elimination of irrelevant sensa through negative prehensions, into something symbolic for a blonde girl asking for a cigarette in a crowded bar. The relevant prehensions crucially include hybrid prehensions, or empathy: successful communication involves putting oneself "in the shoes" of ones interlocutor (Fortescue 2001: 110). The teleology of language use includes the maximalization of "subjective intensity" in the present as well as in the relevant future, the latter including linguistic teleology. The importance of maximalizing contrasts based on some kind of common ground, which Whitehead regards as part and parcel of the striving for "subjective intensity", seems obvious from a linguistic perspective.

1.2.5.3. Contradictions and contrasts

The importance of abductive reasoning in reanalysis and extension – essentially, devising a new linguistic structure to account for ambiguous linguistic input – has been mentioned before. Fortescue (2001: 172), who regards structural change as largely confined to language acquisition, sees abduction as largely a matter of conceptual valuation – abstracting qualia and patterns from a (series of) event(s), and particularly conceptual reversion – the establishment of relevant patterns and contrasts between the structures and qualia thus abstracted, on the basis of diversity and identity: conceptual reversion establishes novelty in the sense that its data are partially identical, partially different from the qualia and patterns that ingress into the event (Whitehead 1929: 36, 352-353). Thus abduction in language creates novelty by synthesizing perceptual data as contrasting on the basis of common ground. Structural change motivated by analogy, such as extension, work in largely the same way: key here is that relations between different parts of a system are regarded as different-yet-similar, contrasting on the basis of some common identical ground.

Previously, reanalysis and extension, and analogous processes in the case of interlingually identified diaforms, have been dealt with in a quasi-Hegelian fashion: a diaform is regarded as contradictory in the sense that it identifies structures of two different languages as somehow the same, and "syntactic borrowing" consists in a negation of the differences between the two structures, just as analogical extension negates the differences between two "identified" paradigms within a single grammar. Abduction or conceptual reversion might also be seen as a thoroughly dialectical process: disparate data contrasting without any common ground of identity are synthesized on the basis of a common ground: quoting Findlay's foreword of Hegel's encyclopedia logic ([1830] 1975: 3):

> Those who expect all thought-advance to be that of the deduction of conclusions from firmly established premisses are quite incapable of dialectical thinking: in dialectic it is the insufficiency of the premises that leads to the more sufficient conclusion.

Hegel's version of the Dialectic, and Whitehead's process philosophy, are incompatible, in the sense that both are founded on incommensurable metaphysical viewpoints: Hegel is an idealist: ideas, which can of course be contradictory, have objective existence in the material world, and the perpetual negation of contradictions in synthesis is a upward progression to the "Absolute Idea". Whitehead's realm of Ideas exists as potentiality alone, and he is firmly committed to the law of noncontradiction (Whitehead 1929: 35-36, Fortescue 2001: 34).

Nonetheless contrasts, based on a ground of common identity, play a key role in Whitehead's teleological view on the universe. As mentioned, Whitehead casts relationships and events in subjective, aesthetic terms, and creativity – the integration and synthesis of the "many" (past objectified occasions) into the "one" (the actual occasion), which by virtue of that synthesis becomes something truly novel (Whitehead 1929: 28) is a primary characteristic of the universe. In that synthesis, the actual occasion strives towards attainment of subjective intensity, depth of experience, by patterned contrasts on the basis of common identity: each part maximally contributing to the whole (Whitehead 1933: 324-325), and "all aesthetic experience is feeling arising out of the realization of contrast under identity" (Whitehead 1929: 396).

As mentioned earlier, Haley (1988: 47-51) regards the similarities uncovered by poetic metaphor as discovered, rather than created, i.e. they are Peircean possibilities actualized and may therefore be compared with Whitehead's eternal objects. Haley (1988: 71-72, 99-100) emphasizes the importance of grounded dissimilarity in metaphor:

> The truth of metaphor is compelling, paradoxically, because it is embodied in a 'lie' – an apparent impossibility which "flags our attention", invites us to consider more carefully, and thus ultimately to sharpen our understanding of possibility. (Haley 1988: 97).

The semantic clash introduced by metaphor functions as a Peircean index in focusing the attention of the reader on the icon introduced into the metaphor (Haley 1988: 14-15). This would seem to root metaphor in analogy:

> Far from crossing the line between reality and unreality, the step from analogy to the level of Peircean "metaphor" per se is a step from analogical isomorphism into an overarching iconic *type*. (Haley 1988: 26).

As mentioned, Fortescue (2001: 60) interprets Whiteheadian symbolism as basically including a metaphorical view on language, and analogy is what perpetuates linguistic structure (Itkonen 2005: 8). Grammaticalization includes the continuous bleaching and fading of metaphors, which end up in linguistic structure as detritus on the bottom of the sea, or, in Langacker's (1977: 106-107) view, languages can be seen as gigantic "expression-compacting" machines, continually attacking the creative input of speakers by phonetic erosion, grammaticalization, etc. and:

> Only the assidious efforts of speakers – who salvage what they can from its output and recycle it by using their creative energies to fashion a steady flow of new expressions to feed back in – keep the whole thing going.

It would thus seem eminently possible to frame linguistic teleology, in structure, expressed particularly as the striving towards one meaning-one form, within a Whiteheadian perspective of maximalizing "subjective intensity". It should be noted that analogy-as-process, actualized for example in extension, obviously does not establish "sameness" from the viewpoint of language as a whole, it established similarity: structurally identical verbal paradigms are nevertheless kept distinct by the phonologically distinct verbs, which of course serves the purpose of language as a whole: to synthesize contrast of meaning with contrast of form – another way of positing the principle of one meaning-one form. As I have argued, whether the structures involved are belonging to different languages, or to the same languages, is irrelevant with regards to the mechanisms concerned.

The same goes for metaphor: with regards to the metaphor "Man is a thinking reed" treated by Haley (1988: 15), "a man is a man" would, obviously, be a tautology, not a metaphor, and neither is one involving promiscuous and irrelevant contrasts: "A man with a nose is a thinking reed with hair on its chest" is not a metaphor, or not a good one, at least. Language, likewise, brings relevant, distinctive contrasts into focus by eliminating irrelevant ones; paradoxically, convergence as the process by which two languages become gradually more similar brings their differences into sharper focus:

> Depth of experience is gained by concentrating emphasis on the systematic structural systems in the environment, and discarding individual variations. Every element of systematic structure is emphasized, every individual aberration is pushed into the background. The variety sought is the variety of structures, and never the variety of individuals (...) In every possible way, the more advanced organisms simplify their experience so as to emphasize their experience so as to emphasize those nexus with some element of tightness of systematic structure. (Whitehead 1929: 452).

1.2.5.4. Advantages of a Whiteheadian framework

The preceding passages may perhaps be regarded as diverting quite far from the issues at hand in this research: namely, the relationship between language contact and (structural) linguistic change. Their relevance, therefore, needs some argumentation.

Throughout this introduction, I have been mostly busy attacking dichotomies of various sorts. The dichotomy between internal and external change being perhaps the most prominent one: I have argued that it makes no sense to distinguish internal and external change in terms of the mechanisms concerned, as they can be seen as essentially identical: the difference between them is that contact-induced change involves structures belonging to a different language – but even the concept of "different language" might involve an abstraction of "language" from linguistic events and prehensions involving linguistic events. Slightly more into the background is a dichotomy between causation and teleology: in the natural sciences, the operation of natural laws cause effects to materialize in the presence of necessary and sufficient conditions – but it is not possible to conceptualize linguistic change in the same way. As a historical process in the strict, Collingwoodian sense – history as the acts of human beings (Collingwood 1993 [1946]: 9) – linguistic history must surely be conceptualized as holistic and multicausal: determining a single cause for a given innovation, to the exclusion of others, is impossible (Aitchison 2001: 134). Physical processes provide human actors with the circumstances they have to deal with – but this is subsumed by the teleological motivation of their actions.

The two concerns are closely related, of course. If humans are seen as the creators of linguistic history, rather than hypostasized languages or linguistic structures, it follows that a history of actions, moreover, teleologically motivated actions, follows from a history of thoughts (Collingwood 1993 [1946]: 117-118, 305-306), as Collingwood (1993 [1946]: 117) characterized Hegel's view:

> Historical transitions are, so to speak, logical transitions set out on a time-scale.

This view is already implicit in regarding logical processes such as abduction, or reanalysis and extension, founded upon perception of analogies, as the prime drivers of internal syntactic change – but it is no big step to include contact-induced structural change within the same category. And if historical transitions are, indeed, ultimately logical transitions, the task of the historian is to re-enact these transitions in his own mind (Collingwood 1993 [1946]: 282).

It is my opinion that the Whiteheadian framework serves very well to accomodate an hermeneutic, and holistic, view on linguistic change. As Fortescue (2001: 55), Whitehead's system enables one to account for both structure and process, *langue* and *parole*, without having to find a place for structure outside of actual usage: structure is only *actualized* in language use, but exists as mere "potentiality" otherwise.

Also, Whitehead's system is irreducably diachronic and teleological: though, to be precise, Whitehead's metaphysic is achronic in that the becoming of an event takes place "outside" of space and time, or rather, includes the gaining of spatiotemporal extension for an event, a linguistic event would always include the comprehension of a linguistic sign as an objectified *past* event. Whitehead's teleology of events gaining determinacy by integrating qualia and patterns as maximalizing contrasts based on a common ground can be related to the way in which linguistic structure serves a teleological aim to serve communicative clarity, to maximize contrast distinctive of meaning, and minimalize irrelevant ones (and thus strive towards the principle of one meaning – one form) all in order *to be understood*, to play a role as an object in a succeeding event. In communication. The teleology of linguistic change proposed by, for example, Anttila (1989) and Esa Itkonen (1978), of poetic metaphor by Haley (1988) and of the universe as a whole by Whitehead all come down to the same thing:

> The teleology of the Universe is directed to the production of beauty (Whitehead 1933: 341)

and

> Beauty is the mutual adaptation of the several factors in an occasion of experience (Whitehead 1933: 324)

this adaptation involving that

> (...) the subjective forms of these prehensions are severally and jointly intervowen in patterned contrast. (Whitehead 1933: 324-325)

Finally,

> All aesthetic experience is feeling arising out of the realization of contrast under identity. (Whitehead 1929: 396)

Whitehead's "aesthetic" view on the universe may appear dense and overly poetical from a cosmological point of view[4] – but extremely familiar from a structuralist/historical linguistic point of view, with its primary emphasis on distinctive features and the teleology of one meaning-one form. The category played by hybrid prehensions, essentially, figuring out what the other person thinks and wants from us, brings in the hermeneutic. The dipolarity of events, with their physical and mental poles, may seem counterintuitive when regarded from a cosmological point of view, but it is extremely appropriate when applied to language. The importance of conceptual prehensions in a linguistic event drive home the point that all history is a history of thought.

Finally, Whitehead's conception of events is holistic: the past is continuously immanent in the present through the prehension of objectified past events by the actual event – the whole universe as we see it is composed of these objectified past events. If the actual event is a thinking human being, with conceptual prehensions at its disposal rather than just the much simpler causal/perceptual events of physical nature, no simple isolation of "cause" and "effect" can come into question. Linguistic change involves teleology and contributing factors – and the task of the historian is to detail these as plausibly and comprehensively as possible.

4 In his book *Unweaving the Rainbow* (Boston 1988), the biologist Richard Dawkins warns against the usage of "bad poetic metaphor" in science, attacking, among others, the religious evolutionary view on the universe of Teilhard de Chardin, which shows some similarity with Whitehead's philosophy. One shudders to think of the reaction he would have to Whitehead - though perhaps, being a philosopher rather than a palaeontologist like Teilhard, perhaps he would get a free pass.

2. THE SOCIOHISTORICAL BACKGROUND OF FINNISH-SWEDISH LANGUAGE CONTACT

2.1. Brief sketch of the history of Finnish

The exact prehistory of Finnish onwards from the Uralic proto-language, thought to have been spoken around 6000-4000 BC in the region of the Volga and Kama rivers in Eastern Russia, is controversial: generally, Uralic is thought to have split up into Proto-Samoyed and Proto-Finno-Ugric, the latter having split into Proto-Ugric and Proto-Finno-Permic, Finno-Permic having split between Proto-Permic, ancestor of the Udmurt and Komi languages, and Finno-Volgaic, from which the two Volgaic languages, Mordvin and Mari, split independently, as well as early Proto-Finnic, the ancestor language of the Finnic and Sámi languages. The modern-day Finnic languages are Finnish, (North) Karelian, Olonets Karelian, Lude, Vepse, Votic, Ingrian, Estonian, Võru, and Livonian, as well as Tornedal Finnish or *Meänkieli* and Finnmark Finnish or *Kven*. The dating of the arrival of speakers of an Uralic language in Finland and the Baltic area in general is highly controversial: generally, it is dated rather early after the break-up of the Uralic proto-language (for discussion, see Carpelan, Parpola and Koskikallio 2002). A new look at the chronology of the break-up of Proto-Uralic, arguing for a significantly more recent proto-Uralic than the dating mentioned above, has been provided by Petri Kallio (2006).

During all of that time, the ancestor languages of Finnish have been in close contact with Indo-European languages. A number of lexical items dating back to proto-Uralic (*vesi* 'water', *suoni* 'vein') and proto-Finno-Ugric (*jyvä* 'grain', *kota* 'tent', *mesi* 'honey') are thought to have been borrowed from Proto-Indo-European (SSA). Recent research by Jorma Koivulehto (1999 [1983]) has led to a late Proto-Indoeuropean or Pre-Germanic/Pre-Baltic etymology for a number of lexical items primarily found in the western Finno-Ugric languages (*kehrä* 'spindle', *puhdas* 'clean', *susi* 'wolf', *tosi* 'true'). This layer of borrowed lexicon would thus bridge the Proto-Indo-European loanword layer and the one of Proto-Germanic loanwords, especially copious in Finnic languages, to a lesser extent in Sámi (see Hofstra 1985). Thus, contacts between Swedish and

Finnish can be regarded as a last step in a long, unbroken continuum of language contacts around the Baltic Sea.

When, in the 12th and 13rd centuries, Finland came under the sway of the Swedish kings, Finnish society was on a tribal stage: the 16th century bishop and writer Agricola mentions the *hämäläiset, karjalaiset* and *suomalaiset* (Häkkinen 1994: 38). A Finnish national consciousness, as well as a coherent literary language, would only emerge much later. The history of the Finnish literary language is generally divided in three parts: Old Literary Finnish, or Old Finnish from the 1540s onward until 1809, when Finland became an autonomous Grand Duchy in the Russian Empire, Old Modern Finnish, the period of reform and expansion of the literary language from 1809 until 1880, and Modern Finnish, from 1880 onward. The history of the literary Finnish language will be sketched in more detail later: suffice to say for now that the focus of this research will be on Old Literary Finnish or, more concise, Old Finnish.

2.2. Direct contact between Finnish and Swedish communities

2.2.1. Swedish-speaking communities in Finland

Currently, Finnish and Swedish have both official status in the Republic of Finland. Officially, municipalities are considered bilingual if the linguistic minority (Finnish or Swedish) makes up for 8 percent of the population, or 3000 in absolute numbers – if the percentage drops below six percent, a municipality is regarded as monolingual. Basing the following on information provided by the Municipal Information Center (*kuntatiedon keskus*, www.kunnat.net, see: *kielisuhde ja ruotsinkieliset kunnittain 31.12.2005*), monolingual Swedish-speaking municipalities are found in the provinces of Österbotten/Pohjanmaa (Ostrobothnia), Åland/Ahvenanmaa – where most municipalities have a Swedish-speaking majority of more than ninety percent, and Varsinais-Suomi/Egentliga Finland. In the latter, the municipalities of Houtskär (87.5% Swedish-speaking), Iniö (71.5%), Korpo (74.1), Västanfjärd (87.9%), and Nagu/Nauvo (74.1%), all in the coastal archipelago, had the largest Swedish-speaking majorities. In Ostrobothnia, the municipalities of Korsnäs (95.1%), Larsmo/Luoto (93.4%), Malax (88.9%), Maxmo (88.3%), Närpes (91.2%), Pedersöre (90.4%), Nykarleby (90.2), Vörå (84.8), and Kronoby (84.5) had the largest Swedish-speaking groups. In Uusimaa/Nyland, large Swedish-speaking groups are found in Ekenäs/Tammisaari (81.7% Swedish-speaking), Liljendal (76.6%) and Pernå (60.0%). Bilingual communities with a Finnish-speaking majority are found in largely the same areas, including the cities of Helsinki (6.2% Swedish-speaking), Espoo (8.6% Swedish-speaking), Åbo/Turku (5.2% Swedish-speaking), and Vaasa (25% Swedish-speaking). In addition, the municipality of Pyttis/Pyhtää in Kymenlaakso province, bordering on Nyland, has a Swedish-speaking minority of 10.5%.

All in all, there were 289.695 primary speakers of Swedish in Finland in 2005, or 5.5%. Åland is considered to have been colonized by speakers of Swedish in the 6th century (Jutikkala and Pirinen 1973: 19, Juttikala 1987: 356), whereas the coastal regions of Ostrobothnia, Nyland and Varsinais-Suomi are generally considered to have been colonized by speakers of Swedish in the twelfth century (Wallén 1932: 3, Juttikala 1987: 357). The percentage of Swedish speakers in Finland has decreased steadily since 1880, at which point they made up 14.3% of the population (Fougstedt 1984: 19-20) – the percentage in earlier centuries is extremely uncertain, but may have been roughly in the same ballpark (Juttikala 1987: 369). The history of the Swedish-speaking areas from the early 17th century until the Industrial Revolution has been depicted in detail by Wallén (1932). By and large, the linguistic border between Finnish and Swedish seems not to have shifted that much during that period. Shifts mentioned by Wallén are, first, the Fennicization of Kymenlaakso province, where currently only Pyttis has a significant Swedish-speaking majority, and which according to Wallén probably started well before 1600 (Wallén 1932: 5, 11, 70, 80-81, Juttikala 1987: 370). As it is, some municipalities in Kymenlaakso province have tiny Swedish-speaking minorities nowadays (Kotka 1.1%, for instance). Another shift is the Fennicization of the coastal municipalities in Satakunta province (Juttikala 1987: 370), mainly Merikarvia (Sastmola) and Ahlainen (Vittisbofjärd) – a Swedish-speaking community continued to exist here until the 18th century (Wallén 1932: 74). In the northern region of Ostrobothnia, a bilingual area emerged in the 17th century around the municipalities of Veteli and Evijärvi through colonization of former marshland from two sides: in what was part of the expansion westwards and northwards from Savo, supported by the Swedish crown (Tarkiainen 1990: 138-140, Bladh and Wedin 2005: 53-55), speakers of Savo dialects took to the area (called the *savolaiskiila* or "Savonic wedge" in Finnish dialectological literature) from the east, but a smaller number of Swedish-speakers from the west colonized the area as well (Wallén 1932: 57). In the 18th century, the area became largely Finnish-speaking (Wallén 1932: 76).

A counterposed development took place in central and western Nyland (Juttikala 1987: 370), with the area of Esbo gradually becoming Swedish-speaking in the 18th century (Wallén 1932: 14-15), as well as the area around Lojo/Lohja (Wallén 1932: 91, 104-105) and Sjundeå/Siuntio (Wallén 1932: 102) in the 18th and 19th centuries, with Vihti to the north of these municipalities becoming a bilingual zone (Wallén 1932: 104-105). On the northeastern borders of Nyland, Swedish-speaking minorities came into existence in Orimattila, Anjala and Elimäki at the end of the 18th century (Wallén 1932: 167).

Varsinais-Suomi has mostly seen an expansion of the Finnish-speaking population during the time treated in Wallén (1932: 72-74, 108-110), with Perniö and Sauvo becoming largely Finnish-speaking in the 17th century (Wallén 1932: 25, 29), and Kakskerta and Kuusisto in the 19th century (Wallén 1932: 100-101), as causes for the gradual Fennicization of coastal Varsinais-Suomi Wallén mentions the isolation of the largely island-based Swedish-speaking communities as well as the good transport connections from the inner mainland to the southwestern coast (Wallén 1932: 108-110). The counterposed development in western and northern Nyland was, according to Wallén (1932: 128-129), stimulated by low land value and low local population density, but also by a striving among speakers of Finnish to send their children to a Swedish-speaking school.

The development in the subsequent period, from the beginning of the Industrial revolution in Finland in the later 19th century until 1950, has been treated by Klövekorn (1960). The main distinctive feature of this period has been a massive influx of Finnish-speakers in the cities, however, this development differed from city to city. Helsinki, set within the Swedish-speaking coastal area of Nyland, became the capital of the Autonomous Grand Duchy after the destruction of Turku by fire in 1827 – until 1870, though, the city remained largely Swedish-speaking (69%), with a rapid expansion of the Finnish-speaking community leading to a Finnish-speaking majority of 54% in 1900 (Klövekorn 1960: 74). The industrial city of Jakobstad (Pietarsaari) in Ostrobothnia saw, after the completion of the nearby Seinäjoki-Oulu railway, a rapid expansion of population, leading the erstwhile almost exclusively Swedish-speaking city to become bilingual – in 2005, 56.1% of its inhabitants spoke Swedish as a first language. There is a clear difference between the municipality of Jakobstad and the surrounding, rural municipalities of Larsmo, Pedersöre and Nykarleby, all of which have a majority of Swedish-speakers of more than eighty percent. A similar influx of speakers of Finnish together with industrialization has occurred in Borgå/Porvoo (Klövekorn 1960: 91, 232-233), Karleby/Kokkola (Klövekorn 1960: 51, 252-256), Vaasa (Klövekorn 1960: 256-257), Kristinestad and Kaskö (Klövekorn 1960: 244-247). There are, however, exceptions as well: the old city of Nykarleby has, due to a large fire in 1858 and competition with neighbouring Jakobstad, remained on the sidelines of the industrial revolution, and remained largely Swedish-speaking (Klövekorn 1960: 247-248).

In tandem with industrialization, the rise of a transport sector (railway lines, etc.) and a services sector led to a growth of the Finnish-speaking community particularly in Nyland – less so in Ostrobothnia, the Swedish-speaking communities of which are hardly connected by railway (Klövekorn 1960: 188-192, also Fougstedt 1984: 25). This development was amplified by the comparatively large farms in Nyland, which, too, caused a need for (Finnish-speaking) labour (Klövekorn 1960: 210-211). Hence also rural communities in Nyland, like Sjundeå/Siuntio, Kyrkslätt/Kirkkonummi and Vihti saw an expansion of the Finnish-speaking community (Klövekorn 1960: 70-71). This is reflected in the language border today as well: whereas Ostrobothnia sports a broad line of almost exclusively Swedish-speaking rural communities, the Swedish-speaking part of Nyland is largely bilingual with significant Finnish-speaking minorities. Thus, Ostrobothnia has a relatively sharp language border, with the exception of the northern Veteli-Evijärvi area, whereas that in Nyland is far more diffuse (Klövekorn 1960:50). Wallén (1932: 270-273) mentions that mixed marriages were comparatively rare in Ostrobothnia, where the Swedish-speaking part is also seperated from the Finnish-speaking part by large wilderness areas.

This situation seems to be reflected in the extent to which the regional dialects of Swedish in Finland have been influenced by Finnish: Thors (1981: 86) mentions that the number of Finnish loanwords is lowest in exclusively Swedish-speaking Åland, somewhat larger in Ostrobothnia and Varsinais-Suomi, larger in the Swedish-speaking areas north of Ostrobothnia proper in Mellersta Österbotten/Keski-Pohjanmaa, larger still in western Nyland and largest in eastern Nyland. Thus, Swedish seems to have received most Finnish loanwords in those areas where the language border was most diffuse: the northern parts of Swedish-speaking Ostrobothnia, i.e. the Veteli/Evijärvi area as well as Nyland.

Terho Itkonen (1964a, 1964b: 229-230) has explained the total loss of final **-k* in some dialectal varieties of Finnish by taking recourse to the effects of Finnish/Swedish bilingualism. The core areas of this phenomenon seem to be the area of Merikarvia and Ahlainen north of Pori (T. Itkonen 1964a: 146), an originally Swedish-speaking area very gradually Fennicized until the 19th century, the far northern areas of Finnmark/Ruija and Västerbotten/Länsipohja in Norway and northern Sweden (T. Itkonen 1964a: 151), Värmland on the Norwegian/Swedish border, inhabited by Finnish émigres from the 17th until the 20th century (T. Itkonen 1964a: 154), the southeastern Häme dialects (T. Itkonen 1964a: 175) as well as the Karelian Isthmus and Ingria, in which case Terho Itkonen assumes Russian rather than Swedish influence (T. Itkonen 1964a: 160. 173). Lea Laitinen (1992: 58) has remarked that a number of possibly contact-induced phenomena regarding the Finnish necessitive modal verb occur in roughly the same areas, namely agreement of verb and subject in person and number in the southern and southeastern Häme dialects as well as in Finnmark, Tornedal and Värmland in Norway and Sweden (Laitinen 1992: 42-43), and the use of a subject marked in the nominative without agreement in person and number, found in western Nyland and eastern Varsinais-Suomi, Värmland as well as the “Savonic wedge” (Laitinen 1992: 48). The same can be said for a variety of phenomena concerning negation (Laitinen 1992: 58), first of all lack of agreement between subject and negative auxiliary, found in Värmland, the Savonic wedge area and surroundings, however, also in eastern Savo dialects and southeastern dialects in case of which Swedish contacts cannot be easily invoked as an explanation (Savijärvi 1977: 183), second, agreement between the subject and the lexical verb of the negative construction in number (*he ei luevvat*), which can be found in the southern and southeastern Häme dialects (Savijärvi 1977: 183). Interesting in this regard is a statement by an inhabitant of Sjundeå in 1847, cited by Wallén (1932: 102):

> Almost all the Finns that one can find here, in the municipality of Sjundeå, speak Swedish too. A consequence of this is that the Finnish dialect which you can hear around here is mixed with Swedish for almost one fourth of it. (translation by me – MdS).

Finally, in his essay on Swedish phonological influence on Finnish dialects, Ojansuu (1906) mentions the easternmost dialects of Varsinais-Suomi as a particular core area of phonological contact-induced change. Based on all this, one might expect contact-induced phenomena in those Finnish dialects spoken near a particularly diffuse language border with Swedish with lots of bilingualism: in Finland, particularly the southern and southeastern Häme dialects of Nyland and Kymenlaakso, the Finnish dialects spoken near the northern edges of the Swedish area of Ostrobothnia, namely, the "Savonic wedge" of Veteli and Evijärvi and surrounding areas, as well as the dialects of Varsinais-Suomi, perhaps particularly the southern and eastern ones near the Swedish-speaking communities of Pargas/Parainen, Kimito/Kemiö and Västanfjärd. As for the Savonic wedge area of Evijärvi, Veteli and surroundings, Ojansuu (1906: 24) mentions how fieldwork research by Aspelin uncovered instances of "language mixing", i.e. pervasive code-mixing in Kaustinen, north of Veteli.

2.2.2. Finnish-speaking communities in Sweden

As mentioned, the Finnic varieties currently spoken in Sweden are likely to have a key importance in the research of contact-induced structural change in Finland. The Finnish inhabitation of the Tornedal area, the western part of which remained under the Swedish crown after 1809, has its roots in the medieval expansion of the *birkarla* (*pirkkalaiset*) from the Häme area to the arctic north, however, influx from speakers of eastern Finnish and Karelian dialects later on led to the emergence of some significant eastern dialectal features on an otherwise western basis (Tarkiainen 1993: 277, Andersson and Kangassalo 2003: 101). The number of Finnish speakers in the Tornedal region was about 30.000-40.000 during the last relevant census in 1930 – the current number is unknown (Wande 1996: 234-235). Aside from the Tornedal region proper and the adjacent community of Vittanki, varieties of Finnish are also spoken more eastward in the areas of Jellivaara and Nattavaara. The dialect of the latter two areas seems to differ in some aspects from that of the Tornedal region. Swedish influence on Tornedal Finnish or *Meänkieli* is particularly apparent in the lexicon: Swedish loanwords are very numerous. Aside from this, however, Wande (1982: 54, 60, 62) lists some possibly contact-induced morphosyntactic features of Meänkieli, namely, the use of a marked accusative case as well as agreement in person and number in necessitive constructions, a markedly higher frequency of postpositions and an expansion of the use of the marked accusative. Additionally, Virtaranta (1982: 305) mentions lack of use of possessive suffixes as well as lack of agreement of the negative verb in the dialect of Kurravaara in the Tornedal region.

Aside from this, speakers of Finnish have lived in central Sweden for a very long time – in late medieval times, Finnish farmers lived in the Mälardalen region and eastern Götaland (De Geer 1985: 47), and the presence of Finns in Stockholm is also thought to have its root far back in the middle ages (Tarkiainen 1990: 24). Finnish inhabitation in central Sweden however, has generally not been continuous, but sustained by successive waves of emigration from Finland. In the late 16th century, conscious Swedish policy had speakers of particularly Savo dialects emigrating to the wilderness areas of Södermanland, Närke and Värmland (De Geer 1985: 49, Tarkiainen 1990: 133, Andersson and Kangassalo 2003: 41). In the Swedish/Norwegian border region of Värmland, Savo dialects have survived until the 20th century. Swedish influence on the Savo dialect of Värmland is apparent in loanwords as well as in the voicing of stops (Andersson and Kangassalo 2003: 56-57) in addition to the morphosyntactic features mentioned above. Fieldwork by Julius Mägiste in the late 1940s showed great anomalies in the case-marking of the object as well as in verb congruence (Andersson and Kangassalo 2003: 60): Värmland Finnish was already rapidly dying by that time, and such phenomena may be due to the common structural features of language death as well as contact-induced change.

In the 1960s and 1970s, a great wave of emigration from Finland to Sweden has led to, currently, about 200.000-300.000 speakers of Finnish living in Sweden (Andersson and Kangassalo 2003: 65). The dialectal background of this group is heterogenous, and it is spread out all over Sweden, with a certain concentration, nevertheless, in the western Mälardalen region as well as the greater Stockholm area. Swedish influence has, in addition to loanwords, led to certain morphosyntactic features particularly in the speech of second- and third-generation immigrants, Andersson and Kangassalo (2003: 86-87) mention, for example, a heightening of the frequency of postpositions, anomalies in the case-marking of the object and an incipient use of articles.

2.2.3. Swedish as a language of the Finnish élite

In the eleventh century, missionary work from Sweden led to a gradual christianization of the, mainly coastal and southwestern, Finnish populace, with as its apex the "crusade" of St. Hendrik which is thought to have taken place around 1157, in as far as the event is actually historical (Jutikkala and Pirinen 1973: 24-26). In 1171 or 1172 a Papal bull encouraged the Swedes to conquer and christianize Finland, which led to southwestern Finland gradually becoming a Swedish bridgehead in Finland – though hampered by competition with the Danes, who pushed to Nyland from their strongholds in Estonia, and by an uprising of the Häme tribes against the rather violent means of conversion employed by bishop Thomas, Swedish power in Varsinais-Suomi, Häme, Nyland and Ostrobothnia, in the latter two cases fortified by Swedish colonization, was consolidated by the mid-13rd century, after a "crusade" by Birger Jarl against Häme (Jutikkala and Pirinen 1973: 28-35).

In Karelia, the Swedes had to compete with the Russians of Novgorod, who had conversion and conquest designs of their own (Jutikkala and Pirinen 1973: 23), and at the end of the thirteenth century Sweden tried to assert control over Karelia by building the city of Viborg on the Karelian Isthmus – outside of Viborg and its immediate surroundings, however, the Swedes gained little of a foothold in Karelia, and the Pähkinäsaari peace treaty, which soon ensued, drew the border of Swedish power from Viborg in the southeast to the Botnic Gulf in the northwest (Jutikkala and Pirinen 1973: 37-39).

While originally Swedish power in Finland was concentrated in the hands of the clergy, around 1250 it shifted to the Swedish crown, with the concomitant emergence of a medieval class society. The nobility was drawn from both Finnish and Swedish stock, with some Danish and German elements as well. The clergy was largely of Finnish origin. (Jutikkala and Pirinen 1973: 40-43). In 1362, the young king Haakon granted Finland the same status and rights (among others, to participate in the election of a King) as other provinces of Sweden (Carlsson 1985: 8, Jutikkala and Pirinen 1973: 50), this was later enshrined in King Christopher's Land Law of 1442 (Jutikkala and Pirinen 1973: 58). Thereby, Finland was not a Swedish colony, but a Swedish province like all others (Carlsson 1985: 7-9).

The period from late medieval times to the 16th century was a good one for the Finnish language. The catholic Church made ample use of the popular tongue – Finnish in Finnish-speaking areas, Swedish in Swedish-speaking areas – in sermons and clerical education, and it is not unthinkable that, to some extent, Finnish was written down even in medieval times, even if nothing has remained of that today (Jutikkala and Pirinen 1973: 68-69, Häkkinen 1994: 12, Huovinen 1985: 68, Nikkilä 1985: 35). The same may well have been the case with legal proceedings (Nikkilä 1985: 37). The two main cities, Åbo/Turku in the southwest and Viborg in the southeast, had large German-speaking minorities or even majorities, and became largely Finnish- and Swedish-speaking only in the course of the 15th century (Jutikkala and Pirinen 1973: 70). Since Finnish (and Swedish) were used to a large extent by the catholic Church, the reformation and adoption of the Lutheran faith executed by King Gustav Vasa in the 1520s (Jutikkala and Pirinen 1973: 76-78) did not lead to radical changes in that respect, however, it did lead to attempts at translation of the Bible and religious literature to Finnish in the 1540s by Bishop Mikael Agricola. This work was of course stimulated greatly by the development of book printing: a royal printing press was founded in Stockholm in 1520, and a translation of the Bible in Swedish completed in 1541 (the New Testament had appeared in 1526) (Häkkinen 1994: 20-22). The final translation of the Bible in Finnish was completed in 1642.

In the beginning of the 17th century, a gradual strengthening of the position of the Swedish language in Finland began. In 1596 and 1597, the Swedish duke Carl, who had his designs on the throne and would, indeed, later become King Carl IX, incited a peasant rebellion against the Finnish authorities, which were supportive of Carl's contender Sigismund. Even if this rebellion, the *nuijasota* or club-war, was suppressed, an invasion in 1599 by Carl himself led to a purge of the local Finnish nobility, which was partially replaced by more reliable noblemen from Sweden – even if many noblemen were later rehabilitated, the nobility of Finland was brought under stronger Swedish political control (Jutikkala and Pirinen 1973: 99). In the mid-17th century, reforms in government structure carried out by Gustav II Adolph led to a strengthening of the position of Swedish, and an influx of Swedish-speaking government personnel to Finland – also, in 1649, Swedish began to be used as a secondary language in education, after Latin, whereas before, Finnish was widely used as such (Jutikkala and Pirinen 1973: 114, Nikkilä 1985: 74). These developments were accompanied by the emergence of a Swedish nationalism, and conscious, though not very radical, attempts at swedishizing Finland. Finally, Sweden as a great power was crushed after the great Northern War in the early 18th century, during which Finland was occupied by Russia from 1713 to 1720 – during this period, most of the local élite and bureaucracy went into exile, and came back swedishized, and, halfway through the 18th century, the government bureaucracy in Finland was almost exclusively Swedish-speaking (Jutikkala and Pirinen 1973: 160-161).

This development did not cease when Finland finally became a Grand Duchy within the Russian empire in 1809, after which Swedish remained the language of Finland's political economy for a very long time. Nevertheless, a Finnish national movement emerged, and a group mainly within the Swedish-speaking élite began to advocate adopting the Finnish language, the so-called fennomanes. This was accompanied by the publication of the Finnish national epic *Kalevala* by Elias Lönnrot, and the founding of the *Suomalaisen Kirjallisuuden Seura* (Society for Finnish Literature) in 1831. The first Finnish-language school was founded in 1858, however, the development of Finnish-language education was rather slow, with there being as much pupils in Finnish-language schools as in Swedish ones only in 1899 (Jutikkala and Pirinen 1973: 131, 247). Within the local government and the court, Swedish and Finnish were declared equal in 1863, and Finland remains bilingual (or rather, with the official status of Sámi in the north, trilingual) until this day (Jutikkala and Pirinen 1973: 238-239), but the decisive breakthrough in favour of Finnish would come with industrialization and the Fennicization of the main cities after 1900.

During the time in which Swedish was on the ascendancy in Finland, command of Swedish became a necessary precondition for entering the higher strata of society – hence Wallén (1932: 129) mentions how speakers of Finnish strove for their children to enter Swedish-language schools. Similarly, mixed marriages in the cities seemed to have mainly involved Finnish-speaking women and Swedish-speaking men, since the woman would be taken up in the social group of the man (Klövekorn 1960: 153). This would mean that until the great turnaround in the early 20th century, there likely was a continuous, piecemeal language shift from Finnish to Swedish among those people climbing up on the social ladder, with concomitant bilingualism and possibly contact-induced change in both directions.

2.3. The history of Literary Finnish

2.3.1. Old Finnish: birth and consolidation

The oldest surviving texts in Finnish all date from the 1540s: the Codex of Westh, which consists of liturgical fragments possibly of different origin, the liturgical Uppsala Codex B28, the Uppsala Liturgical Fragment, a version of the Paternoster included in the work *Cosmographia* by the German Sebastian Münster (1544), and the *Abckiria* (1543) and *Rucouskiria* (1544) by Mikael Agricola (?1510-1557), Bishop of Åbo/Turku. Interestingly, some of these older fragments, for example the Uppsala Liturgical Fragment and the Paternoster in *Cosmographia* – which may date back to Catholic times – have some strong East Finnish dialectal features (nonetheless, Penttilä, cited in Nikkilä 1985: 59, has suggested that the Uppsala Liturgical Fragment is largely West Finnish, with some East Finnish surface features likely introduced by copyists). This could well reflect the status of Viborg as Finland's second city, and an important centre of religious education. This might be particularly the case with the East Finnish features found in Agricola's work, as Agricola, after all, studied in Viborg (Häkkinen 1994: 439-441).

Agricola's oeuvre consisted, besides the two works mentioned above, of, among others, a translation of the New Testament (*Se Wsi Testamenti*, 1548). A striking feature of Agricola's work is its linguistic diversity, reflecting his own probable dialectal background (he was born in the municipality of Pernå/Pernaja in eastern Nyland) as well as his time in Viborg and the status of the Southwestern dialects spoken in Turku, the main centre of the country at that time (Häkkinen 1994: 440-441). Furthermore, it is quite possible that parts of his translations were done by colleagues and assistants (Häkkinen 1994: 441). Some striking features of Agricola's work have been regarded as an indication of Swedish being his mother tongue or at least his primary tongue, notably by Heikki Ojansuu (1909: 164: Ojansuu later changed his mind on this question), in this regard, Ojansuu mentions, for example, a frequent use of postpositions instead of cases (Ojansuu 1909: 164) and various anomalies concerning the negative verb, including lack of agreement but also agreement of the lexical verb (Ojansuu 1909: 167). It should be noted that similar quite possibly contact-induced features do occur in Finnish dialects, and indeed, the current consensus, argued for forcefully by Rapola (1969: 33-35) is that Agricola was a native speaker of Finnish. In his overview of the controversy, Ikola (1988: 34-35) mentions that Pernaja/Pernå was, probably, mainly Swedish-speaking at the time of Agricola's birth, nonetheless, Ikola argues that a number of putative sveticisms in Agricola's works may be dialectal features of Finnish (Ikola 1988: 49-50) and concludes that, most likely, Agricola was a native bilingual (Ikola 1988: 63).

Religious literature began to expand at the end of the 16th and during the 17th century, with, for example, Jaakko Finno's *Virsikirja* (1583), a collection of religious songs. A landmark was the publication of a Bible translation in 1642, on which two different committees had been working during the previous forty years. The translators of the Bible strove for a more consistent style than Agricola's – this also meant a consolidation of the Southwest Finnish dialectal base of the emergent literary language, at the cost of the East Finnish features found here and there in Agricola's work and earlier fragments, and a purging of the more obvious sveticisms in Agricola's work (Rapola 1969: 43, Häkkinen 1994: 445). Also strongly Southwest Finnish are the texts of Jaakko Finno; Hemminki Maskulainen, who published a collection of religious songs in 1605 and a translation of the medieval *Piae Cantiones*, a collection of religious songs and school songs, in

1616; and Eerik Sorolainen, who, in addition to his work on the Bible translation committee, published two collections of sermons in 1621 and 1625. In 18th century religious literature, however, other dialects were represented as well, notably in the sermons published by Johan Wegelius in 1747 and 1749 – Wegelius worked in Oulu and Tornio – and the religious songs published by the Ostrobothnian priest Abraham Achrenius in 1769, and by his son Antti in 1790.

Not all of the religious literature of the Old Finnish period is translated literature – for example, the religious songs of father and son Achrenius are original. However, the core and main reference point of the religious literature published during that period is the Bible, a translated document. The legal literature published in the Old Finnish period is mostly translated as well – the translations of King Christopher's Land Law by Martti around 1580, Ljungo Tuomaanpoika in 1601, Abraham Kollanius in 1648, the translations of Magnus Erikssons City Law by Tuomaanpoika in 1609 and Kollanius in 1648, the translation of Gustav II Adolph's military law by Hartikka Speitz in 1642, the clerical law translated by Henrik Florinus in 1688 and finally the reformed Swedish law translated by Samuel Forseen in 1759. Wordly, non-translated literature only emerged in the latter part of the 18th century, with, for example, Kristfrid Ganander's and Juhana Frosterus's work as well as the periodical *Suomenkieliset Tieto-Sanomat* published in 1775 and 1776 by Antti Lizelius. As Häkkinen (1994: 472) points out, in case of religious texts such as the Bible, translators often sought as literal a translation as possible. The same goes, mutatis mutandis, for legal literature (Pajula 1955: 277). This quite easily leads to the proliferation of constructions which may have little or no equivalent in spoken language, and, because of the eminent role of the Bible as the cornerstone of the Old Finnish literary language, we might expect, for example, significant stylistic influence of Biblical language on original religious literature as well. Thus, contact-induced morphosyntactic constructions which have arisen through striving for as isomorphic a translation equivalent as possible in the conscious process of translation can be expected to live a life of their own – as is the case, for example, with the ablative- or elative-marked agent appearing in combination with the Finnish passive until well into the 19th century in written language (Häkkinen 1994: 360). This construction is extremely rare in spoken Finnish dialects (Itkonen-Kaila 1992: 158) though a somewhat similar construction has arisen in the easternmost dialects of Finnish as a result of direct contacts with Karelian and, indirectly, Russian (Nau 1995: 150-151). However, from Agricola's texts onwards, it has been common in literary language, having arisen as an isomorphic translation equivalent of foreign patterns – originally, Swedish model patterns have been thought to have played a main role here (Petander 1893: 21, however, Itkonen-Kaila (1992: 148) stresses the role that Latin and German model patterns may have played, particularly in Agricola's texts).

However, making inferences about the occurrence or non-occurrence of a given pattern in the spoken Finnish of the 17th and 18th century on the basis of dialectal material collected only in the 19th and 20th centuries is an extremely hedgy matter. As Häkkinen (1994: 441-442) points out, the cities where the Old Finnish literary language was created – mainly, Turku and Viborg – had, more likely than not, an extremely heterogenous dialectal basis, and, additionally, they were foci of language contacts between Finnish, Swedish and German – as medieval Finnish towns had a significant Low German component – as well, whereas early dialectal research in the 19th century focused, in particular, on rural dialects thought to have been relatively untouched by the results of language contact, which were thought to be pernicious.

Also, in addition to direct contacts between Swedish and Finnish, the influence of particularly religious and Biblical language on the spoken Finnish in the 17th and 18th century should not be underestimated. The pervasiveness of contact-induced change of this kind has been argued for particularly by Detlev Fehling (1979: 356):

> I do not subscribe to the superficially plausible argument that the influence of the written word must have been slight in communities where writing was a rare practice. For what was lacking in quantity may easily have been compensated by intensity. I think that even where only a single written document existed, parts of which every member of the community knew by heart – a Bible translation, a law code, or an epic poem of national significance – its influence need not have been much less powerful than that of the daily flood of our newspapers. In two or three generations any part of its syntax could become familiar enough to penetrate daily speech.

Influence of Biblical language has been taken into account in Finnish dialectal research (Nuolijärvi 1988: 124-128), to name some examples, the future construction *tahdon tehdä* is primarily restricted to literary language, but occurs, albeit rarely, in spoken language as well – according to Ikola (1949: 225) due to the influence exerted by religious language. The same has been argued for for part of the sporadic occurrences of the ablative/elative-marked agent with a passive in Finnish dialects by Itkonen-Kaila (1992: 158).

2.3.2. Old Modern Finnish: Reform

The 19th century was, as mentioned, a period of great expansion for the Finnish language in various domains. From the mid-century onwards, Finnish became a language used in schools, and the equal status of Finnish and Swedish as languages of courts and government was enshrined as law in 1863. Concomitantly, the amount of literature published on the Finnish language itself grew rapidly: this included a series of Finnish grammars (by Reinhold von Becker in 1824, by Gustav Renvall in 1840, Gustav Eurén in 1846, and two monographs on Finnish syntax, the first by Jahnsson in 1871 and the latter, strongly based on Jahnsson's, by Setälä in 1880) and dictionaries, like Elias Lönnrot's Finnish-Swedish dictionary (1866-1880).

At the background of these developments was the emergence of a Finnish national movement, stimulated greatly by the publication of the Finnish national epic *Kalevala* in 1835, and in an extended version, 1849 by Elias Lönnrot. The folk poetry on which the *Kalevala* was based lived on, at that time, in the easternmost reaches of the Finnish language area, and aside from Lönnrot, others like Carl Axel Gottlund noted down and published folk poetry which they encountered during their fieldwork. This led to an increased interest in the East Finnish dialects, whereas the basis of the literary language until that time had been the Southwestern dialects, particularly those around Turku. Turku itself lost its status as the capital of Finland after a disastrous fire in 1827, after which the capital was relocated to Helsinki. Stimulated, then, by the national/romantic movement, the focus on East Finnish dialects brought about by the publication of folk poetry (Carl Axel Gottlund, famously or rather infamously, argued that anyone should write as he speaks, which, in his case, was a rather idiosyncratic version of the Savo dialect (Häkkinen 1994: 447)) and the emergence of linguistics as a scholarly discipline – which included prescriptive as well as descriptive linguistics – led to a period of conscious reform of the Finnish literary language, in which East Finnish features were introduced and constructions regarded as "Swedish" eschewed. Another spirited advocate of East Finnish forms was Reinhold von Becker, who introduced many East Finnish constructions in the *Turun Wiikko-Sanomat*, a paper he published from 1820-1831 (Häkkinen 1994: 447). The result of this reconstruction of the Finnish literary language would eventually be a hybrid language, with both West and East Finnish elements.

Aside from ortographic reforms, the 19th century saw the end of such contact-induced morphosyntactic patterns as, for example, the use of inverted word order in subordinate clauses (Häkkinen 1994: 473), the elative/ablative agent in combination with the Finnish passive (Häkkinen 1994: 360-361) and the use of the demonstrative pronoun *se* and the numeral *yksi* as definite and indefinite articles (Häkkinen 1994: 357). An indication of the attitude towards constructions thought to be foreign in origin is a quote from Renvall (cited in Cannelin 1926: 79, my translation):

> In some cities and in many places in the countryside as well language is such mumbo-jumbo, that it is not Finnish, neither Swedish, but an anarchic mixture of both which clearly proves how ugly a language can become, if it is unthinkingly composed of different substances, either two different languages or two different dialects. Try, for example, the company of Finnish

> women in Turku! What a barbaric pig's latin for a language: for example *onk syster ollu visitin pääl, tul helseman minun päällen, se on farlit seilata tormiss yli haavin* and so on.

It is not surprising that this purist bent of prescriptive linguistics was reflected profoundly in descriptive linguistics as well. Hence Rapola (1930: 81) argues that the value of Finnish literature which had appeared before the *Kalevala* was generally underestimated, since its linguistic base was regarded as a hideous West Finnish dialect, riddled with sveticisms. An example of this attitude is Ojansuu's (1909: 159, translation by me) opinion, that:

> Only during the great reform of the 19th century the Finnish language was liberated from those foreign tumours, which had penetrated it during the previous centuries and which were, for a great part, quite integrated in the literary language, and even borrowed into those dialects, which had been originally quite free from the Swedish "oxidation"

Partially, this has led to a tendency within dialectal research as well as research of Old Finnish to regard constructions as borrowed from Swedish too enthusiastically, without paying attention to the role Latin, Greek and German source languages played, in, for example, Agricola's work. Recent research has sometimes led to a reconsideration of these explanations.

For instance, the elative/ablative agent was regarded by Petander (1893: 21) in case of Sorolainen's writings, and Saarimaa (1934: 294) in case of Aleksis Kivi's writing as a Swedish calque, whereas Itkonen-Kaila (1992) has stressed the possible roles of German and Latin source patterns as well. Similarly, the tendency of earlier prescriptive grammar to eschew verb-fronting of any kind as a result of calqueing Swedish inversion has been criticized by Lindén (1963). Also, the scarcity of research literature dealing with Swedish influence on Finnish itself may, as Häkkinen (2003: 45) notes, another consequence of the strong prescriptive bent of early research.

2.3.3. Conclusion

Ascertaining the dialectal spread of a given, putatively contact-induced, innovation in Finnish varieties is an important diagnostic tool in uncovering its origin: some dialects, notably those spoken in Sweden and Norway, as well as the northern Ostrobothnian dialects, the eastern dialects of Varsinais-Suomi and the southern and southeastern dialects of Nyland are known to be quite prone to Swedish contact influence. However, this is by no means a straightforward issue.

First of all, the particular historical circumstances in which the Finnish literary language emerged – the importance of translated literature in Old

Finnish, and particularly the eminent position of the Bible translation – mean that contact-induced constructions may indeed have perpetuated themselves throughout the older history of written Finnish without having any equivalent in spoken language. Also, we know very little of the spoken language of the 17th and 18th century Finnish cities – that which has lain, mostly, at the basis of the written language. Dialectal research, commencing in the 19th century, has focused mainly on rural dialects, thought to present a picture of pure, untouched Finnish, even if there are, partly anecdotical, reports of heavy language-mixing in various areas. It is therefore extremely risky to extrapolate on the basis of the picture of Finnish dialectal variation of the 19th and early 20th century towards earlier times. Additionally, the occurrence of a given construction in spoken language does not necessarily indicate direct contacts between Finnish and Swedish, but may have arisen due to influence of written, particularly religious language, as has, in a few cases, been argued in the research literature. One would imagine such influence to be strongest in the centres of education and alphabetism, though it should not be underestimated elsewhere. At the same time, the Finnish cities of the 17th and 18th century were also the places in which direct contacts between Finnish, Swedish, and particularly earlier also Low German can be expected to have been the most intense.

Hence, it is important to treat the dialectal spread of given features critically: the presence of a given form in a dialect does not necessarily mean its equivalent in literary language has been derived from it: it may have been the other way around, or, quite possibly, the two may have arisen independently, one through direct contacts between speakers, the other through conscious striving after an isomorphic translation. The strongly prescriptivist research literature of the 19th and early 20th centuries, an exponent of the purist period of language reform, should be dealt with cautiously – however, it provides invaluable source material on a subject on which, otherwise, scarce material is available.

3. CORPUS AND RESEARCH OBJECT

3.1. The corpus

In this research, I will focus primarily on legal translations from the Old Finnish period. The reason is, first of all, that a great deal of research has been done on religious texts, for example, Agricola's translations (Ojansuu 1909, Schmeidler 1959, Gläser 1973, Savijärvi 1977, 1988, Kiuru 1993, Itkonen-Kaila 1991, 1992 and 1997) and the first Bible translation (Ikola 1949, 1950) but comparatively little research has been done on the corpus of legal translations of that time. One could mention here Pajula's history of Finnish legal language (Pajula 1960) and his study of Martti's 16th century translation of King Christopher's law (Pajula 1955), Rapola's study of the phonology of Abraham Kollanius' 1648 translations of King Christopher's and Magnus Eriksson's laws (Rapola 1925), as well as Inaba's paper on the dative-genitive case in Martti's translation (Inaba 2000a) and Elsayed's on the use of modal verbs in Old Finnish legal translations (Elsayed 2000). Another reason is that the core of religious literature in the Old Finnish period – Agricola's translations, as well as the 1642 Bible translation – has a multiplicity of source texts, Agricola using, in addition to the Swedish 1526 New Testament, German, Greek and Latin source texts as well. This makes posing a connection between a given linguistic construction and a specific source model extremely difficult, as Itkonen-Kaila (1997) points out in detail. As I have argued here, there are enough other difficulties and pitfalls in pinpointing the role of language contact in a given linguistic innovation during the Old Finnish period, and, as Inaba (2000a: 111) remarks, in case of legal translations, there is a more straightforward connection between source text and translation.

The primary texts which constitute the corpus of Old Finnish legal texts will be detailed below. First of all, there is Martti's translation of King Christopher's 1442 law, henceforth M, which has not been dated exactly, but probably dates from the 1580s (Häkkinen 1994: 98, Pajula 1955: 326, Rapola 1967: 136-137). The identity of the translator is uncertain – Pajula (1955: 342-383) argues that the translator was, in fact, Jaakko Finno, and that Martti, who was the preacher of the Finnish congregation in Stockholm during the later part of the 16th century, was the copyist of an individual manuscript. The idea that Finno was the original translator of King Christopher's law has been criticized by Rapola (1960: 199-200, 1967: 137). Martti, in any event, lived probably from 1510 to about 1585, and hailed from the northern part of Southwest Finland – between Turku and Rauma (Tarkiainen 1990: 50). Seven manuscripts of Martti's translation survive until this day (Pajula 1955: 58-76), indicating that it was quite widely used (Häkkinen 1994: 98). One of the manuscripts, the Stockholm codex B 96, has been published in 1905 in an edition by E.N. Setälä and M. Nyholm (Airila), in 1930, M. Airila and H. Harmas published a comparison of the Stockholm codex B 96 and the other surviving manuscripts. Setälä and Nyholm's 1905 edition has been published in an electronic form by the Research Institute for the Languages of Finland (*Kotimaisten kielten tutkimuskeskus, KKT*), which will be used here.

A second translation of King Christopher's law, together with Magnus Eriksson's City Law dating from the mid-14th century, was completed by Ljungo Tuomaanpoika, chaplain of Kalajoki, in northern Ostrobothnia, in respectively 1601 and 1609, which were published by Wilhelm Lagus in 1852 and by Matti Ulkuniemi in 1975. Ulkuniemi's edition was published electronically by KKT, which will be used here. I will henceforth designate Ljungo's 1601 translation of King Christopher's Law as L1, and his 1609 translation of Magnus Eriksson's City Law as L2. In the preface of his translations, Ljungo sharply criticizes an earlier translation (Rapola 1967: 137) which indicates he was familiar with Martti's possibly rather widely copied text. Finally, in 1648, Abraham Kollanius, a lawyer from Karkku, Satakunta, completed his translation of both law texts – King Christopher's Land Law (hence K1) and Magnus Eriksson's City Law (hence K2). Additionally, Kollanius' translation of the City Law includes a translation of the chapter dealing with the Church Law (*Kyrkobalken*) from the medieval *Upplandslagen* (Pajula 1960: 58). According to Pajula (1960: 61), Kollanius may have had Martti's translation at his avail as well, even if he himself strongly denied using any earlier translations. Neither Ljungo's, nor Kollanius' translations appeared in print, even if, with Ljungo's translation, printing was begun (Rapola 1967: 138). In case of Kollanius' translation, intentions to print were squashed after a control committee expressed dissatisfaction with the quality of the translation (Häkkinen 1994: 98, Rapola 1967: 139), however, as Rapola (1967: 139-140) remarks, Kollanius' translation was a step ahead of its predecessors in terms of ortographic and linguistic consistency. Kollanius' translation was published in 1926 in an edition by Rapola, which, also, has been published electronically by KKT, and it is the electronic version which will be in use here.

The source texts of these translations have been written in the mid-14th and 15th centuries, with the *Upplandslagen* even older (confirmed by King Birger Magnusson in 1296), and the Land Law and City Law themselves are linguistically rather heterogeneous compilations based on earlier law texts, namely the regional County laws (*landskapslagarna*) such as the Uppland law (*Upplandslagen*) and the West Gothian law (*Västgötalagen*). Thus King Christopher's 1442 Law and Magnus Eriksson's City Law of almost a century before are Old Swedish rather than the early Modern Swedish that was spoken during the time the translations were made. The number of surviving manuscripts of either law is very large, and the manuscripts differ slightly among themselves in ortography, dialectal features, etc (Pajula 1955: 20-21). It is not certain, therefore, which exact source text Martti's and Ljungo's translations were based on – the first printed version of King Christopher's law appeared only in 1621, and Kollanius likely benefited from a later edition printed in 1638 or 1643 (Pajula 1960: 58). From 1827 to 1877, Carl Johan Schlyter published a large edition of all medieval Swedish laws. King Christopher's Land Law, in Schlyter's edition has, as well as his edition of the *Upplandslagen* and fragments of the City Law have been published electronically by the Nordic institute of the University of Lund. Here, I will use the electronic versions of the Church Chapter of the *Upplandslagen* (UL) and of King Christopher's law (KrL) published by the Nordic Institute of the University of Lund, whereas I will use Schlyter's version of Magnus Eriksson's City Law (MEL). For the 1734 translation of *Sweriges Rikes Lag, Ruotzin Waldacunnan Laki* (RWL, 1759), a reprint of the printed 1780 version was used. The birth of RWL was troubled: though Samuel Forseen, provincial secretary of Turku, finished translating the text in 1738, it was not printed until 1759. On his death in 1744, Forseen left the task of correcting and publishing the work to his son-in-law E.J. Paleen; eventually the translation was printed (and the printing financed by Georg Salonius. (Häkkinen 1994: 99).

Table 3:1. *The corpus of examined texts.*

SOURCE: King Christopher's law, 1442 (KrL).	SOURCE: Magnus Eriksson's City Law, approx. 1360 (MEL).	SOURCE: Church chapter of the Uppland County Law, latter part of the 13rd century (UL).	SOURCE: Reformed Swedish Law (*Sweriges Rikes Lag*) of 1734 (SRL).
Martti (M), approx. 1580.			
Ljungo (L1), 1601.	Ljungo (L2), 1609.		

Kollanius (K1), 1648.	Kollanius (K2), 1648	Kollanius, 1648 – incorporated in K2.	
			Translated by Samuel Forseen, *Ruotzin Walda-cunnan Laki* (1759)

In references to the texts, I will use approximate English translations of the chapter titles, namely, the following:

Table 3:2. *Chapters of the examined texts.*

Number:	KrL:	MEL:
1	King's Chapter	King's Chapter
2	Marriage	Marriage
3	Inheritance	Inheritance
4	Land	Land
5	Building	Building
6	Trade	Trade
7 (MEL)		Ships
7 (KrL), 8 (MEL)	Court Chapter	Courthouse Chapter
8 (KrL), 9 (MEL)	Peace Oath	Peace Oath
9 (KrL), 10 (MEL)	Capital crimes	Capital crimes
10 (KrL), 11 (MEL)	Purposeful murder	Purposeful murder
11 (KrL), 12 (MEL)	Accidental murder	Accidental murder
12 (KrL), 13 (MEL)	Purposeful wounding	Purposeful wounding
13 (KrL), 14 (MEL)	Accidental wounding	Accidental wounding
14 (KrL), 15 (MEL)	Theft	Theft
16 (MEL)		Gambling

Number	RWL:
1	Marriage
2	Inheritance
3	Land
4	Building
5	Trade
6	Crimes
7	Punishment
8	Forfeit of goods
9	Courthouse Chapter

There are slight differences in the numbering of paragraphs between the Finnish translations and the source texts, and between the translations themselves. In case an example sentence of M is given with equivalents in other translations, the paragraph number indicated will be that in M; in case there is no example given from M but one from L1, L2 and K1 or K2, the indicated paragraph number will be that in Ljungo's translation.

It should be noted here that, on the one hand, this corpus makes for an excellent possibility of observing contact-induced linguistic change: first of all, translators of foreign literature during the 16th and 17th centuries strove for as literal a translation as possible, for example by consistently copying word order patterns (Häkkinen 1994: 472, Pajula 1955: 273-277). Also, the translators were possible not fluently bilingual – thus Rapola (1967: 139) remarks that Abraham Kollanius was turned down for a position as notary, ostensibly for his lack of command of Swedish. It should be noted here that the contact situation in question is an anachronistic one: the Swedish of the source texts is Old Swedish, and probably quite different from the Swedish the three translators would be otherwise acquainted with. Pajula (1955: 277-296) lists a number of occasions, in which Martti misunderstood or mistranslated Old Swedish legal terms. What this means is that Old Finnish legal language may be regarded as a kind of interlanguage – strongly shaped by influence of the source language, Old Swedish, but not necessarily very representative of the Finnish of that time. This means that, on the other hand, one must be cautious in drawing conclusions about contact-induced change within Finnish as a whole on the basis of this corpus.

3.2. Alignment and case-marking in Modern and Old Finnish

3.2.1. Subject and object case-marking

In Modern Standard Finnish, three grammatical cases, Nominative, Partitive and Genitive may all be used to mark the subject: whereas the partitive may be used to designate the subject in certain intransitive, existential constructions, the genitive is used with a small class of necessitive expressions which will be under scrutiny in chapter 5:

Hän *ui* *järvessä*
He-NOM swim-3SG lake-INESS
'He swims in the lake'
Hänen *täytyi* *uida järvessä*
He -GEN had to-3SG swim-INF lake-INESS
'He had to swim in the lake'
Järvessä *ui* *kaloja*
Lake-INESS swims-3SG fish-PART PL
'There's fish swimming in the lake'

The concept of a genitive subject is, nevertheless, not uncontroversial. Penttilä (1963: 641) regarded both the genitive subject and the infinitive complement of necessitive clauses as *hänen täytyi uida järvessä* as forming an adverbial, hence necessitive clauses would be subjectless. Ikola (1971: 29), on the other hand, regarded the genitive subject and the infinitive complement to form, as an embedded clause, the subject of the necessitive auxiliary. Auli Hakulinen et al. (2004: 500-501) nevertheless opt for the nominal argument of the auxiliary to be a genitive subject.

For case-marking of the direct object, the partitive or accusative is used. The choice of the partitive depends both on the semantics and definitiness of the object as well as on the semantics, aspect and aktionart of the verb – typically, the partitive marks the object of irresultative, negative or frequentative verbs, and is used as the object case of divisible nouns or mass nouns, whereas the accusative is typically used with resultative verbs in positive sentences with definite nouns. In Hopper and Thompson's (1980: 262) view, the accusative thus signals a higher grade of transitivity.

Negation, demanding the partitive in Finnish, is connected to a low grade of transitivity as well (Hopper and Thompson 1980: 277).

The phonological surface form of the accusative, nonetheless, is distinguished from the genitive and nominative only in the lexical subclass of personal pronouns (as well as the interrogative pronoun *kene-*, referring to a person), where its marker is *-t*. In the singular, the marked form of the accusative is *-n*, like the genitive; in the plural, *-t*, identical with the nominative. Additionally, in a number of constructions (namely, those where no nominative subject is possible, i.e., passive constructions, imperative constructions and those using a genitive-marked subject) the accusative is unmarked (*-ø* in the singular, *-t* in the plural). Nonetheless, in these constructions, the object form of personal pronouns remains marked:

Hän syö kalan
He eat-3SG fish-ACC (marked)
'He eats the fish'
Hän ei syö kaloja
He NEG eat fish-PART PL
'He does not eat the fish'
Hänen täytyy tappaa koira
He-GEN must kill-INF dog-ACC (unmarked)
'He must kill the dog'
Hänen täytyy tappaa minut
He-GEN must kill-INF me-ACC (marked)
'He must kill me'
Koira tapetaan
Dog-ACC (unmarked) kill-PASS
'The dog is being/will be killed'
Minut tapetaan
me-ACC (marked) kill-PASS
'I am being/will be killed'

The concept of an accusative object is not uncontroversial either. Though the *-n* accusative, at least, is historically distinct from the genitive case, having developed from an earlier *-m* (Hakulinen 1979: 98), Auli Hakulinen et al. (2004: 1186) recognize an accusative only with personal pronouns (and the interrogative pronoun *kene-*). The *-n* and *-ø* accusatives would thus be genitives and nominatives, respectively. I will nevertheless stick to the term "accusative" here, particularly for simplicity's sake: instead of four object cases (nominative, genitive, accusative and partitive), the appearance of which is based on both morphosyntactic and (in case of pronouns) lexical criteria, the concept of an accusative case enables us to distinguish two object cases, the partitive and the accusative, occurring mainly on the basis of syntactic criteria, in mutually exclusive environments.

Table 3:3. *Subject cases.*

NOMINATIVE	- ø	Most transitive and intransitive constructions
GENITIVE	-*n*	closed class of necessitive constructions
PARTITIVE	-*tA*, -*A*	intransitive, existential constructions

Table 3:4. *Object cases.*

PARTITIVE	-*tA*, -*A*	negative clauses, irresultative verbs, divisible nouns, etc.
UNMARKED ACCUSATIVE	- ø (singular) -*t* (plural) -*t* (personal pronouns)	passive, imperative and necessitive constructions
MARKED ACCUSATIVE	-*n* (singular) -*t* (plural) -*t* (personal pronouns)	

Old Finnish differs from this in some respects. First of all, the usual accusative marker for personal pronouns in Old Finnish is -*n* (identical with the genitive), rather than -*t*. The dialectal background of these two markers is different: West Finnish dialects generally use -*n* on personal pronouns, whereas the -*t* pronominal accusative marker has an East Finnish background (Rapola 1969: 74, Inaba 2000b: 48). Second, Old Finnish tends to employ marked accusative objects with necessitive constructions as well. This, too, is common in West Finnish dialects (Häkkinen 1994: 362-363). Finally, a reanalysis of the object of passive constructions as a subject took place throughout the period of Old Finnish with concomitant changes in the case-marking of pronominal objects (Häkkinen 1994: 325-326).

3.2.2. Alignment

Finnish differs in some important respects from Nominative-Accusative alignment. Particularly, the case-marking of subjects of existential clauses conforms to that of the object, rather than the subject: the partitive case is used in negated clauses, as well as with mass/divisible nouns (Hakulinen et al. 2004: 850-851), and in the rare case a personal pronoun may occur as subject of a possessive clause (syntactically, a subset of existential clauses with the possessor being a local adverbial – Hakulinen et al. 2004: 852-853), it shows the *-t* accusative (T. Itkonen 1974: 385-386, 1993 [1979]: 311). Existential clauses are:

> (...) intransitive sentences which, without foregoing presuppositions, express the existence of the subject, its coming into existence, its cessation of existence, or an essential change in state – usually from the standpoint of location in its widest sense. (T. Itkonen 1993 [1979]: 309).

Givón (2001a: 191) notes that it is not rare, cross-linguistically, for existential subjects to differ in their properties, in as far as grammatical relations and case-marking are concerned, from other subjects.

The most common verb of existential clauses is *olla* 'to be', though a few others may occur as well, with the theme of existential clauses being usually a local adverbial, with the subject placed after the verb (Hakulinen et al. 2004: 850).

Kadulla	*on*	*auto*	
street-ADESS is	car		
'There's a car on the street'			
Kadulla	*on*	*autoja*	
street-ADESS is	car-PL PART		
'There are cars on the street'			
Kadulla	*ei*	*ole*	*autoa*
street-ADESS NEG	is	car-PART	
'There's no car to be seen on the street'			

Compare the non-existential clauses:

Auto	*on*	*kadulla*	
car	is	street-ADESS	
'The (specific) car is on the street'			
Auto	*ei*	*ole*	*kadulla*
car	NEG	is	street-ADESS
'The car is not on the street (but it may be somewhere else)'			

As mentioned, personal pronouns, in the rather marginal constructions where they may occur as subjects of existential clauses, take the accusative ending -*t*:

Minulla		*on*	*sinut*
I-ADESS	is	you-ACC	
'I have you'			

Thus, in terms of case-marking, the existential subject behaves like an object, rather than an intransitive subject (Laitinen and Vilkuna 1993: 25) – a circumstance which leads Fred Karlsson (1982: 109) to introduce the term "ject" for the existential subject. This would seem unnecessary if one, with Terho Itkonen (1974, 1975, 1993 [1979]), would depart from applying the framework of Nominative-Accusative alignment, and regard Finnish as some kind of ergative, or, perhaps partially, active/stative language. The fact that existential subjects occur with a nominative-like -∅ ending, rather than with an accusative *-n*, with the exception of personal pronouns, does not speak against their identification with objects in terms of case-marking, as in Modern Finnish, the object is unmarked and nominative-like in clauses where either no nominative subject is possible (passives, imperative clauses) or where the subject occurs in the genitive case (necessitive clauses).

This system Comrie dubs the "antiergative" (Comrie 1975: 115-116, Hopper and Thompson 1980: 254): where in ergative languages, ergative case-marking on the subject correlates with transitivity and the presence of an (usually unmarked) object, in Finnish, the object marker correlates with the presence of an (unmarked) subject. Dixon (1979: 75) would rather regard the system of Finnish object-marking as a mirror-image of ergative languages where ergative subject-marking is only used if confusion between agent and object is otherwise a possibility (Dixon 1979: 72-73), and criticizes the term anti-ergative, which he regards as disregarding the crucial difference in ergative languages between transitive and intransitive subjects (Dixon 1979: 75-76, footnote).

In any event, as existential clauses have no arguments than their subjects, it seems possible to regard noun subjects of existential clauses as well as marked with a zero accusative (T. Itkonen 1993 [1979]: 309). Thus, after Terho Itkonen (1975: 50), the distribution of grammatical cases in Modern Finnish is like this:

Table 3:5. *Alignment in Finnish*

CLAUSE	SUBJECT	OBJECT
transitive, agentive subj.	nominative	accusative or partitive
intransitive, agentive subj.	nominative	-
intransitive, non-agent. subj.	nominative	-
existential, non-agentive subject	accusative or partitive	-

Terho Itkonen compares this with the "traditional" ergative system of alignment, which would be based on an opposition between transitive subjects and intransitive subjects/objects, rather than between transitive/intransitive subjects and existential subjects/objects:

> (...) It may be said that the crucial border in Finnish is not one separating a transitive subject from an intransitive subject and the object; rather, it is one separating the subject of "non-existential" or "normal" sentences from both the subject of "existential" sentences and the object, with concomitant differences in the form of the finite verb. (T. Itkonen 1993 [1979]: 307)

Table 3:6. *Ergative alignment.*

CLAUSE	SUBJECT	OBJECT
transitive, agentive subj.	ergative	absolutive
intransitive, agentive subj.	absolutive	-
intransitive, non-agent. subj.	absolutive	-
existential, non-agentive subject	absolutive	-

As Terho Itkonen (1993 [1979]: 312) states, Finnish differs from ergative languages, aside in drawing the line between subject and subject/object case, also in its assignment of case-markers: the Finnish nominative is unmarked, whereas among the existential subject/object case-markers, the accusative may be marked or unmarked, and the partitive is always marked. In the most typical ergative languages, however, the transitive subject case (ergative) tends to appear marked, whereas the intransitive subject/object case (absolutive) is unmarked (Dixon 1979: 62, 72, Givón 2001a: 208). This leads Terho Itkonen to describe the Finnish case-marking system as "an inverted ergative system" (T. Itkonen 1993 [1979]: 312). The distribution being strictly taken syntactic, namely, based on the isolation of one particular intransitive sub-clause (existential clauses), rather than on semantic criteria (as would be an active/stative based on agentivity/non-agentivity (Dixon 1979: 76, Givón 2001a: 202)), the moniker seems an elegant one.

In fact, an active/stative or, in T. Itkonen's terminology, "ideal ergative" subsystem seems to be found in case of necessitive verbs such as *täytyy*, *pitää*, which occur with subjects marked in the genitive case, or, more marginally, in the nominative case. In Standard Finnish, the dividing line seems to be made on syntactic criteria, with subjects of *pitää* and existential infinitival complements occurring with nominative case-marking, and others with genitive case-marking, but in dialectal varieties of Finnish, the distribution seems to approach an active/stative system with agentive subjects tending to prefer genitive case-marking, and non-agentive ones preferring nominative case-marking (T. Itkonen 1993 [1979]: 314-317). The subject-marking of necessitive clauses will be subject of chapter 5 below.

4. THE PASSIVE

4.1. The passive in modern Finnish

The main share of the category of grammatical voice in modern Finnish is formed by the impersonal passive, signifying agency by an unspecified human, or at least animate, agent (Hakulinen et al. 2004: 1256) – this appears to be typical for impersonal passives (Siewierska 1984: 199). In imperfect tenses, the passive is formed by the marker *-tAAn*, which is inflected in mood and tense (but not in person). Perfect passives are formed with a copular *olla* and a passive participle bearing the marker *-ttU*:

kaupunki tuhotaan — ’the city is being destroyed’ (present imperfect)
city is destroyed
kaupunki tuhottiin — ’the city was destroyed’ (past imperfect)
kaupunki on tuhottu — ’the city has been destroyed’ (present perfect)
kaupunki oli tuhottu — ’the city had been destroyed’ (past perfect)
kaupunki tuhottaisiin — ’the city would be destroyed’ (conditional)
kaupunki tuhottaneen — ’the city may be destroyed’ (potential)

The passive in Finnish occurs with intransitive as well as transitive verbs, which may not be uncommon cross-linguistically, and indeed seems to be common for non-promotional passives (i.e. passives where the patient argument retains features of the object) (Shibatani 1985: 834, Givón 2001b: 128). The single explicit argument the Finnish passive may take is its object. Like the object of an imperative or necessitive verb in Finnish, it is usually marked with the zero accusative. In negative sentences, however, it is marked with the partitive case, and with personal pronouns as well as the interrogative *kene-* ’who?’, a *-t* accusative appears:

mies *tapetaan*
man-ACC (∅) kill-PASS
’The man is being killed’
hänet *tapetaan*
he-ACC (-t) kill-PASS
’He is being killed’
häntä *ei* *tapeta*

he-PART NEG kill-PASS
'He is not being killed'

As shown above, the marker *-tAAn* is a composite marker, the first element of which is the actual passive marker *-tA* (or *-ttA*, *-dA*, depending on the vagaries of Finnish morphophonology). The second, *-Vn*, is an impersonal ending which is omitted with negated verbs (Hakulinen et al. 2004: 1255). Historically, the passive marker seems to have been derived from a causative or reflexive verbal derivational marker **-ttA*, with the impersonal *-Vn* having developed from a 3rd person singular marker **-sen* – possibly a medial marker, in which function it still occurs in South Estonian (Posti 1980: 112-113). The Finnish passive has cognate structures in all Finnic languages (Laanest 1982: 240).

As mentioned, the Finnish passive implicitly refers to a human or animate agent, but it is not possible in modern Finnish to specify an overt agent by an oblique nominal phrase or otherwise. In that respect, the Finnish passive is rather prototypical crosslinguistically, overt agent phrases being, in many languages, much less frequent than their omission and confined often to especially written language (Siewierska 1984: 35, 229, Itkonen-Kaila 1974: 210, Givón 2001b: 126). The object retains its accusative or partitive case-marking, the zero accusative being normal in Finnish when a nominative subject cannot be specified (i.e. in imperative and necessitive phrases as well) (Comrie 1975: 115-116). Following from its unambiguous status as an object, there is no morphological agreement in modern Finnish between the passive verb and its single argument:

häntä *ei* *tapeta*
he-PART NEG kill-PASS
'He is not being killed/will not be killed'
heitä *ei* *tapeta*
they-PART NEG kill-PASS
'They are not being killed/will not be killed'
Not:
**he* *eivät* *tapeta*
they-NOM NEG PL kill-PASS

This applies as well in the perfect tense, which is formed by a combination of the auxiliary *olla* 'to be' and the passive participle (marker *-ttU*). The auxiliary *olla* remains in its basic 3rd person form *on* 'is':

hänet *on* *tapettu*
he-ACC be-3SG kill-PASS (singular participle)
'He has been killed'
heidät *on* *tapettu*

they-ACC	be-3SG	kill-PASS	

'They have been killed'
Not:

**He*	*ovat*	*tapetut*
They-NOM	be-3PL	kill-PASS (plural participle)

As Comrie (1977: 50) points out, there is no object promotion visible in the Finnish passive: the object retains the standard features, with regards to case-marking, lack of agreement, etc., which objects in Finnish have in the absence of a nominative subject. It does not gain any of the typical features of a grammatical subject. Typical for the Finnish passive is Subject Demotion: in standard Finnish, no agent can be specified in connection with the passive (though it is nonetheless implicitly there). The fact that passivization in Finnish is not restricted to transitive verbs would, according to Shibatani (1985: 834) also support an analysis in which Subject Demotion, or agent defocusing, is regarded as central. All in all, the Finnish passive seems a very good example of the prototypical non-promotional passive as described by Givón (2001b: 128) in, for example, features such as lack of object promotion, lack of agent phrases, and lack of restriction of passivization to only transitive verbs.

4.2. The passive in Old Finnish

With regards to the nature of the single argument of the passive verb in Modern Finnish, Old Finnish (and to a lesser extent, dialectal Finnish) is somewhat divergent, in that it clearly shows signs of object promotion, i.e., the reanalysis of object to subject. Also, an oblique agent phrase occurs in Old Finnish. The latter has been known from Agricola's times until well into the 19th century – the agent, being part of an adverbial phrase, was usually marked with the ablative case, more rarely with the adessive or the elative case (Häkkinen 1994: 360). Thus, in Agricola's 1548 New Testament translation:

Luke 17:20

Coska	*hen*	*nyt*	*Phariseusilda*
when	he-NOM	now	Pharisee-ABL PL

kysyttiin
ask-PASS IPF
"And when he was demanded of the Pharisees..."

In dialectal Finnish, this phenomenon is extremely rare. Itkonen-Kaila (1992: 157-158) mentions that a large part of the examples mentioned in earlier literature seem to be proverbs, possibly influenced by literary or religious language. Aside from this, the construction appears to occur sporadically in some dialects bordering Swedish-speaking areas (Itkonen-Kaila 1992: 158). It is therefore likely that the agent phrase came into existence as a translation equivalent in literary language alone. Traditionally, Swedish, which may employ an agent phrase using the preposition *av*, in combination with an (impersonal) passive, has been regarded as the source language (for instance, Petander 1893: 21). However, also German (which uses a prepositional phrase with *von*) and Latin (which uses an ablative-marked agent preceded by the preposition *ab*) could have functioned as models (Itkonen-Kaila 1992: 148). Pinpointing the origin of the phrase is complicated by the fact that it is extremely rare in dialectal Finnish. It should be mentioned, nevertheless, that a somewhat similar construction, in which the agent is marked by the adessive case, occurs in the easternmost dialects of Finnish. According to Nau (1995: 150-151) this construction may have risen under the influence of neighbouring Karelian, and, indirectly, Russian.

In Old Finnish, pronominal objects associated with the passive appeared in the nominative case. This usage of the nominative, rather than the *-t* accusative, occurs still in western Finnish dialects (Lehtinen 1985: 271):

Western dialects:	*hän*	*tuodaan*	*tänne*
	he-NOM	bring-PASS	here
	'He will be brought here'		
Standard Finnish:	*hänet*	*tuodaan*	*tänne*
	he-ACC	bring-PASS	here
	'He will be brought here'		

Additionally, person and number marking on passive verbs occurs regularly in South Estonian (Laanest 1982: 241, Lehtinen 1985: 270) and, to some extent (namely, with the 1st and 3rd person plural) in Old Finnish as well, e.g. (Hakulinen 1979: 241):

he	*tapetijt*
they-NOM	kill-PASS PL
"they were killed"	

This construction is unknown in spoken Finnish and generally considered to have developed as a translation equivalent of foreign-language source constructions (Kangasmaa-Minn 1980: 22, Lehtinen 1985: 285, Häkkinen 1994: 251). The source language in question would be Greek or Latin, rather than Swedish, which has an impersonal *-s* passive (Itkonen-Kaila 1997: 36).

This, of course, would mean no genetic connection exists between the South Estonian personal passive and its equivalent in Old Finnish.

However, according to Lauri Hakulinen (1979: 241), the presence of person/number markers in Old Finnish as well as the nominative case-marking of a pronominal object may be, at least in the case of the 3rd person, a remnant of an older personal passive, rather than a contact-induced innovation. This hypothesis found acceptance with Ikola (1959: 43). Hakulinen nevertheless regarded Agricola's 1st pers. plural passive forms, such as *me rangaistamme* 'we are punished' (Mod. Finnish *meidät rangaistaan*) as quite possibly devised by Agricola himself. In any event, the generally accepted analysis of the passive marker as a combination of a causative **-ttA* and an originally medial person marker **-sen* (or, maybe, **-sen* for the singular and **-set* for the plural, both of which are found in South Estonian (Posti 1980: 113)), would make such an analysis possible. In this scenario, a reanalysis of an original grammatical subject of a medial verb form as the grammatical object of an impersonal passive must have taken place – and must have left untouched parts of the Western dialects of Finnish, as well as the older literary language. The likely causative/reflexive origin of the passive may make positing such a reanalysis necessary anyway (Lehtinen 1984: 33, 36-37).

The question is here whether Western dialects and Old Finnish retain the original state of affairs or are themselves based on an innovation, partially reversing the earlier one. In the latter case, one might regard the occurrence of nominative subjects with the Finnish passive as a Swedish grammatical borrowing. However, the origin of the construction is, according to Lehtinen (1985: 275), quite a bit more problematic: the loss of accusative case-marking seems to occur particularly in those areas where the pronominal accusative marker is *-n*, rather than the *-t* of modern standard Finnish (and eastern dialects). Therefore, analogy with common nouns, which, as mentioned, are marked with the zero accusative rather than the *-n* accusative as objects of passive verbs, seems a more likely explanation. Thus the zero marker on the pronoun would be a "zero accusative", rather than a nominative signifying an underlying reanalysis from object to subject. Of course, the presence of Swedish model patterns may have nonetheless functioned as a background condition stimulating the innovation, and their role may have been more salient in older literary texts (Häkkinen 1994: 325).

Although personal marking on passive verbs in the present imperfect tense has been totally confined to Old Finnish, agreement between the object and the verb occurs considerably more widely in the case of the present and past perfect passives, which are formed with the auxiliary *olla*:

minä	*olen*	*kutsuttu*
I-NOM	be-1SG	invited-PASS PARTIC

vs. Standard Finnish:

minut	*on*	*kutsuttu*
I-ACC	be-3SG	invited-PASS PARTIC

This rather widely used instance of agreement between the passive and its single argument – here, a subject rather than an object – may be a sveticism (for example Schlachter 1986: 108, a counterposed viewpoint has been put forward by Ikola 1959: 45, who regards subjecthood and person/number agreement as the original state of affairs with the Finnish passive). It should be kept in mind, though, that the present perfect passive with a singular common noun as object is inherently somewhat ambiguous: in a sentence such as *poika on kutsuttu* 'the boy has been invited', the noun can be analysed both as the object of the passive verb form, and as the grammatical subject of the auxiliary. In the latter case, the participle *kutsuttu* would function as a nominal predicate rather than as a component of a finite verb form. As no surface difference proceeds from either of the two competing analyses, we have a fine example of syntactic reanalysis here. The reanalysis would be extended to pronominal subjects as well, and as a difference between accusative and nominative case-marking does occur here, an innovation in surface structure is consequently produced.

It should be noticed here that a construction in which the passive participle functions as an adjectival, nominal predicate, and agrees with the subject in person and number, is quite possible in modern Finnish (Hakulinen et al. 2004: 528-530). Hakulinen et al. emphasize the fact that a construction such as:

talo	*on*	*saneerattu*
house	is	renovated

is ambiguous in modern Finnish: both the unambiguous passive construction *talot on saneerattu*, where the lack of agreement with the plural noun makes clear that the plural noun is an object, and the unambiguous *talot ovat saneerattuja*, where a predicate agrees in person and number with a plural subject, are grammatical (Hakulinen et al. 2004: 529). The difference between the two is a rather subtle semantic one: the nominal predicate construction points to a state, the passive one to a finished activity (by an unmentioned human agent) (Saarimaa 1971: 150, Hakulinen et al. 2004: 529). At the same time, the tendency for reanalysis of passive objects as passive subjects in these types of clauses is real enough, and a source of worry for prescriptive literature such as E.A. Saarimaa's (1971: 150-151). Conditions for disambiguation include marked number and person on the subject/object noun, and negation (in which the object, in passive clauses too, is marked with the partitive case). Another condition may be lexicalization of the passive participle as an adjective, and occurrence of adverb modifiers of the passive participle (Hakulinen et al. 2004: 1273). As will be shown below, the number of unambiguous *objects* of perfect passive constructions in the corpus is low (except in RWL in the case of negated clauses). Thus, while the existence and grammaticality of both perfect passive and nominal predicate constructions with passive participles does provide us with a potential problem in tracing a possibly contact-induced reanalysis, the lack of unambiguous passive objects does strongly indicate the existence of such a reanalysis.

In any event, going with Aikhenvald's (2003) position of language contact as a background condition stimulating "internal" reanalysis and extension, or with Harris' and Campbell's (1995: 51) caveat that, distinct from syntactic borrowing, language contact may be a catalyst for internal mechanisms of change, foreign model pattern may function more as a "magnetic pole" stimulating one analysis over the other, rather than a source from which language material gets transferred. This notwithstanding, I am unsure whether it is sensible to distinguish syntactic borrowing from contact-induced reanalysis and extension in this sense, as argued in 1.2.4.4.

Finally, a more marginal and, as a passive, recent periphrastic passive construction should be mentioned, involving a nominal verb form, the s.c. agent participle, which is formed with the marker *-mA*. The agent participle usually functions as an adjective, denoting an action performed on the head word by an agent, which is specified obligatorily:

Pekan *maalama* *talo*
Pekka-GEN paint-AGENT house
'The house painted by Pekka'
Minun *maalamani* *talo*
My-GEN paint-AGENT 1SG house
'The house painted by me'

This construction, which was rare in written Finnish until the 19th century, perhaps mainly because of the *lack* of any foreign-language equivalents (Häkkinen 1994: 319, Itkonen-Kaila 1992: 141-142) in a case of 'inverted' covert interference, can be employed as a translation equivalent of a passive prase which specifies an agent, by using the agent participle as a nominal predicate, e.g.:

Talo *on* *Pekan* *maalama*
House-NOM is Pekka-GEN paint-AGENT
'The house is painted by Pekka'

Eeva Lindén (1964: 246) mentions that this construction, inm which the agent participle is used as a nominal predicate, is often used as a translation equivalent of Swedish model patterns.

4.3. Distribution of the passive in the corpus

The following table depicts the amount of finite passive constructions gathered from the corpus, distributed according to its object (∅ = Zero Accusative object, P = Partitive object, ? = object whose case-marking could not be determined, 0 = lack of an object). Passive infinitives have been left out – as the majority of them are used with an auxiliary necessitive *pitää,* they are taken into account in chapter 5.

The numbers in italics depict percentages. As can clearly be seen, the distribution of objects with various case-markings is similar throughout the corpus, with the exception of the partitive, which seems to be significantly more common in Kollanius' translations as well as in RWL than in Martti's and Ljungo's older translations.

Table 4:1. *Distribution of the passive in the corpus.*

	M	L1	L2	K1	K2	RWL
∅	503	504	374	369	363	708
	49.9	*53.8*	*44.8*	*42.7*	*39.4*	*42.1*
P	63	46	32	104	106	157
	6.2	*4.9*	*3.8*	*12*	*11.5*	*9.3*
?	27	15	14	16	6	25
	2.7	*1.6*	*1.7*	*1.9*	*0.7*	*1.5*
0	415	371	415	375	447	792
	41.2	*39.6*	*49.7*	*43.4*	*48.5*	*47.1*
n	1008	936	835	864	922	1682

As a general feature of passive constructions in the corpus, it should be noted that pronominal objects are marked with the zero accusative, rather than with the *-t* accusative. As pronominal objects in Old Finnish are otherwise, as in the West Finnish dialects, marked with *-n* accusative, rather than the *-t* accusative (Rapola 1969: 74), Lehtinen's (1985: 275) explanation of a general substitution of *-n* with -∅ for passive objects would be applicable here as well. Some examples:

(1) Inheritance, 11
M: *caiken hänen colmannexens iongan* ***hän naitettin***
all-ACC her-GEN third-ACC 3SG to which she-∅ marry-PASS IPF
ottakan hänen perillisens
take-IMP her-GEN heir-3SG

L1: *caicken waimon colmannexen iohonga* ***hän naitettin*** *åttauat waimon perilliset*
K1: *caiken sen colmannexen, johon* ***waimo*** ***oli annettu***
woman-∅ give-PASS PLPF
'All of the third part, to which she was married, should be taken by her heirs'

(2) Peace oath, 24
M: *sijtteqn* ***hän*** *syypääxi* ***löyttin***
when he-∅ guilty-TRANSL find-PASS IPF
L1: *sittä quin* ***hän*** *syypäxi* ***löythän***
when he-∅ guilty-TRANSL find-PASS
K1: *cuin* ***hän*** *syypäxi* ***tehtin***
when he-∅ guilty make-PASS IPF
'When he is found guilty'

4.4. Swedish source constructions

The Swedish passive resembles the Finnish in that an impersonal imperfect form (the *-s* passive) co-occurs with perfect tense constructions formed by the usage of a copular 'to be' (*vara*) and a perfect participle: in Germanic languages, the perfect participle always bears passive voice if the verb is transitive (Wessén 1970b: 163-164). The patient of the passive verb, however, remains in the nominative, and, in case of perfect tense constructions, shows, in Old Swedish, number and person agreement with the auxiliary:

(3) Peace Oath, 26
MEL: *ella nokot aff thöm förra sagdh*
or something of those before said-PARTIC
æru eller vrskild
be-PL or distinguished-PARTIC
'Or any such thing as has been said or mentioned before'
(4) Church Chapter, 2
UL: *Sißæn præstins hus æru væl boin*
Then the priest's house-PL be-PL well built
'Then the priest's house has been built well'

The impersonal *-s* passive originally arose through agglutination of the reflexive pronoun *sik* to the verb stem, and is common to all Scandinavian languages (Wessén 1970b: 187). It occurs in both the present and the past imperfect tense, but may occur as an infinitive as well, in forms that may be homophonous:

(5) Purposeful murder, 12
MEL: *Aff them botum, ther fore konu drap*
Of those fines which for a woman's slaying
bötas *som ær twægilt*
fine-PASS which are twice as high
'Of those fines, which are taken for the murder of a woman, which are twice as high'
(6) Purposeful wounding, 22
MEL: *Thetta skal* ***bötas*** *epter twæggia manna witnum*
This must be fined-PASS INF with two men's testimony
'This must be fined with the testimony of two men'

In addition to the *-s* passive and periphrastic constructions with *vara* 'to be', a periphrastic construction using *varda* 'to become' occurred as early as Runic Swedish. At the end of the Old Swedish period, constructions using *bliva*, a borrowing from Low German, slowly replaced those employing *varda* (Wessén 1970b: 185). Constructions using *varda* or *bliva* tend to signify a change of state, whereas those using *vara* tended to signify an ongoing situation (Wessén 1970b: 185-186):

(7) Purposeful murder, 13
MEL: *Komber thaes manz arffue som draepin* ***wardh***
Comes that man's heir who killed-PARTIC was
'If the heir of the man who was killed arrives'
(8) Purposeful wounding, 6
MEL: ***Wardher*** *man hoggin i hand*
Is someone cut-PARTIC in hand
'If someone's hand is cut'

The following tables show the distribution of Old Swedish source constructions of Finnish imperfect passives using *-tAAn/ttiin* and (periphrastic) perfect passives using a copular *olla* and a participle with the ending *-ttU,* taken from a sample of the corpus. The samples used are: M, Building; L1, King's Chapter as well as Marriage and Inheritance; K1, Court Chapter and Peace Oath, L2, Trade; K2, Church Chapter (with UL as source text); RWL, Courthouse Chapter.

Table 4:2. *The passive and its Swedish source constructions.*

M	Imperfect		Perfect	
	-s	49	*-s*	1
	vara	4	*vara*	73

	varda	26	*varda*	1
	other	29	other	6

L1	Imperfect		Perfect	
	-s	65	*-s*	0
	vara	7	*vara*	57
	varda	11	*varda*	0
	other	18	other	7

K1	Imperfect		Perfect	
	-s	70	*-s*	0
	vara	5	*vara*	43
	varda	9	*varda*	2
	other	17	other	2

K2	Imperfect		Perfect	
	-s	42	*-s*	0
	vara	2	*vara*	38
	varda	12	*varda*	0
	other	17	other	2

RWL	Imperfect		Perfect	
	-s	185	*-s*	213
	vara	0	*vara*	0
	varda	13	*varda*	0
	varde (opt.)	27	*varde* (opt)	0
	other	42	other	12

The unsurprising result is that *-s* passives tend to be translated mainly as imperfect (present and past imperfect, though overwhelmingly more often present) passives in Finnish, and that periphrastic passives using *vara* tend to be translated as periphrastic passives using *olla*. This is of course to be expected, regarding the similarity in tenses between the impersonal and periphrastic passives in Finnish and Swedish. Constructions using *varda*, however, tend to be usually translated with imperfect passives. In RWL, a large number of constructions using *varda* and a perfect participle are optatives, which are translated with a passive imperative in Finnish:

(9) Courthouse Chapter, 1:12
SRL: *varde* *Domaren ... sielf* *straffad*
become-CONJ judge himself punished-PARTIC
til lif eller ära
with life or honour
RWL: *Rangaistacon* *Tuomari ... itze hengen*
Punish-PASS IMPER judge self life-GEN
eli cunnian *puolesta*
or honour-GEN with regards to
'May the judge himself be punished, with his life or his honour'

(10) Courthouse Chapter 5:2
SRL: *och varde* *then ... til Höfrätten* *sänd*
and become-CONJ it to high court sent-PARTIC
inom Michels dag
before St. Michael's day
RWL: *lähetettäkön* *se ... Howrättijn,* *ennen Mickelin päiwää*
send-PASS IMPER it to high court before St. Michael's day
'And let it be sent to the High Court before St. Michael's day'

What this establishes, however, is that an interlingual identification between the *-s* passive and the Finnish imperfect passive on the one hand, and between the Swedish periphrastic passive using *vara* and the Finnish equivalent construction using *olla* 'to be' is possible.

4.5. The object of the negated passive

An important difference between subjects and objects (as well as subjects of existential clauses) in Finnish is their behaviour under the scope of negation: as mentioned earlier, objects and existential subjects in negative sentences are marked with the partitive case (Hakulinen et al. 2004: 890). There are sporadic exceptions to this case: Almqvist (1987: 39) finds a small number of accusative objects with negated clauses in a corpus of written modern Finnish, and Ojansuu (1909: 161, see also Häkkinen 1994: 361) mentions that an accusative with negated clauses does occur to some extent in Agricola's Old Finnish writings.

Partitive object marking occurs normally with passive verbs as well, both with negative clauses and under other, aspectual conditions which would govern a partitive case in positive clauses, for example: (Hakulinen et al. 2004: 1259):

isoäiti	*vietiin*	*sairaalaan*
grandmother-∅[5]	take-PASS IPF	hospital-ILL

'Grandmother was taken to the hospital'

vs.

isoäitiä	*ei*	*viety*	*sairaalaan*
grandmother-PART	NEG	take -PASS PARTIC PF	hospital-ILL

'Grandmother wasn't taken to the hospital'

It should be noted here that negation in Finnish employs a negative auxiliary *e-*, with person and number marking. Voice, tense/aspect and mood are marked on a non-finite form of the lexical verb, invariably preceded by the negative verb. An exception is the imperative, in which mood is doubly marked: by usage of a different stem (*äl-*) as the negative verb, and, in some cases, a suffix (*-kO*, in Old Finnish also *-kA)* on the lexical verb. In case of the impersonal passive, the negative auxiliary appears invariably in its basic 3rd pers. sing. form *ei*:

5 Hakulinen et al. (2004: 1186) do not recognize a "zero accusative" case, but rather opt to analyze *–n* and -∅ accusatives as genetives and nominatives, respectively, reserving the designation "accusative" for the *–t* accusative of personal pronouns.

häntä ei tapeta (indicative present) 'He will not be killed'
häntä ei tapettu (indicative imperfect past) 'He wasn't killed'
häntä ei ole tapettu (present perfect) 'He hasn't been killed'
häntä ei ollut tapettu (plusquamperfect) 'He hadn't been killed'

Through contact with Swedish, as well as with other languages, one could expect features of object promotion to appear, and one would expect, in the case of the negated passive, that the partitive object would be substituted with a nominative subject.

It should be noted in this context that there has been a tendency in some Finnish dialects in close contact with Swedish-speaking areas for the negative auxiliary to lose number and person marking - total loss of number marking, with the singular paradigm of the negative auxiliary being generalized to plural persons as well, seems to occur in mainly the Southwestern and Ingrian dialects (Savijärvi 1977: 181), with total loss of person and number marking occurring in the Southwestern dialects, the extinct Finnish of Värmland, and rarely in some Eastern dialects (Savijärvi 1977: 182, 188). Thus, there has been a tendency for the 3rd person sing. basic form of the negative auxiliary to appear as a negative particle. In Old Finnish, a similar tendency appears, as well as, in some cases, the appearance of person and number marking on the lexical verb) (Ojansuu 1909: 167, Savijärvi 1977: 196-197, 222; 1985, Forsman-Svensson 2000: 140-142). However, negation, and concomitant partitive case-marking of the object, seems to be more a semantic feature of the whole clause than something governed primarily by the negative auxiliary (Hakulinen and Karlsson 1988: 182-183): some adverbs bearing negative meaning, such as *tuskin* 'hardly', may cause partitive case-marking as well as the negative auxiliary, and the negative auxiliary does not necessarily cause partitive case-marking in sentences where the underlying tone is generally positive, e.g., starting with such phrases as *eikö meidän pitäisi* 'shouldn't we?'. Also, Savijärvi's (1977: 64) examples of negated passive clauses in the Southwest dialects seem to show partitive objects.

In any event, one would expect object promotion to show first of all in periphrastic, perfect passive constructions, which are formed with the auxiliary *olla* 'to be', which almost invites a reanalysis whereby the passive participle is reanalyzed as a nominal predicate, and the object of the passive verb as the subject of a copular *olla.* As mentioned, this reanalysis does occur widely in spoken Finnish with perfect passive constructions (Hakulinen et al. 2004: 1260).

The following tables show the distribution of case-markers with negated passives, divided between imperfect (e.g. present and past imperfect) and perfect (e.g. periphrastic, present perfect and past perfect/plusquamperfect) passives, the latter employing an auxiliary *olla.*

Table 4:3. *Negated passives and case-marking.*

M:

n=88	∅	P	0	?
imperfect	10	24	6	10
perfect	9	2	21	6

L1:

n=84	∅	P	0	?
imperfect	14	17	4	3
perfect	19	0	24	3

L2:

n=59	∅	P	0	?
imperfect	9	17	12	2
perfect	12	0	7	0

K1:

n=88	∅	P	0	?
imperfect	10	30	6	4
perfect	10	2	24	2

K2:

n=56	∅	P	0	?
imperfect	2	23	1	3
perfect	10	1	15	1

RWL:

n=111	∅	P	0	?
imperfect	1	42	11	5
perfect	21	11	15	5

Though the numbers involved here are small, they do provide a consistent picture: zero accusative/nominative objects occur particularly with perfect-tense passives, virtually exclusively so in all the texts except RWL. With imperfect-tense passives, there seems to be variation in M, L1 and L2 with the zero accusative/nominative being an only slightly more marginal alternative of partitive case-marking. In K1, K2 and particularly RWL, partitive case-marking seems to be more common with imperfect-tense passives. This would support a primary role played by the auxiliary *olla* in furthering a reanalysis from object to subject, e.g., object promotion.

Some examples with perfect-tense passives:

(11) King's Chapter 4
M: *iold* ***eikä se*** *ole ennen lailla* ***woitettu,***
if NEG he-∅ be before law-ADESS win-PASS PARTIC
eli ***sorttu*** *oikeudella*
or convict-PASS PARTIC justice-ADESS
L1: *iollei* ***se*** *ennen* ***ole*** *ruodzin kirioitetulla lailla* ***voitettu,*** *ia oikeudella duomittu*
'If he has not been found guilty by law, and sentenced by court'

(12) Trade, 3:
L2: *Iollei se ole käsketty myytä*
If-NEG it-∅ be order-PASS PARTIC to be sold
'If is has not been ordered to be sold'

(13) Ships, 13
K2: *ja* ***se eij ole*** *ulwos* ***wiety***
and it-∅ NEG be out bring-PASS PARTIC
'and it has not been brought out'

(14) Trade, 15
K2: *Joll****eica händä*** *sencaldaisesta* ***ole käsitetty***
If-NEG he-PART such-ELAT be catch-PASS PARTIC
'If he has not been caught for such a reason before'

(15) Inheritance 22:1
RWL: *Jos* ***se ei ole ylöskirjoitettu***
If it-∅ NEG be write-PASS PARTIC
'If it has not been written'

(16) Building 27:4 4
RWL: *Jos* ***ei uutta peldoa ole tehty***
If NEG new-PART field-PART be make-PASS PARTIC
'If a new field has not been made'

Notably, variation between partitive and zero accusative/nominative subject-marking seems to be partially free, with both alternatives occurring in virtually identical contexts:

(17) Building, 34
M: *ios **hän** mös sihen **ei** **sidhota***
if he-∅ also there-ILL NEG bind-PASS
'If he isn't found guilty of that either'

(18) Building, 44
M: *ioldei **händä** laillisesti **sidhota***
if-NEG he-PART legally bind-PASS
'If he isn't legally found guilty'

(19) Peace Oath, 4
K1: *nijn **eij** **ole** **Walasyy** **rikottu***
thus NEG be Peace Oath-∅ break-PASS PARTIC
'Thus the Peace Oath is not broken'

(20) Peace Oath, 13
K1: *Sijnä **eij** **ole** walan **syytä** **rikottu***
There NEG be Peace Oath-PART break-PASS PARTIC
'There, the Peace Oath is not broken'

It would be interesting to see whether case-marking is affected by the semantics of the object/subject as well. If the variable case-marking with passive objects found in the corpus is indeed indicative of an ongoing process of object promotion, one might expect the transition from object to subject to primarily affect those objects which are, by their semantic nature, prototypical subjects: namely, human and animate objects[6.] In other words, if an underlying restructuring from object to subject, with concomitant changes in case-marking, takes place, we might expect more loss of object case-marking for those objects that are prototypical in a subject position, whereas non-prototypical subjects would retain their object case-marking more often.

As the following table shows, closer analysis partially indicates this: there seems to be an association of nominative/zero accusative arguments and human or animate referents with negated passives, and of partitive arguments and inanimate referents with negated passives, in Martti's and Ljungo's translations. In Kollanius' translations, however, such an association does not show, and in RWL, only quite weakly.

6 Cross-linguistically, this might not be so obvious as it seems, though. Hidalgo (1994: 176-177) mentions that the inverse seems to occur in Spanish, with a promotional passive occuring with non-topical (inanimate, indefinite, etc.) patients, and a non-promotional impersonal clause with definite patients.

Table 4:4. *Negated passives, animacy and case-marking*

		hum./anim.	inanim.	chi sq.	sign. at 0.05
M	Ø	13	6	3.9	yes
	P	10	16		
L1	Ø	20	13	8.3	yes
	P	3	14		
L2	Ø	7	14	4.3	yes
	P	1	16		
K1	Ø	4	16	1.8	no
	P	12	20		
K2	Ø	3	9	1	no
	P	10	14		
RWL	Ø	8	14	3.3	no
	P	9	44		

However, the sample sizes we are dealing with here are all quite small – and, probably, too small to base any firm conclusions on.

There may, however, be a confounding factor at work here which itself is not related to the grammatical categorization of the single argument of the passive. In Finnish, conjunctions often fuse with a following negative auxiliary, a fusion generally accompanied by apocope: thus *että* 'that' becomes *ettei* 'that not'. The conjunction *jos* 'if' had a number of fused, negative counterparts in Old Finnish: *jollei, jolleica, joldei, jossei* and *ellei* are all found in the corpus. Mostly, these are based on apocope forms of conjunctions such as *jolla, jolta, jossa,* and *ellä*. Now, with Martti and Ljungo (but not Kollanius or RWL), there seems to be a correlation between the occurrence of a fused conjunction *jollei* 'if not' or equivalents, and zero accusative/nominative case-marking of the single argument of the passive:

Table 4:5. *The negative conditional conjunction jollei and case-marking.*

		jollei	other	chi sq.	sign.at 0.05

M	Ø	8	11	2.8	no
	P	5	21		
L1	Ø	16	17	9.1	yes
	P	1	16		
L2	Ø	12	9	8.3	yes
	P	2	15		
K1	Ø	3	17	1.2	no
	P	9	23		
K2	Ø	1	11	0.5	no
	P	4	20		
RWL	Ø	1	21	0.2	no
	P	4	49		

The numbers nonetheless involved are very small, and the distribution reaches statistical significance only in Ljungo's text. It might be possible to hypothesize that *jollei* and equivalents were not seen by Martti and Ljungo as containing a negative auxiliary, but rather as lexical equivalents of Old Swedish wtan 'if not, unless', which precedes a grammatically positive sentence, the factuality of which depends on the factuality of the main clause.

Here is a case in which Martti and Ljungo (of course, perhaps mistakenly) seem to use *jollei* in a clause which seems to be meant as positive (as it is with Kollanius as well in KrL):

(21) Court Chapter, 43

M: *maxakan 3 mrka colmie iakohon,* ***iollej*** *hän sanans synä cohta oienna ia iällens eli takaperin otta.*

L1: *maxakan 3 marca col: kerd:* ***iollei*** *hän sanans sijnä*
if-NEG he word-3SG there
cohta oienna ia takaperin åtta.
immediately rectifies and withdraws

K1: *maxacaan colmet marca, colmehen osahan,*
jos *hän cohta sanansa ojenda, eli tacaperin otta.*

if he immediately word-3SG rectifies or withdraws
KrL: *böte III mark til treskiptis* ***om*** *han siin ordh genast raetter eller j geen kallar.*
'Let him pay three marks in three parts, if he immediately rectifies or withdraws his words.'

In the following two cases, Ljungo uses a negative *mutoin iollei*, where Martti uses a positive conditional clause with *jos*:

(22) Court Chapter, 25
M: *mwtoin* ***ios*** *hän laissa wanno walallansa, nÿn ettej hän lakia*
except if he law-INESS swears oath-ADESS
tiedhä sÿnä asiasa
L1: *mutoin* ***iollei*** *hän käräiäs wanno idze walallans etei hän*
except IF-NEG he court-INESS swears himself oath-ADESS
lakia sijnä asias tiedhä
KrL: *wtan han for thinge swær meth een edhe sinom ath han ey lagh om thet maal weeth*
'except if he swears by an oath in court, that he does not know the law on this issue'

(23) Purposeful murder, 6
M: *nijn tule hänen saadha cwkaudhen päiuät mennä kuningan tÿgö, ia 14 öätä mennä kuningan tÿköä pois, ia ei enämbä,*
mwtoin ***ios*** *hän nautitze kuningan armoia*
except if he receives king-GEN mercy-PART
L1: *nin hänellä on Cwkauden päivät Kuningann ethen tulla, ia 14 ötä Kuningan tyköä mennä ia ey enämbätä,*
mutoin ***iollei*** *hän Kuningan armoia nautitze*
if-NEG he king-GEN mercy-PART receives
KrL: *tha ægher han maanada dagh haua fore konung koma, oc XIIII nætter fraan konunge fara, oc ey lenger, wtan han konungs nadh nyute meth fridzbreff hans*
'he shall have a month to travel to the king, and fourteen days to travel back, and no more, except if he has received mercy from the king.'

Additionally, there are some cases in which Martti and Ljungo combine a negated *jollei* with another negative verb in the same clause:

(24) Inheritance, 12
M: *quitengin* ***ioldei*** *cansalapsett* ***ei*** *ole tiedholle*
however if-NEG sibling-PL NEG are knowledge-ALL
tulluet, ia ios Isä eli äiti ei ole eläillä, joka ei tappanut eli murhannut
come-PARTIC
L1: *jos ey täysiä sisarita ole taidholla tullet, jos* ***ei*** *isä eli äiti*
if NEG father or mother
ei ***ole*** *elehillä ioca ei tappanut eli murhannut*

NEG is alive
KrL: *æn ey æru samsytzkan til weetz komen, oc æn ey ær fadher eller modher lifuandis til som ey draapo eller myrdho*
'If no siblings are yet able, and if they have no living father or mother, who has not committed murder'

(25) Building, 31
M: *nÿtt ios se quin maan eli kihlacunna ÿcteitzellä asupi köÿhtÿ nijn*
ettei *hän maan eli kihlacunnan*
THAT-NEG he land-GEN or district-GEN
oikeut ***ei*** *woi vlgos tehdä*
right-PART NEG can uphold
KrL: *Nu æn then som a almenningiom landz eller heredz boor, kan fatikdom henda, swa ath han formaa ey landz skyld vppehalda*
'if he who lives on the common lands of the land or parish is so impoverished, that he cannot comply with the rights of the land or the district'

(26) Capital crimes, 11
M: ***ioldei ei*** *enämbi löÿtä nijn*
IF-NEG NEG more find-PASS
KrL: *vindz ey mera ath*
'if nothing more is found'

In the latter two cases, however, M's independent negative verb is absent in five other manuscripts (Airila, Harmas 1930: 165, 274), while in the first it is absent in four (Airila, Harmas 1930: 72). In L2, similar cases occur as well:

(27) Trade, 31
L2: ***Jollei eij*** *hän woij maxa, käykän työhön Kuninghalle ia Caupungille, quin ennen on sanottu*
'If he cannot pay, let him go to work for the King and the City, as has been said before.'

(28) Ships, 6
L2: ***Jollei ei*** *paatti catoa maxakan quitengin 6 marca col . ker :*
'If the boat does not disappear, then he should nevertheless pay six marks threefold.'

This said, it should be noted that double negation in general occurs to some extent in the corpus, notably, with Kollanius as well:

(29) Marriage, 2
K2: *Jos* ***eij*** *se cuin neljäkymmendä marca maxaman pitä,* ***eij*** *woi maxa, mengähän työhön*
'If he who must pay forty marks cannot pay, then let him go to work.'

(30) Trade, 19:
L2: *Nin **eij** **ej** pidhe yhtän Cauppa Sunnun takina tehtämän*
thus NEG NEG must any trade-PART sunday-ESS be done
'thus no trade must be done on Sundays'

(31) Theft, 14
L2: Löytä mies aion suolaises wedes eli ierffues,
*Kussa **ei** oikea åmistaia **eij** lässä ole*
where NEG right owner NEG present is
'If a man finds wreckage in salt water or in a lake, where the right owner isn't present'

Thus, it's possible to hypothesize that the presence of *jollei* and a (sporadic) "bleaching" of the negative meaning inherent in the fused conjunction, perhaps influenced by its frequent usage of Old Swedish *wtan*, was a minor factor promoting zero accusative/nominative case-marking with passive verbs. This said, the occasional occurrence of an independent negative auxiliary in combination with *jollei* may perhaps be seen as a consequence of the general, occasional presence of double negation in the corpus, rather than as a sign of loss of negativity with *jollei.* Also, it should be noted that, even where the usage of *jollei* seems to be clearly inappropriate as the sentence seems to have been intended as positive, it normally does seem to cause partitive case-marking on the direct object. Thus, the paucity of the, albeit interesting, indicators *jollei* may have been subject to loss of negative meaning, as well as the small amount of negated passives in general, make it difficult to substantiate whether the presence of *jollei* may have been a factor in the loss of case-marking with the partitive.

4.6. Agreement

Another parameter indicating subjecthood in Finnish is agreement between the subject and the main verb in person and number. In Finnish, this presupposes nominative case-marking, rather than genitive or partitive case-marking, on the part of the subject. In case of passive verbs, agreement would seem to be a good indicator of object promotion. As mentioned, in Agricola's texts, agreement in person and number appears to an extent even with present/imperfect passive verbs (Hakulinen 1979: 241), however, such forms do not appear in the corpus used here. Also, the corpus shows only sporadic occurrences of 1st and 2nd persons - they seem to occur only in a few instances of direct speech, as well as a few instances where oaths are directly quoted. This leaves only agreement in number as an avenue of research. This means, additionally, that negated sentences cannot be expected to show any traces of agreement: the 3rd person plural form of the negated auxiliary, *eivät*, was marginal up until the 19th century, and Old Finnish generally used an unmarked *ei* with plural subjects (Häkkinen 1994: 345).

The following table shows occurrence of number agreement with plural arguments and periphrastic passives (that is, perfect passives, using an auxiliary *olla*), pitted against occurrences of non-agreement with such passives. Partitive objects have been taken into account as non-agreeing. Also, in a number of cases, a periphrastic passive may exhibit plural marking without the presence of an explicit plural subject: these include in particular cases where the relative pronoun *kuin* functions as a subject, as in the following example:

(32) King's Chapter, 5
L1: *Sijttä mahta hän länit lainata, waldakundans hallita, ia caicki tehdä,*
quin   *ennen*   *sanottut*   *ouat*
REL   before   say-PASS PARTIC   be
'which have been mentioned before'

Table 4:6. *Perfect passives and agreement.*

	M	L1	L2	K1	K2	RWL
agr.	32	37	20	22	22	57
non-agr.	1	4	1	0	2	2

The numbers indicate that agreement in number is clearly the normal case, whenever such agreement is applicable. Number, however, may be marked inconsistently throughout the texts: usually, both the auxiliary and the passive participle show plural marking:

(33) Marriage, 17
L1: *ios*   *huomen lahiat*   *olit*   *annetut*
if   dowry-PL   be-PL   give-PASS PARTIC PL
'If the dowry was given'

Sometimes, only the passive participle shows plural marking. Cases like these includes negative clauses:

(34) Peace Oath, 43
L1: *Jollei*   *he*   *ole*   *tauoitetut*
if-NEG   they-PL   be   caught-PASS PARTIC PL

'If they are not caught'

(35) Marriage, 18

K1: *On*	*ne*	*maasta*	*annetut*
Be	they-PL	land-EL	give-PASS PARTIC PL

'If land is given'

Finally, there are some cases where the auxiliary is marked in the plural, but the passive participle remains unmarked for number:

(36) Trade, 26

L2: *iotca*	*sen*	*pälle*	*pandu*	*ouat*
REL-PL	it-GEN	upon-POSTP	place-PASS PARTIC	be-PL

'who have been assigned to it'

Lack of agreement with plural arguments occurs only sporadically. As mentioned, plural partitive objects were taken into account here: it seems these, too, are quite rare. Not all cases of non-agreement occur with partitives:

(37) Peace Oath, 44

L1: *nin*	*on*	*kuningan*	*wala*	*sakot*	*rikotu*
thus	be	king-GEN	peace oath-PL	break-PASS PARTIC	

'Thus the King's Peace Oath is broken'

The picture is thus clearly that, wherever the conditions for number agreement occur in the text (i.e. with plural arguments), agreement does occur. This clearly indicated object promotion in case of periphrastic passives. It is interesting to contrast this with negated passives, which, as mentioned, still show partitive case-marking to some extent even with periphrastic passives. Most of these have, in fact, singular arguments: plural partitive arguments appear to be quite rare. Like negation, plural nominative/zero accusative arguments force disambiguation: the underlying linguistic analysis of the argument as subject or object becomes visible in surface structure. There might be underlying semantic reasons for the fact that this disambiguation seems to have swung into the direction of object promition more often in the case of plural arguments than with negated sentences: the Finnish partitive, after all, entails some features concerning countability and species: typically, the partitive is the object and subject case for mass nouns, divisible nouns and the like, as well as the object case for negative clauses. Perhaps the greater degree of individuation for nominative/zero accusative arguments marked in the plural may have been a factor in actuating object promotion to a greater degree here.

Thus object promotion, which seems to have its focus in the reinterpretation of the single argument of the periphrastic passive, seems to occur most clearly in contexts where some other factor forces the issue: negation, which demands a partitive object but a nominative subject (in non-existential clauses) and plurality, which demands agreement with a subject but does not allow agreement with an object. In other cases, the analysis followed is variable: something clearly seen with negated imperfect passives, which may take both nominative and partitive-marked arguments. As Harris and Campbell remark, this ambiguity is a hallmark of processes of reanalysis and extension:

> After reanalysis, typically extension alters one aspect of the surface manifestation before others. At this point, a surface structure has some of the structurally ambiguous aspects that it had before reanalysis, but also one (newly extended to it) that is unambiguously characteristic of the new analysis, and often at least one that is characteristic of the old. For this reason, speakers must be able to see both analyses at once. (Harris and Campbell 1995: 59)
>
> The recognition that a speaker uses multiple analyses during the period of actualization provides a natural acount of the apparently contradictory data that are found in real changes. (Harris and Campbell 1995: 83)

The data concerning object promotion with the Old Finnish passive strongly support that, unless one analysis is forced by some syntactic circumstance, the argument of the passive is in a way both subject and object, at the same time.

4.7. Periphrastic passives with *tulla*

A common passive construction in Old Finnish employs the verb *tulla* 'to come' as an auxiliary, combined with a translative form of the passive perfect participle:

työ	*tulee*	*tehdyksi*
work-NOM	become-3SG	do-PASS PARTIC TRANS

"The work gets done"

The construction does occur in Finnish dialects. The translative participle is used mainly in the Southwestern dialects as well as those of Ostrobothnia (though widely in eastern dialects as well), whereas in the dialects of Häme a similar construction employing a partitive passive occurs (Ikola, Palomäki and Koitto 1989: 454). Though not very frequently, the construction is a part of modern Standard Finnish as well, where, as in dialectal Finnish, it seems to designate a somewhat fortitious, accidental occurrence (Ikola 1978: 41-42, Ikola, Palomäki and Koitto 1989: 454, Häkkinen 1994: 468). As Häkkinen mentions (1994: 468), the construction seems to be mainly used in Old Finnish as a translation equivalent of source constructions employing *bliva* (in Swedish) or *werden* (in German).

In the corpus, the construction is somewhat marginal in M, but occurs more frequently in the other texts, as the following table shows. Source constructions have been checked with the translations of KrL as well as with the source text of RWL:

Table 4:7. *The periphrastic passive with tulla and source constructions.*

	number of constructions	*varda* as source construction
M	10	3
L1	32	21
L2	43	
K1	51	43
K2	48	
RWL	67	*varda*: 43 *bliva*: 11

What this shows is that *varda* (and, in RWL, *bliva* as well) were the main source constructions for periphrastic passives employing *tulla* for all texts excluding M. Some examples:

(38) King's Chapter, 31
M: *hän* *fangitan* *ia* *täydhellisilla*
he-NOM catch-PASS and complete-ADESS PL
toimituxilla *ia* *Todhistailla* ***tule***
act-ADESS PL and witness-ADESS PL become-3SG
woitetuxi
win-PASS PARTIC TRANS
L: *ios hän kynni åtethan ia täydellä toimella ia todistoxella laillisesti* ***tule woitetuxi***
K: *Saadhan hän kijnni, ja täydhellä toimella, sekä todhistoxilla* ***tule*** *laillisesti* ***woitetuxi***
KrL: *warder han faangen oc meth fullom skælom oc witnom laglica tilwnnen*

'If he is caught and found legally guilty, with witnesses'

(39) Purposeful Wounding, 15
M: *mwtoin ios hän* ***tule***
unless if he-NOM become-3SG
nijn ***lyödhyxi***
thus beat-PASS PARTIC TRANS
K: *Mutoin jos hän nijn* ***tule mändätyxi*** *eli* ***hakatuxi***
KrL *wtan hon warde swa baardh eller huggen*
'Unless he gets beaten in such a fashion'

(40) Crimes, 12:1
RWL: *Jos mies eli waimo surma toisen wäijywäisesti ja salaisesti ;*
tulcon *murhajan pää pois*
become-IMPER murderer-GEN head off
lyödyxi, *mies*
strike-PASS PARTIC TRANS man-NOM
teilatuxi, *ja waimo*
broken on the wheel-PASS PARTIC TRANS and woman-NOM
lawosa ***poltetuxi***
pyre-INESS burn-PASS PARTIC TRANS
SRL: *Varde mördaren halshuggen, mannen steglad, och qvinnan i båle bränd*
'If a man or a woman murders another secretly, may the murderer's head be cut off, the man broken on the wheel, and the woman burnt on the pyre.'

4.8. Agent phrases

As mentioned earlier, the passive of Modern Finnish implies a human agent which is not mentioned explicitly in the text, and the Finnish passive does not allow for an agent to be expressed by an adverbial phrase. Agent phrases employing an ablative agent occur extremely rarely in some dialects bordering Swedish-speaking areas (Itkonen-Kaila 1992: 158), whereas adessive-marked agents occur sporadically in Eastern dialects, possibly through Karelian influence (Nau 1995: 150-151).

In literary Old Finnish, however, ablative agent phrases (to some extent agent phrases using the elative cases and certain postpositions as well) occurred quite frequently until the end of the 19th century (Häkkinen 1994: 360, 478). The exact origin of agent phrases is difficult to determine: according to Itkonen-Kaila (1992: 148), Latin (with agent phrases using the preposition *ab*) as well as German (with agent phrases using the preposition *von*) may have played an important role in addition to Swedish (which employs the preposition *av* in agent phrases).

In the corpus, agent phrases are fairly rare, though they occur to a somewhat bigger extent in RWL, as the following table shows:

Table 4:8. Agent phrases in the corpus.

	M	L1	L2	K1	K2	RWL
agent phrases	7	7	6	3	3	48

It seems to me that the low number of agent phrases in the older translations is more a consequence of the nature of the text than any indication of the translators' idiolect. Thus I counted as many agentive phrases (namely, three) in the short confirmation by Carl IX in the preface of K1 (which was not otherwise taken into account) as in the whole body of the text. Cross-linguistically, personal passives without an over agentive phrase appear to be more common than those employing agent phrases (Siewierska 1984: 30, 35). A situation somewhat analogous to the borrowing of the agent phrase in Old Finnish appears to occur in some Dravidian languages, notably Kannada, which employs both an impersonal passive with object promotion, and an impersonal one with optional object promotion (in case of non-human patients) (Sridhar 1990: 214-215). Both constructions appear to be rare and restricted to formal language (the personal passive more so than the impersonal), notably translated texts from English or Hindi, even so, agent phrases are rarer than the lack of an overt agent (Sridhar 1990: 214). A similar situation, with the passive occurring rarely, in formal style and often translated texts, but agent phrases even rarer, occurs in Tamil (Asher 1985: 151-152) and Telugu (Krishnamurti and Gwynn 1985: 225). The law translations, which show their roots in orally transmitted law in their brief, formulaically repeated sentences, may simply not be a fruitful soil for agent phrases to appear.

A few examples of agent phrases, taken from RWL, follow. The sample compared with the Swedish source text (namely, the Courthouse Chapter) shows virtually exclusively phrases employing *av*.

(41) Courthouse Chapter 8:2 4

RWL: *Hengen asiat,* *jotka* *Ala-oikeuxilda*
Capital crimes which lowercourts-ABL
tutkitut *ja* *tuomitut*
investigated-PASS PARTIC and judged-PASS PARTIC
owat
are

SRL*: Lifssaker, som af Underrätterna ranskade och dömde äro*
'Capital crimes, which have been investigated and judged by lower courts.'

(42) Courthouse Chapter 10:21

RWL: *mutta* *tuomittacon* *caiken edestä* *sildä*
but judge-PASS IMPER for everything that-ABL
Oikeudelda
court-ABL
SRL: *men varde dömd för altsammans af then Rätt*
'But let (him) be judged by that court'

(43) Courthouse Chapter 10:26

RWL: *Nijn myös ne (...) coetellan* *ja* *tuomitan*
thus also those investigate-PASS and judge-PASS
nijldä (...)
those-ABL
SRL: *Så ock the (...) pröfves och dömes af them*
'Thus also those will be investigated and judged by those (...)'

4.9. Overview

Contact with Swedish seems to have stimulated the development of a promotional passive in Old Finnish, partially through restructuring of the old non-promotional passive, partially through the usage of a competing construction with *tulla* and a passive participle bearing translative case-marking as an equivalent of Swedish source constructions with *varda* and *bliva*. Parameters signifying subjecthood, and thereby presence of object promotion, are lack of partitive case-marking in negated clauses, and agreement with the subject in person and number. As to the former, the present/imperfect passive with the marker *-tAAn* shows strong variation between nominative and partitive case-marking, which would suggest simultaneous presence of both possible analyses: the argument as object and as subject. Nominative case-marking, though, is at most a marginal remnant in case of periphrastic perfect passives, with the exception of RWL. Agreement in person and number in Old Finnish occurs marginally with the present/imperfect passive, i.e., somewhat in Agricola's texts, but not at all in the corpus studied here. With perfect periphrastic passives, though, agreement in number is the normal case – though it can be marked in a variety of ways. Finally, the presence of agent phrases, though sporadic with the exception of RWL, may be taken as another sign of the development of a promotional passive (Givón 2001b: 128). It should be noted that all of these somewhat conflict with each other: for example, nominative and partitive case-marking both occur with periphrastic passives in RWL, but, with few exceptions, wherever it can occur, agreement in number does occur. Again, this would indicate that both possible analyses of the single argument of the passive are present in the background, one of them being realized in structural environments which "force the issue" – but perhaps some structural environments provide a stronger stimulus for object promotion to become manifest than others.

Leaving aside, for a moment, the passive construction employing *tulla* and a participle bearing transitive case-marking, the usage of which as a translation equivalent of constructions employing *varda* and *bliva* in Swedish seems to be a straightforward incidence of covert interference, and the marginal occurrence of agent phrases, it should be noted that, taken by itself, the development of a promotional passive out of the periphrastic passive is a perfect example of reanalysis and subsequent extension. The construction *poika on kutsuttu* 'the boy is invited' can be taken as [*poika*]OBJ [*on kutsuttu*]PASS PERF or as [*poika*]SUBJ [*on*]COP [*kutsuttu*]PASS PARTIC without any modification in the surface structure, and, from the variation observed in the material of this study, it seems both analyses are present. However, syntactic contexts such as non-3rd person singular arguments – *minä olen kutsuttu* vs. *minut on kutsuttu* 'I am invited', or negation – *poika* (NOM) *ei ole kutsuttu* 'the boy was not invited' vs. *poikaa* (PART) *ei ole kutsuttu*, or plural arguments – *pojat ovat kutsutut* vs. *pojat on kutsuttu* 'the boys were invited', force the issue one way or another. This point was driven home by Esa Itkonen, who compares reanalysis and extension in language and the hypothetico-deductive method in science as both manifestations of reasoning where, to avoid circularity, the hypothesis, or linguistic analysis, must be proven fruitful in leading to new predictions, or being extended to non-ambiguous contexts:

> Taken in itself, abduction is an instance of circular thinking. The law which has been abduced has, as yet, no genuine support. To acquire such support, it must allow the deduction of new predictions about other (types of) data. Only if such predictions are made, and only if in addition they turn out to be true, has the law been (tentatively) confirmed. (E. Itkonen 2002: 414)

> The hypothetico-deductive method applies to events that occur in the outside world. Reanalysis and extension applies to language which is a normative practice; that is, extension as an analogue of deducing new predictions is not about new events to be discovered, but about new actions to be performed by the speaker him-/herself. Moreover, the analogue of deducing (new) true predictions consists in performing (new) actions that will be accepted by the linguistic community. New predictions are discovered to be true but new actions are accepted to be correct. (E. Itkonen 2002: 416).

However, regarding the above case of reanalysis and extension as reanalysis and extension *as opposed to* syntactic borrowing, or conversely, as a case of syntactic borrowing *as opposed to* such "internal mechanisms of change" as reanalysis and extension – surely it is possible to regard the change from object to subject with accompanying subject-properties such as nominative case-marking in negated clauses, agreement in person and number, etc. as borrowed from Swedish as well – would leave, in my opinion, part of the picture out of view. As structural changes are instantiated through cognitive operations by speakers, some of which may be bilingual, and are then accepted and spread throughout a speech-community, a model which regards syntactic borrowings as reanalysis/extension performed upon a diamorph within a single bilingual competence would capture both, and would allow us to regard such structural changes as, by establishing isomorphism between the two interlingually identified constructions, establishing iconicity (the principle of one meaning – one form) between structure and meaning:

From

poika	*on*	*kutsuttu*	-----	*pojken*	*är*	*inbjuden*
subj-ACC	be	PASS PARTIC		subj-NOM	be	PASS PARTIC

'The boy is invited'

To

poika	*on*	*kutsuttu*
pojken	*är*	*inbjuden*
subj-NOM	be	PASS PARTIC

'The boy is invited'

We see here that the *reanalysis* of an object as a subject – which as such leaves no traces in surface morphosyntax – can equally be regarded as the *transfer* of subjecthood within a given contruction from a source language, and that the change as a whole serves to establish a more iconic relationship between meaning and form. In order to gain a holistic view on a certain change, the dichotomy between internal and external changes, even that appearing in a typology between reanalysis/extension on the one hand and syntactic borrowing on the other hand, must be abandoned. Structural change is always internal, in that it always proceeds through cognitive processes performed by a speaker on the language he speaks. They are always external, in that single changes can be never isolated from extralinguistic factors in general, and, with bilingualism and multilingualism being ubiquitous, are extremely difficult to isolate from language contact. Distinguishing "internal" from "external" changes may have made sense in the effort to isolate subsystems of language more or less impervious to contact-induced change and thereby reliable guides to genetic relationships, but with this effort seeming more difficult than ever as the transfer of just about any structural linguistic feature has been documented somewhere, and with the dichotomy hampering our understanding of contact-induced processes such as the development of a promotional passive documented in this chapter, we may be better off scuttling it.

5. NECESSITIVE CONSTRUCTIONS[7]

5.1. Introduction

Here, I will examine the case-marking of the subject in various necessitive constructions in Old Finnish legal texts. In Standard Modern Finnish, the most common necessitive verbs – which take a genitive-marked subject, an unmarked accusative object and remain unipersonal (marked for 3rd pers. singular), and thus does not agree with the subject – are *täytyä*, *pitää*. *tarvita* and *tulla*. The verbs *täytyä* and *pitää* signal obligation to do something, *tarvita*, which usually appears in negative sentences, signals dispensation from obligation. Necessitive *tulla* is uncommon in spoken Finnish, but common in written language (particularly legalese). Whereas, usually, the subject is marked with the genitive, the subject appears in the unmarked nominative case when the infinitival complement is an existential verb form, however, in spoken varieties of Finnish, a nominative subject appears somewhat more widely, particularly with intransitive infinitival complements (Laitinen 1992: 11). The genitive subject, again, is most frequent with prototypical agents, particularly personal pronouns (Laitinen 1992: 271, Ikola, Palomäki and Koitto 1989: 358). This has led Terho Itkonen (1993 [1979]: 314-317, see also Laitinen and Vilkuna 1993: 25) to regard the case-marking associated with necessitive *pitää* as an "ideal ergative" or active/stative subsystem within the general "inverted ergative" alignment system of Finnish.

In older literary Finnish as well, personal pronouns appear usually with genitive case-marking as the subjects of necessitive constructions (Häkkinen 1994: 347). Thus:

Sinun *pitää* *laittaa* *lehmät* *talliin*
You-GEN must put-INF cow-ACC PL stable-ILL
'You must put the cows in the stable'
Illalla *lehmät* *pitää* *olla* *tallissa*
Evening-ADESS cow-NOM PL must be-INF stable-INESS
'At evening, the cows must be in the stable'

7 An earlier version of this section appeared as an article as De Smit (2005)

However, this picture is complicated somewhat with regards to Finnish dialects. As Laitinen (1992: 42, 50) points out, in various dialects (Southern Häme, Tornedal, Finnmark, Värmland) the originally unipersonal necessitive verb may agree in person and number with the (nominative) subject, whereas in other dialects (the eastern Southwestern dialects, the Savo dialects in Ostrobothnia, Värmland), the verb remains unipersonal, but takes nominative-marked personal pronouns as subjects. These dialects are spoken generally in the vicinity of Swedish-speaking communities and according to Laitinen (1992: 42, 50), these phenomena may have been caused by contact influence from Swedish (see also Saukkonen 1965: 123, Wande 1982: 62, Kangassalo, Nemvalts and Wande 2003: 157). Two examples by Terho Itkonen (1974: 392) from the dialect of Tuusula in Nyland:

Emäntä *piti* *ottaas* *sem* *pois* *minult*
Landlady-NOM must take-INF it-ACC away me-ABL
"The landlady had to take it away from me"

Em *miä ymmärräm* *mikä minun on ku*
NEG-1SG I understand what I-GEN is as
miä täyryn *aina* *itkee*
I must-1SG always cry-INF
"I don't know what's wrong with me, as I always have to cry"

In the following, I will deal with the variation between genitive- and nominative-marked subjects with the two most frequent necessitive verbs – *pitää* and *tulla* – in the corpus. I will explore the idea that the variation between nominative and genitive-marking with *pitää* could be explained, in case of Ljungo's and Martti's translation, by assuming a merger of the agent of *pitää* and an active infinitive complement, and the patient of *pitää* and a passive infinitive complement, leading to a redistribution of case-markers which somewhat resembles accusative case-marking.

5.2. Distribution of the necessitive verbs *pitää* and *tulla*

In the three texts surveyed, the most common necessitive verbs by far are *pitää* and *tulla*. Both necessitive constructions are still extant in modern Finnish as well, though *tulla* seems restricted in particular to legalistic usage (Ikola, Palomäki and Koitto 1989: 247-248). The dialectal basis of necessitive *pitää* seems to be the Eastern Finnish dialects, whereas in the Western dialects, it is competing with *täytyä* (Laitinen 1992: 39). I have found only two instance of necessitive *täytyä* in the older texts, namely, one in K2, where it occurs together with *pitää*, and one in L2:

(44) King's Chapter, 10
K2: *Nämä neljäkymmendä Marca* **täyty** *ia* **pitä**
These forty marks-ACC (unmarked) must and must
cadhentoistakymmenen miehen cansa nijldä ulwos arwattaman,
twelve-GEN man-GEN with those-ABL extract-INF PASS
jotca syypäät owat
who guilty be-3PL
'These forty marks must be extracted from those who are the guilty parties, by (a jury of) twelve men'

(45) Ships, 12
L2: *Käypi että heidhen* **täyty** *vlos heittä,*
Happens that they-GEN must throw out
heittäkän ensin hänenä calunsa vlos ioca luuata
throw-IMPER first his wares out who without permission
siselle sälytti
kept inside
'If it so happens that they must throw out wares, throw out first the wares of him who kept them inside without permission'

In RWL, *täytyä* occurs somewhat more widely, though still fairly rarely:

(46) Building, 22:5
Härkä, hewoinen, coira, eli mikä eläin se ikänäns on, joca
Ox, horse, dog or what animal it ever is, which
tarttuwaiseen tautijn cuole, eli tapettaa **täyty**
contagious-ILL disease-ILL dies, or be killed must
'An ox, a horse, a dog, or whatever animal, which dies of a contagious disease or must be killed'

(47) Building, 28:5, 5
nijn **täyty** *lähimmäisten naaburein hänelle awuxi*
thus must closest-GEN neighbours-GEN him-ALL help-TRANS
tuleman
come
'Thus must his closest neighbours come to help him'

The infinitival complement of *pitää* in the surveyed texts is generally a form of the 3rd infinitive with instructive case-marking – *hänen pitää tekemän* – a construction currently rare in Finnish dialects, occurring mainly in the Southwestern dialects (Ikola, Palomäki and Koitto 1989: 357), but very common in older Literary Finnish. The infinitival complement of *tulla* is generally a 1st infinitive – *hänen tulee tehdä.* With very few exceptions, the object of the infinitival complement is marked by the marked accusative or partitive (and not the zero accusative) case throughout the three documents, as it commonly is in older Literary Finnish (Häkkinen 1994: 362-363) as well as the western Finnish dialects (Laitinen 1992: 74).

In Old Swedish, the most common deontic expressions are formed by either conjunctive verbs or modal verbs, namely, *scal*, *ma* and *a* (Ståhle 1958: 1-3, Wendt 1997: 86). The modal verb *scal* seems to denote a more categorical order than *a* (Mattson 1933: 27-29), though the difference between the two seems to have a dialectal basis as well, *scal* being the most common in Old Swedish law texts, whereas *a* occurs in, particularly, the *Upplandslagen* and the *Östgötalagen* (Ståhle 1958: 3, Wendt 1997: 88). Finally, *ma* often denotates a dispensation from a given norm in positive sentences, and a prohibition in negative sentences (Mattson 1933: 23, Ståhle 1958: 1-2, Wendt 1997: 88).

In all three old Finnish texts, *pitää* seems to be the most common[8], occurring 478 times (or 72,2%) of 662 times in M, 522 (or 72,9%) of 726 times in L1 and 540 (or 77,9%) of 693 times in K1, the rest being occurrences of *tulla.* In L2, *tulla* is quite marginal, with *pitää* occurring 377 (95,9%) of 393 times. K2 (which includes part of the *Upplandslagen*) has a much larger share of *tulla,* with *pitää* occurring 436 times out of a total of 523 (83,4%). In RWL, *tulla* appears to be rather marginal as well, comprising only 6.4 percent of the analyzed examples. A breakdown of the numbers is presented in Appendix A.

Most commonly, constructions with *pitää* have equivalents with *scal* in the source text (84,8% in M, 86,8% in L1 and 80,6% in K1), whereas constructions with *tulla* usually have source patterns with *a* (3rd pers. sing. *aegher*) (71,8% in M, 72,7% in L1 and 79,1% in K1). Thus, Kollanius seems to use *pitää* somewhat more widely than the two earlier translators. Most of the occurrences of *tulla* in K2 seem to be based on *a*/*aegher* constructions in the translated Church Law chapter of the *Upplandslagen:* 52 constructions of *tulla* seem to have *a*/*aegher* as a source construction, and ten some other construction (*scal/sculu*, *maa*, etc.), whereas 38 occurrences of *pitää* seem to have *scal/sculu* as a source pattern, with 25 having another source pattern.

The existence of a diaform, or interlingual identification, between necessitive *pitää* and *scal*, Modern Swedish *ska*, is widely known and thought to have led to some changes in the use of *pitää* over time, notably,

---

8 I attempted to analyze all necessitive constructions in the three texts. Though it is possible I overlooked some, I am confident my corpus is representative of the texts as a whole. In case of multiple infinitival complements with different objects or even different voice-marking, these infinitival complements were taken into account as elliptical. Thus, the number of necessitive constructions in the corpus is somewhat higher than the number mentioned here, which designates instances of either *pitää* or *tulla* with an ascertainable Swedish source construction.

its non-implicative use in the Western Finnish dialects (Laitinen 1992: 218), the use of *pitää* without an infinitival complement in Western Finnish (Laitinen 1992: 139-140) and its use as a future auxiliary in older Literary Finnish (Ikola 1949: 199-205), though surely the construction itself is of indigenous origin (Laitinen 1992: 117-139). Like *pitää,* necessitive *tulla* has cognates in other Balto-Finnic languages, although, in case of Finnish, Swedish *tillkomma* has been thought to have facilitated its development as a necessitive construction (Saukkonen 1965: 152, Häkkinen 1993: 220).

5.3. Subject-marking and transitivity

Looking now at the relative frequency of nominative and genitive case-marking of the subject with *pitää* and *tulla* in the three texts (see the table in Appendix A), we find that nominative case-marking is generally much more frequent with *pitää* than with *tulla*, and also, much more frequent with the first two writers, Martti and Ljungo, than with Kollanius. Pirkko Forsman-Svensson (1992b: 56-59) noted a similar phenomenon: where, in her corpus of both religious texts and legal proclamations, nominative subjects occurred quite widely with *pitää* (more than a fourth of all cases with the religious texts, and more than half of all cases with the legal proclamations), *tulla* overwhelmingly preferred genitive subjects. As the number of occurrences of *tulla* in RWL is, as mentioned, quite low, not one example with nominative case-marking could be found.

Also, with Kollanius, a strong tendency to use a nominative subject in the absence of a direct object can be noted – with *pitää,* there are 53 occurrences of a nominative subject without a direct object, whereas 21 nominative subjects occur with an object marked one way or another. In K2, there are 64 occurrences of nominative subjects without a direct object and 22 with an object marked in the accusative or partitive. However, genitive subjects co-occur with direct objects 190 times and without a direct object 89 times in K1, with direct objects 127 times and without a direct object 85 times in K2. This may well reflect a tendency to use nominative subjects with intransitive sentences – as mentioned, well known in spoken Finnish. The same tendency can be found in RWL and also, though much weaker, with Martti: nominative subjects co-occur with direct objects 45 times, and without them 47 times, genitive subjects co-occur with direct objects 130 times, and without them 60 times. However, it is much harder to see the same tendency at work in Ljungo's translations. In L1, nominative subjects of *pitää* co-occur with direct objects 66 times, and without them 50 times, whereas genitive subjects co-occur with direct objects 125 times, and without them 76 times. In L2, nominative subjects of *pitää* co-occur with direct objects 62 times and without direct objects 63 times, genitive subjects of *pitää* co-occur with direct objects 79 times and without direct objects 36 times.

Table 5:1. *Marked object and absence of direct object with nominative and genitive-marked subjects.*

	obj	M	L1	L2	K1	K2	RWL
nom.	1	45	66	62	21	22	18
	0	47	50	63	53	64	80
gen.	1	130	125	79	190	127	122
	0	60	76	36	89	85	79
chi sq.		10.02	0.86	9.01	38.4	28.8	47.4
sign. ($p <= 0.05$)		yes	no	yes	yes	yes	yes

As the table above shows, the tendency for nominative-marked subjects to occur in the absence of a direct object and for genitive-marked subjects to occur with a direct object is strongest in K1. With K2 and RWL, nominative-marked subjects occur without direct objects even less, but genitive-marked subjects without direct objects are more common. M and L2 seem to have a very similar distribution: genitive-marked subjects occur most frequently with a direct object, however, nominative-marked subjects occur with and without direct objects almost equally often. With L1, however, there does not seem to be any correlation between subject-marking and the presence of a direct object.

The same result is attained if nominative and genitive subject-marking is plotted against transitivity, intransitivity and existentiality with the three translations of King Christopher's law:

Table 5:2. *Genitive and nominative subject-marking and transitivity. Chi-square was calculated with intransitive and existential constructions grouped as one. Percentages in italics.*

	M - Nom.	M - Gen.	L1 - Nom.	L1 - Gen.	K1 - Nom.	K1- Gen.
Trans.	58 *63*	144 *75.8*	81 *69.8*	141 *70.1*	31 *41.9*	218 *78.1*
Intrans.	25 *27.2*	41 *21.6*	29 *25*	60 *20.9*	29 *39.2*	57 *20.4*
Exist.	9 *9.8*	5 *2.6*	6 *5.2*	0 *0*	14 *18.9*	4 *1.4*
Chi Sq.	4.9		0		37	
sign.	yes		no		yes	

5.4. Subject-marking and lexical categories

The distribution of various nominative- and genitive-marked subjects with L1 (see the table in Appendix B), in case of *pitää*, proves an interesting picture. Nominative-marked subjects outnumber genitive-marked subjects 18 to 2 when the subject is a plural demonstrative pronoun (*ne*) and 44 to 3 when it is a plural noun, whereas singular nouns occur much more frequently with genitive case-marking (81 to 23), and the same can be said for the singular demonstrative pronoun *se* (19 to 1). All in all, it seems that nominative case-marking of the subject of *pitää* with L is most frequent in case of plural nouns and pronouns, but much less frequent in case of singular nouns and pronouns. Numerals and quantifiers prove a less clear picture, doubtlessly due to their low frequency. The one plural pronoun which occurs most commonly with genitive case-marking (18 to 2) is the 3rd pers. plur. personal pronoun *he* (the 1st pers. personal pronoun *me* occurred once, with genitive-marking).

Some examples from L1:

(48) King's Chapter, 3
Ensimmäisen valitzemuxen änen ***pitä***
first-ACC choice-ACC vote-ACC must
Wplandin ladmannin *<pitämän>* ***pitätämän,*** *ia* ***ne***
Uppland-GEN lawman-GEN SG hold-INF hold-PASS INF and those-NOM
iotca
that-NOM
hänen cansans ouat, ***nimitetyt Kuningasta valitzeman.***
him-GEN with be-3PL appointed-NOM PL king-PART choose-INF
'The lawman from Uppland must cast the first vote, and those appointed that are with him must elect the King'.

The first necessitive construction here shows a genitive-marked singular noun subject with possible hesitation, apparently, as to the voice marking of the infinitival subject, the second, with the necessitive modal verb elliptically removed, a nominative-marked plural pronoun subject. The following sentence from L1 has a nominative plural noun with a nominative quantifier *kaikki* attribute as subject:

(49) Court Chapter, 21
Caicki todistos miehet *kuningan edes*
All witness-NOM PL king-GEN before
pispan, ladmannin kihlakunnan domarin ia
bishop-GEN SG lawman-GEN SG county-GEN judge-GEN SG and

heiden lautamiestens *edesä* ***pitä wannoman*** *ennen quin he*
their jury member-GEN PL before must swear-INF before that they
todistauat
testify-3PL
'All witnesses must swear before the king, bishop, lawman, county judge and their jury members before they testify'

(50) Building, 51
Kuningan ***nimitös miehet*** ***pitä*** *sen* ***tietämänn***
King-GEN jury member-NOM PL must it-ACC SG know-INF
kukin länisäns, Ne iotca ei tege quin
each district-INESS those-ACC PL who-NOM PL NEG do as
sanottu on,
said is
pitä hänen iulgistaman *ensimäises maan käräiäs*
must he-GEN SG proclaim first-INESS country-GEN court-INESS
Mickel messun iälkin
St. Michael's day-GEN after
'The King's jury members must know whoever in their districts who do not do as said, and must proclaim them on the first country court after St. Michel's day.'

In the second sentence above, the subject of the first verb, a noun, is marked in the nominative plural, whereas that of the second verb, a singular personal pronoun, is marked in the genitive singular. Probably, a plural personal pronoun was originally intended here.

With M, the same redistribution of case-markers may be discerned: *ne* occurs most frequently with the nominative with a frequency of 22 to 0, plural nouns occur in the nominative with a frequency of 21 to 2, singular nouns occur in the genitive with a frequency of 81 to 23, and *se* occurs in the genitive with a frequency of 19 to 2. With M, numerals (with the exception of *yksi* 'one') seem to favour nominative case-marking, whereas the quantifier *kaikki* occurs roughly as regularly with both. The 3rd pers. plural personal pronoun *he* occurs only with its genitive/accusative *-n* form. Here, as well as with L1, the subject marking of *tulla* cannot be explained in a similar fashion: genitive subjects are more frequent throughout.

A few examples from M:

(51) Marriage, 2
Nytt ios tahto mies waimo kihlat,
Now if wishes man-NOM woman-? engage-INF
nijn ***pitä miehen*** *ioca hänen naitta* ***tykän oleman,***
then must man-GEN which her-ACC wed-INF present be-INF
ia ***neliä todhistaiat,*** ***caxi*** *miehen puolest* ***toiset***
and four witness-NOM PL two man-GEN on the part of other-NOM PL

caxi *waimon*
two woman-GEN
'Now, if a man wants to become engaged with a woman, the man who weds her must be present, as well as four witnesses, two on the part of the man, the other two on the part of the woman'.

In the sentence above, the immediate subject of the necessitive verb has genitive case-marking (*miehen*), but subjects later on, which bear numeral attributes, does not; similar cases can be found elsewhere in M as well:

(52) Court Chapter, 40
Nijn ***pitä kuningan,*** *eli* ***nee*** *quin kuningan*
So must king-GEN or those-NOM PL which king-GEN
puolest pitäuet eli ouat, sen ***ilmoittaman*** *kiriallans*
on behalf of hold-INF or are-INF that report-INF letter-ALL
'Thus the king, or those who on behalf of the king are holding it, must report it by letter'

The following example from M shows an interesting reversal in that the noun phrase governed by the copular infinitival complement *oleman* bears genitive case-marking, but the subject does not:

(53) Theft, 15
Se *quin todhista* ***pitä oleman, wahuan Taloin miehen***
He that testify-3SG must be-INF strong-GEN home-dwelling man-GEN
'He that testifies must be a person of fixed residence'

With K1 and K2, as well as with RWL, there appears to be no such correlation between case-marking and lexical categories: genitive subjects are more frequent here even with *ne* and plural nouns, though nominative subjects do seem to be more frequent themselves with plural nouns than with singular nouns. Thus correspondences like the following, where M and L1 have unmarked plural forms whereas K1 has forms on *-n* are not atypical:

(54) Court Chapter, 20
M: ***ne pitä*** *sekä* ***todhistaman*** *että* ***wannoman*** *lähimäises käreiäs sen iälkin.*
L1: ***ne pitä*** *sekä* ***todhistaman*** *että* ***wannoman*** *lähimäises käreiäs sen iälkin.*
K1: ***Nijdhen pitä*** *lähimmäisesä Käräjäsä sen jälkeen, sekä* ***wannoman*** *että* ***todhistaman****.*

(55) Peace Oath, 18
M: *Nijn* ***pitä*** *sen* ***kihlacunnan nimitöxen tietämän****, ios hän kosti sen edest eli tuli mw wirhi waihellens.*

L1: *Nin **pitä** sen **kihlakunnan lautamiehett tietämän**, ios hän kästi sen edestä, eli tuli mw rijta heidhen waihellens,*
K1: *Sen **pitä** Kihlacunnan **Lautamiesten tietämän** mingä tähdhen hän costa, elickä tulico muu eripuraisuus heidhän wälillensä.*

In L2, the distribution of genitive- and nominative-marked subjects is less clear, though the same tendency for plural nouns and pronouns (with the exception of personal pronouns) to take nominative case-marking can be discerned – of 22 plural noun subjects, 20 take nominative, and 2 genitive case-marking. However, L2 seems to prefer nominative case-marking across the board, in contrast to L1. It should be noted here that Ljungo had the translation of Martti at his avail (Rapola 1967: 137), and that the distribution of case-markers in L1 could be based partially on Ljungo copying the patterns of M. Then L2 would be more indicative of Ljungo's "own" idiolect.

As Appendix A shows, 45,6% of subjects of *pitää* in L2 are marked in the nominative, whereas 42% are marked in the genitive, while in L1, 31,1% of subjects are marked in the nominative and 53,9% of subjects are marked in the genitive. So singular nouns, for example, are overwhelmingly marked in the genitive case in L1 (81 vs. 23), but considerably less overwhelmingly so in L2 (26 vs. 24) – of course, the much smaller size of L2 may obscure relationships here. Interestingly, personal pronouns occur with nominative case-marking much more often in L2 than in L1 – in L2, we find 6 occurrences of *he* in the nominative and 25 of *he* in the genitive, in L1, 2 occurrences of *he* in the nominative and 25 of *he* in the genitive. With *hän*, 10 occur in the nominative in L2 against 46 in the genitive, whereas in L1, only 2 occurrences of the nominative were found against 61 in the genitive. Strikingly, relative pronouns are found much more often as subjects, and overwhelmingly with nominative case-marking, in L2 than in L1. The reason may very well be a relatively greater occurrence of *joka* in L2 than in L1 – the other relative pronoun, *kuin*, originally a comparative conjunction but pressed into service as an uninflecting relative pronoun in Old Finnish and the Southwestern dialects, possibly after the model provided by Swedish *som* (see the next chapter), occurs in both texts (and has not been analyzed as to case-marking).

Indeed, sometimes nominative-marked personal pronouns occur in transitive necessitive constructions with a direct object – which would be extremely unexpected on the basis of the dialectal occurrence of nominative/genitive case-marking (Laitinen 1992: 11, 271). Examples from L2:

(56) Land Chapter, 4

että	***hän***	*saman*	*tontinn*	*ia*	*maan*	***mymän***	***pitä***
that	he-NOM	same-ACC	lot-ACC	and	land-ACC	sell-INF	must

'that he must sell the same lot and land'

(57) Trade, 10
hän ***pitä*** *sen* *laillisesti yles* ***taridzeman***
he-NOM must it-ACC lawfully offer-INF
'he must offer it lawfully'

(58) Trade, 31
että ***hän*** *sen* *hänelle* ***mymänn pitä*** *iulki elickä salaa*
that he-NOM it-GEN him-ALL sell-INF must openly or secretly
'that he had to sell it to him secretly or openly'

Also, sometimes personal pronouns may appear marked in the genitive or the nominative case in virtually identical contexts, as here in L2:

(59) Trade, 32
ionga ***he*** *sieldä* ***ostaman*** ***pitä***
which-ACC they-NOM there-ABL buy-INF must
'which they must buy there'

(60) Trade, 32
sen ***heiden*** ***pitä*** ***åstaman***
that-ACC they-GEN must buy-INF
'that they must buy'

This could be interpreted as signifying an ongoing, wholesale shift in L2 from genitive-case marking to nominative case-marking in necessitive constructions, or, the restructuring of the active/stative system with *pitää* to the nominative/accusative (or, to be precise, "inverted ergative") system of the vast majority of Finnish verbs. This does not seem to be implied by the dialectal background of Ljungo – who was born in Liminka, quite far from any current occurrence of nominative-marked subjects in necessitive constructions. Rather, in L2, one might suppose direct influence from the Swedish source text (where the subjects of the equivalent, and interlingually identified, constructions are marked in the nominative) and the Swedish which Ljungo doubtlessly spoke and understood. According to Laitinen (1992: 42, 50) Swedish influence may have both led to the emergence of nominative subject-marking with a unipersonal verb and to the emergence of agreement between the necessitive verb and the nominative-marked subject. In L2, I found only one case of agreement in number between subject and *pitää*:

(61) Ships, 5
mutta nijn että ***Kuningas*** *ia* ***Caupungi*** *oikeudens*

but so that King-NOM and city-NOM right-ACC
***pitäuät saman**, ios Jutun Jsändä hänelle tahto hengen suodha*
must get-INF if accuser-NOM him-ALL wishes life-ACC grant
'But in such a way that the King and the city will get what they are entitled to, if the accuser wishes to grant him his life.'

In RWL, sporadic examples of agreement appear to occur as well, such as the following from the introductory chapter:

(62) *että he tästedes* ***pitäwät*** *sen saman*
that they henceforth must it-ACC get-INF
'That they must henceforth receive it'

If we regard the large frequency of nominative-marked subjects throughout L2 as a manifestation of a shift from genitive-marked to nominative-marked subjects as a result of identification between *pitää* and its Swedish model pattern and a remodelling of case-marking with *pitää* after that model pattern, it must nevertheless be noted that in L2, genitive-marked subjects appear to cling on most stubbornly if they occur with direct objects. This could indicate a subtle interplay between contact-induced linguistic change and the dialectal basis of the material on which this contact-induced linguistic change acts: a shift from genitive subjects to nominative subjects occurs most readily where, in Finnish dialects, nominative-marked subjects are most permissible, and genitive subjects persists the longest where they would occur most frequently in dialectal Finnish.

5.5. Word order and subject case-marking

Though, as mentioned, the marking of nominative and genitive subjects in M seems to correlate, albeit weakly, with the presence of a direct object, as well as with lexical categories as in L1, there seems to be another determiner of case-marking in M. As Appendix C shows, genitive subjects of *pitää* in M seem to generally occur in verb-initial clauses, whereas in subject-initial clauses, nominative and genitive subjects seem to occur about as frequently, i.e. 51% percent of those subjects preceding the auxiliary *pitää* are marked with the nominative and 49% with the genitive, however, of those subjects succeeding *pitää*, 78,9% are marked with the genitive and 21,1% are marked with the nominative. However, most of the nominative subjects in subject-initial clauses seem to occur in clauses without a direct object. This correlation is much weaker with L1, with 43,8% nominative subjects and 56,2% genitive subjects in SV clauses, clauses against 32% nominative subjects and 67,6% genitive subjects in VS clauses. In L1, most of this distribution seems to result from intransitive clauses: the word order pattern SVI shows 22 genitive subjects and 26 nominative subjects, but the pattern VSI 43 genitive subjects and 14 nominative subjects. In K1, there seems to be no correlation at all – if anything, genitive subjects are slightly, though surely not significantly, more common in SV clauses (82,4% against 17,6%) than in VS clauses (77,6% against 22,3%). It should be noted that, in M, word order itself is strongly determined by the word order of the Swedish source text: the subject-initial word order pattern SVOI in M seems to correspond 52 times to an identical word order pattern in the Swedish source text and 10 times to another pattern, whereas the verb-initial word order pattern VSOI seems to correspond 88 times to an identical word order pattern in the Swedish text, and 24 times to a different pattern.

I would tend to explain this state of affairs in M as an archaism. As Laitinen (1992: 117) notes, the consensus view on the origin of the necessitive construction with *pitää* is that originally *pitää* – which aside from it's specific use as a modal auxiliary may mean 'hold' – was an independent intransitive verb, which later began to be combined with transitive infinitives, and then with an adverbial phrase in the dative-genitive which designated the agent of the action denoted by the infinitive:

työ *pitää*
work-NOM hold-3SG
'let's go to work'
työ *pitää* *tehdä*
work-NOM must do-INF
'the work must be done'
työ *pitää naisten* *tehdä*
work-NOM must women-GEN PL do
'the work must be done by women'

Then, the dative-genitive adverbial would have been reanalyzed as the subject of *pitää*, and the original subject as the object. Laitinen notes that a difficulty of this view lies in the fact that there seem to be no traces of an earlier use of the object of the infinitival complement as the subject of *pitää* (Laitinen 1992: 119). Nevertheless, it is tempting to see an echo if this old adverbial nature of the genitive-marked subject in correspondences such as the following in M:

(63) Peace Oath, 11
Sen ***pitä*** *kihlacwnnan* ***nimitöxen tietämän***
that-ACC must county-GEN jury-GEN know-INF
ios se sama *iollen* *hän* *kosti* *teki* *hänelle*
if the same to whom-ALL he avenged-3SG did-3SG him-ALL
wahingon *taicka toinen*

damage-ACC or another-NOM
KrL: *thet* ***scal heredznempd wita*** *huat helder then sami som han hempdis aa giorde gerningena a han eller annar*
'The county jury must know whether the person he took vengeance on did him harm, or whether it was somebody else'

(64) Peace Oath, 22
kihlacunnan ***nimitös*** *samas kihlacunnas* ***pitä***
county-GEN jury-NOM same-INESS county-INESS must
vlos ***etzimän,*** *ia* ***tietämän*** *mikä totuus on, sijnä asias*
find out-INF and know-INF what truth-NOM is that-INESS matter-INESS
KrL: ***Heredz nempd*** *j sama herade* ***scal wtleta*** *oc* ***wita*** *hwat sannast ær om thet maal*
'The county jury in the same county must find out and know what the truth is in that matter'

In other words, supposing for now that, by and large, M, like Ljungo in L1, seems to redistribute case-markers on the basis of number and lexical category, we may nevertheless posit another, weaker factor guiding case-marking in a tendency with M to mark subjects following the auxiliary verb with the genitive case, perhaps reinforced by traces of the old adverbial nature of the subject of *pitää*, whereas no such 'reinforcement' occurs with subjects preceding the auxiliary, the word order itself being determined, by and large, by that of the Swedish source text.

5.6. Explaining the redistribution of case-markers in M and L1

However, the distribution of case-markers in L1 may not be explained in such a fashion. Indeed, the distribution of nominative and genitive subjects with Ljungo, with nominative subjects appearing especially with plural nouns and plural pronouns, and to an extent numerals and quantifiers as well, is reminiscent of that what we would expect of accusative-marked objects. As mentioned accusative marking in Finnish varies between -ø (in verbal forms without an unmarked subject: imperatives, passives, etc.) and -*n* in case of singular nouns – the accusative thus being homophonous with respectively the nominative or the genitive – and is -*t* in case of plural nouns (thus identical with the nominative plural marker -*t*). Quantifiers and numerals with a plural referent (hence excluding *yksi* 'one') appear with unmarked -ø as direct objects:

Table 5:3. *Modern Finnish accusative and Ljungo's subject-marking of pitää.*

	Subject of *pitää* in Finnish dialects	Accusative in Mod. Finnish	Subject of *pitää* in L and M
singular nouns, dem. pronouns	*-n* (trans. verbs), *-ø* (intrans. verbs)	*-n* or - *ø*	*-n* or - *ø*
plural nouns, dem. pronouns	*-n* (trans. verbs), *-t* (intrans. verbs)	*-t*	*-t*, rarely *-n*
quantifiers, numerals	*-n* (trans. verbs), - *ø* (intrans. verbs)	- *ø*	- *ø* or *-n*
personal pronouns	*-n*	*-t* (*-n* in Old and dialectal Finnish)	*-n*

Hence, there seems to be reason to investigate whether Ljungo, in L1, reanalyzed the subject of *pitää*, with its varying genitive and nominative case-marking, as an object, and redistributed his case-marking accordingly.

A number of caveats are, however, immediately apparent. First, in Modern Finnish the accusative has a unique suffix only with personal pronouns and the interrogative pronoun *kene-*; in Old Finnish, not even there. Finnish 17th century grammars (namely, Petraeus' of 1649 and Martinius' of 1689), built on the model provided by Latin, nevertheless discern an accusative case – comprising both the accusative (sing. *-n*. plur. -*t*) and the partitive (*-A*, *-tA*) (Wiik 1989: 13, 49). Petraeus seems to group some clear instances of the genitive, elative and illative case as well under the accusative (Wiik 1989: 19). Though it may well be that Ljungo – who was, as a cleric, of course acquainted with Latin grammar, as Martti was – was aware of the accusative as a category in Finnish noun declension, I am hesitant to argue that Ljungo (or Martti) consciously reanalyzed instances of genitive and nominative as instances of accusative case-marking and hence redistributed case-marking.

Second, though a large part of subjects of *pitää* seem to follow the rules of accusative case-marking, not all of them do. Though singular nouns occur in L1 with genitive case-marking with a frequency of 81 to 23 (hence very significantly higher than the general frequency of genitive vs. nominative case-marking in L1, 201 to 116), there are still 20 singular nouns left without the *-n* we would expect according to the accusative hypothesis, and likewise, there is a small number of plural nouns and pronouns which occurs with unexpected genitive case-marking. The case of the 3rd pers. plural pronoun *he*, the only plural noun/pronoun to occur most often in the genitive, could be explained on the basis of the "accusative hypothesis" (though admittedly also by a general tendency of personal pronouns to occur with genitive case-marking as the subject of *pitää*): in older Literary Finnish, *-n* was the normal accusative ending for both singular and plural personal pronouns (Rapola 1969: 74, Inaba 2000b: 48), with the, originally East Finnish accusative forms on *-t* only making their breakthrough in the 19th century – even if plural accusative pronouns on *-t* are found to some extent in the oldest Finnish texts. Thus the accusative form of he is, with L and the other two translators as well, *heidän*, homophonous with the genitive form[9].

Third, the hallmark of objecthood in Finnish – and one of the parameters used to determine object promotion in the preceding chapter – is partitive case-marking in negative clauses. As Appendix A shows, however, partitive subject-marking with pitää is quite marginal.

A fourth problem is that the redistribution hypothesis seems not applicable at all with *tulla*. Even though the lower general frequency of *tulla* complicates getting a reliable picture on the relative frequencies of nominative and genitive subjects, it is immediately obvious that genitive subjects are here more common even with plural nouns and pronouns (see Appendix B).

However, The redistribution hypothesis does seem to find some support, at first sight at least, from the oldest Finnish texts. Though the accusative ending of personal pronouns is, as mentioned above, commonly *-n* throughout the period of old Literary Finnish, accusative personal pronouns with *-t*, originally an Eastern dialectal form which later became current in Standard Finnish, can be found to some extent in texts of Agricola, as well as some other contemporary texts (Hakulinen 1979: 99). Now, as Inaba (2000b: 79-80) has remarked, unambiguous accusative personal pronouns on *-t* as subjects of necessitive *pitää* may be found, albeit rarely, in some 16th century texts, mainly in Westh's liturgical texts as well as the Uppsala liturgical fragment (Ups), both dating from the 1540s, and extremely

9 I have found one occurrence of an object form of *he* with *-t* in M, but none in L1.

sporadically in Agricola's works as well (Inaba, p.c.). These accusative subjects seem to occur, according to Inaba, only with non-agentive subjects (Inaba 2000b: 80).

A few examples from the Uppsala liturgical fragment (Ups):

(65) (p. 105, John 19:35): *Ia hän tiethä että hän sano*
and he-NOM know-3SG that he-NOM speak-3SG
totta
truth-PART
senpälle että ***teijdhät*** *möss* ***vskoma*** ***pithä****.*
thus that you-ACC also believe-INF must
'and he knows that he tells the truth—that you also may believe'

(66) (p. 113, 1 Peter 2:15): *että* ***teijdhät*** *hyuäin tödhen*
that you-ACC good-GEN PL works-GEN PL
cansa
with
pitäpi *niinen hwlluin ja taitamattoidhen ihmisten*
must those-GEN mad-GEN PL and incapable-GEN PL man-GEN PL
swntukitzeman.
mouth-ACC close-INF
'For it is God's will that by doing right you should put to silence the ignorance of foolish men'

The interpretation of the genitive phrase and the object of the last sentence is a bit tricky – I would interpret *swn* as the object of the sentence, rather than as a verbal prefix, even if it seems fused to the subsequent verb.

The occurrence of apparent accusative subjects with *pitää* in these texts, however, may be explained in a different way. The texts show a mixture of East and West Finnish forms, and possibly an editor with an East Finnish dialect replaced all occurrences of *teidän, heidän* (the West Finnish genitive/accusative form) with *teidät, heidät*, without taking heed of whether the pronoun was a genitive or an accusative (Tapani Lehtinen, p.c.). And if Inaba's remark that the *-t* accusative with pronouns seems to be only used with non-agentive subjects of *pitää* (though the subject of example 77 above seems to be agentive) holds, the occurrence of the case-marker could be framed within the "perfect ergative" or active/stative analysis of *pitää* by Terho Itkonen (1979): the accusative is shared between non-active subjects and all objects just like the zero accusative, partitive and, occasionally, pronominal *t*-accusative is the common case-marker of objects and existential subjects in the Finnish verbal system as a whole.

5.7. Differences in subject-marking between *pitää* and *tulla*

Explaining why Martti and Ljungo have redistributed the case-markers in a manner reminiscent of the object, with the crucial exception of partitive case-marking in negative clauses, involves, first of all, an explanation of why this reanalysis seems not to occur with *tulla*. One possible explanation may rest in the particular semantics of necessitive verbs and their subjects. The subject of a strongly deontic – signifying externally imposed necessity rather than internal necessity – modal verb basically represents two roles at the same time: that of the agent of the action signified by the infinitival complement, and that of the patient of the imposition of someone else's will (Häkkinen 1994: 347, Laitinen 1992: 108, Elsayed 1997: 108), and, of course, in order for someone else's will to be imposed upon, one must have a will, a capability of agentivity of its own, which is one of the reasons for the division in Finnish dialects between genitive-marked agentive subjects of preferably transitive clauses and nominative-marked non-agentive subjects of typically intransitive claused – the *-n* marker is applied only to referents to which deontic force is applicable (Laitinen 1992: 183-184). As Ikola (1949: 174-176) remarks, even in case of the incipient grammaticalization of necessitive *pitää* as a future tense in the first Finnish Bible translation of 1642, *pitää* is never used if the course of action is determined by the logical subject alone, but only when another force imposes itself on the logical subject.

Thus it seems that in the semantic role of the subject of necessitive *pitää*, there was a potential for its reanalysis as the patient, and the application of the accusative to its case-marking. However, it seems to me that necessitive *tulla* is used considerably more widely than a purely deontic sense – in the examined texts, it appears also in constructions where its meaning would be close to 'have the right to'. Some examples from M:

(67) Court Chapter, 4
ia ***hänen tule saadha*** *colmannexet,*
and he-GEN must receive-INF a third-ACC
caikesta kihlacunnan sacko penningeistä sijtä kihlacunnasta
all-ELAT county-GEN fine money-ELAT PL that-ELAT county-ELAT
'and he shall receive a third of all fines from that county'

(68) Peace Oath, 14
Sillä että sijnä ***caickein tule*** *rauha* ***saadha***
Because that there-INESS all-GEN must. peace-? receive-INF
'Because there all must have peace'

And here from RWL:

(69) Inheritance, 2:2
älköt *nautitco* *cuitengan*
NEG-IMPER enjoy-IMPER nonetheless
enämbätä *eli wähembätä, cuin heidän isäns eli äitins*
more-PART or less-PART than their father or mother
olis ***tullut*** *saada, jos hän eläis .*
be-COND must-PARTIC PF get-INF if he live-COND
'Nevertheless, they will not enjoy more or less than their father or mother would have inherited, had they lived.'

In Ljungo's translation of (68) case-marking has been reversed, with M's subject taking, as a goal/benefactor, allative case-marking, and M's object being the subject of an intransitive *olla*:

(70) *sillä* *että* *nijsä* *sijois*
Because that those-INESS place-INESS PL
tule *caickille* ***rauhan*** ***olla***
must all-ALL peace-GEN be-INF
'Because in those places, all must have peace'

The use of necessitive *tulla*-constructions with subjects which are, rather than the object of deontic pressure, benefactors of a certain action, seems to be tied in closely with the usage of *tulla* as a translation equivalent of Old Swedish *a*, Modern Swedish *äga*, which had a meaning 'to own' and 'have a right to' in addition to it's modal meaning (OSSGL). As Inaba (2000a: 122-123) points out, there are a number of instances in M in which the Old Swedish equivalents of *äga* 'to own, to have a right to' has been translated with *tulla* and a beneficary marked with the allative or dative-genitive (*-n*) case. *Tulla* as a necessitive modal verb has a basis in Finnish dialects as well as in other Finnic languages – but it seems to me that the development of the necessitive *hänen tulee tehdä*-construction may well have been partially caused by the use of the dative-genitive case to denote a beneficiary in cases like the ones mentioned above, and perhaps in particular as a translation equivalent of Old Swedish *äga*-constructions.

It is interesting to note in this regard that the word *kuningas*, the referent of which should of course not be the object of any deontic pressure by a worldly power, seems to be strongly associated with *tulla* in necessitive clauses, rather than *pitää*: with L1, I have found 17 occurrences of *kuningas* or *kuninkaan* as an argument of *tulla,* but only four as an argument of *pitää*, and with M, the numbers are 19 to 0. Thus, it may well be that the tendency for the use of *tulla* outside a purely deontic context, with the genitive-marked subject in the role of goal or benefactor and hence marked with a dative-genitive, may have been a factor causing *tulla* to be exempt from the accusative reanalysis possibly governing the division between unmarked and -*n* endings in M and L1.

5.8. Reanalysis of subject as object? Active and passive infinitives

There is good reason to remain hesitant as to whether the obvious redistribution of case-markers in case of *pitää* has followed a reanalysis of subject to object, even if such a reanalysis seems not to be totally impossible on the basis of the semantics of *pitää* (as opposed to those of *tulla*), and evidence, albeit fragmentary and problematical evidence, for such a reanalysis could be mustered from other Old Finnish texts. Particularly the absence of partitive subject-marking seems to be a strong contraindication for assuming an underlying reanalysis, rather than a redistribution of case-markers for some other reason. This said, it should be noted that, with the exception of partitive marking with negation, subject and object marking with *pitää* seem to have virtually totally merged: as normal in Old Finnish, the marked accusative (-*n*, -*t*), as opposed to the unmarked accusative, is used for the object of the infinitival complement of *pitää*.

The solution lies in comparing the case-marking of the agent of *pitää* and an active infinitival complement (which may sport an additional object itself) with that of the patient of *pitää* and a passive infinitival complement (which is necessarily its only argument). Infinitives with passive voice-marking do not occur in modern Standard Finnish, but were common in the literary language until the 19th century (Häkkinen 1994: 309) and seem to be not unknown in dialects (Hakulinen 1979: 254, Laitinen 1992: 148-149). In modern Standard Finnish, passive verbs have only one modifier, namely its object: with nouns, the object is unmarked for case, however, pronouns retain accusative case-marking (-*t*) with passive verbs as well. However, as mentioned in the previous chapter, in the period of older Literary Finnish an ongoing reanalysis of the object of the passive verb as its subject took place, with concomitant loss of case-marking in case of personal pronouns (Häkkinen 1994: 325-326). The picture provided by the three Old Finnish legal translations as to the subject- or object-marking of the modifier of passive verbs is extremely messy. Recall examples 17 and 18, in which we see a partitive-marked object and a nominative-marked subject in virtually identical negated passive clauses:

(17) Building, 34

M: *ios* ***hän***	*mös*	*sihen*	*ei*	*sidhota,*	*quin nÿtt on sanottu,*
if he	also	that-ILL	NEG	bind-PASS	

'if he is not proven guilty of that as well'

(18) Building, 44
M: *ioldei* ***händä*** *laillisesti sidhota,* *warielkan*
IF-NEG he-PART legally bind-PASS
'if he is not legally proven guilty'

But regardless of the variable analysis as object or subject, the grammatical subject of a necessitive clause with a passive infinitival complement is clearly the patient of the action designated by that complement: it undergoes the action described therein, and does not execute it. Another, unmentioned but implicit agent does. The grammatical subject of a necessitive clause with an active infinitival complement may or may not be the agent of the action designated by that complement. The semantical differences between *pitää* and *tulla* sketched above, with the grammatical subject of *pitää* bearing a double role as agent of the infinitival complement (if this infinitival complement is transitive and active, of course) and patient of the deontic pressure inherent in the construction, and with the grammatical subject of *tulla* being subject to weaker deontic pressure, and not infrequently being the benefactor of the action described in the infinitival complement, would seem to imply that passive infinitival complements would co-occur with *pitää* much more often than with *tulla*. And this seems to be indeed the case, as Appendix A shows: with M, passive infinitival complements make up more than a third of those infinitival complements associated with *pitää*, but less than a fifth of those associated with *tulla*, with L1 and K1, the numbers are similar. In L2, I have not found instances of necessitive *tulla* with passive infinitive complements at all, and in K2, only 4 (against 125 occurrences of *pitää* with a passive infinitival complement in K2). In RWL, passive infinitival complements appear not to occur with *tulla*.

Now, looking at the case-marking of the patient of *pitää* when associated with a passive infinitival complement, it seems clear that the marking of that patient by and large conforms to 'marked accusative' (i.e. singular *-n*, plural *-t*) case-marking in M and L1, with overt nominative or zero accusative case-marking (i.e., singular *-ø*) a marginal alternative. Examples from M:

(71) King's Chapter, 3
Caikein näinnen lakicundamiesten änellä,
All-GEN those-GEN lawman-GEN PL voice-ADESS
ia nijdhen quin nämä nimittänet ouat
and those-GEN that these-NOM have appointed
pitä kuningan *wlos* ***walittaman***
must king-ACC choose-PASS INF
'And by the votes of all those lawmen, and those that they have appointed, the King must be elected.'

(72) King's Chapter, 10

M: *ne* ***huomen lahiatt*** ***pitä*** ***annettaman***
those morning gift-ACC PL must give-PASS INF
hänen *Radhins* *suosiolla*
his-GEN council-GEN consent-ADESS
'The dowry must be given with the consent of his council'

So, surface case-marking of the patient of *pitää* with a passive infinitival complement is by and large the same as that of the agent of *pitää* with an active infinitival complement in M and L1. In both of these texts, an overt nominative singular (-*ø*) is more marginal, but does occur to an extent, more often in L1 than in M, as in the following sentence from L1, which shows two instances of marked accusative case-marking and one of indisputable nominative/zero accusative case-marking:

(73) Capital crimes, 15

nin ***pitä*** ***miehen*** *wiruelle* ***pandaman***
thus must man-ACC stake-ALL placed-PASS INF
ia ***waimon*** *tulesa* ***poltettaman*** *ia* ***irthainen***
and woman-ACC fire-INESS burn-PASS INF and loose-NOM
calu *sen* *vikapän* *pitä* ***iaettaman***
good-NOM that-GEN criminal-GEN must divide-PASS INF
'And thus the man must be broken on the wheel, and the woman be burned in fire, and the loose goods of that criminal must be divided'

It should be stressed here that the analysis of the objects of necessitive constructions with passive infinitives as accusative-marked is not the only possible one: because of the fact that the accusative case-markers -*t* and -*n* are homophonous with the genitive singular and nominative plural case-markers, it is also possible to analyze the objects of necessitive *pitää* with passive infinitive constructions as vacillating between genitive (singular) and nominative (plural). The distribution of case-markers in L1 and M is by and large the same as that of *pitää* with active infinitival complements: L2 has a larger proportion of overt nominative subject/objects in these construction, and in K1 and K2, as well as RWL, nominative/zero accusative case-marking is much more frequent with passive infinitival complements (see Appendix B). This is particularly interesting in light of the fact that, with active infinitival complements, nominative case-marking is relatively more marginal with Kollanius. When looking at the patient of *pitää* and a passive infinitival complement, it seems that M has only one case of unambiguous genitive case-marking (i.e., a plural genitive -*n*, where accusative case-marking would have -*t*). One other such case can be found in K2. All other cases of apparent genitive case-marking concern personal pronouns, which, as mentioned, are usually marked with -*n* as objects as well in Old Finnish.

All other occurrances with Kollanius seem thus analyzable as grammatical objects with either marked accusative (*-n* singular, *-t* plural) or nominative/zero accusative (singular) case-marking – a situation very much in accordance with the analysis of the genitive case as a marker of manipulability, referred to above: the patient of a passive infinitival complement is, obviously, not involved in carrying out the action described, neither volitionally, nor under strong deontic pressure.

The two cases of plural genitive case-marking with passive infinitives are the following:

(74) Building, 9
M: ***Wara Seippäin*** ***pitä pandaman*** *askelen*
spare pole-GEN PL must place-PASS INF step-ACC
wluos aidhast, nijn ettei Sika eli lammas tartu
outside fence-ELAT so that-NEG pig-NOM or sheep-NOM get stuck-3SG
wälille.
in between
'Spare poles must be placed a step beyond the fence, so that pigs and sheep do not get stuck in between'
(75) King's Chapter, 15:
K2: ***Caickein*** *jotca caupungin yhteytehen*
those-GEN PL that-ACC PL city-GEN citizenry-ILL
otettahan, ***pitä*** *erinomaisesti Caupungin kirjahan* ***kirjoitettaman***
take-PASS must particularly city-GEN book-ILL write-PASS INF
'Those that are accepted as part of the citizenry must be registered'

Aside from this, partitive case-marking of the subject/object occurs in negative clauses, whereas, with active infinitival complements, the partitive occurs only twice, in both cases in negative, existential clauses – with RWL, partitive case-marking is somewhat more common.

Though variation between marginal nominative case-marking and more general *-n* marking does occur with M, the use of the *-n* genitive with plural referents, occuring marginally with active infinitival complements, occurs but once. With Ljungo, the picture is similar to that provided by Martti: singular nouns, as the patients of necessitive constructions employing *pitää* and a passive infinitival complement, are marked with *-n* or *-ø*, personal pronouns with *-n*, plural nouns and demonstrative pronouns with the case-marking usual for the nominative and accusative in the plural (*-t*). I have not found cases of plural genitive-marking with Ljungo. With Kollanius, as well as with RWL, as mentioned, the patient in these cases is generally marked with nominative/zero accusative case-marking, and I have found only one case of plural genitive case-marking with subjects of *pitää* in K2. In Kollanius' texts and RWL, accusative case-marking occurs as a marginal alternative to more normal nominative case-marking with singular nouns (most of the accusative cases in Appendix B being plural *-t,* which may be interpreted as nominative as well). Particularly interesting, however, is the circumstance that with Kollanius, personal pronouns seem to vacillate between genitive/accusative (*-n*) and nominative case-marking, in virtually identical contexts.

Some examples from K1:

(76) Inheritance, 11
Nijn pitä ***hän,*** *nincuin edhespäin tapoisa*
thus must he-NOM as further on murder-INESS PL
eroitetan ***rangaistaman,*** *ja eij wirwen nenähän*
specify-PASS punish-PASS INF and not stake-GEN nose-ILL
pandaman
place-PASS INF
'Thus, as specified later on in (the chapter concerning) murders, he must be punished, but not be broken on the wheel'

(77) Purposeful murder, 35
Sijtten pitä ***hän*** *Käräjähän* ***wietämän***
Then must he-NOM court-ILL bring-PASS INF
'Then he must be brought to court'

(78) Theft, 1
Nijn pitä ***hänen*** *Käräjähän* ***wietämän***
Thus must he-GEN/ACC court-ILL bring-PASS INF
'Thus he must be brought to court'

(79) Theft, 11
Nijn pitä ***hänen*** *aitahan eli*
Thus must he-GEN/ACC fence-ILL or
puuhun ***sidhottaman***
tree-ILL bind-PASS INF
'Thus he must be bound to a fence or a tree'

This variation does not occur with active infinitival complements: K marks personal pronouns consistently with *-n* there. With RWL, similar vacillations may be found:

(80) Crimes, 1:3 3
nijn ***pitä*** *hän ajettaman ulos waldacunnasta*
thus must he-NOM chase-PASS INF out realm-ELAT
'Thus he must be chased out of the realm.'

(81) Courthouse, 17:4 4

nijn ***pitä*** *hänen molembain rijta-weljein, eli*
thus must he-ACC both-GEN parties-GEN or
heidän asianajajains läsnä ollesa, cuuldaman
their lawyers-GEN present be-INF INESS hear-PASS INF
'Thus he must be heard, with both parties, or their lawyers, being present'

Strikingly, Kollanius occasionally uses nominative- or genitive-marked nouns in negative clauses, where an analysis as object would demand partitive case-marking, and the same occurs in RWL as well:

(82) Theft, 34
K1: ... *Sillä ettei* ***yxikään löyndö***
Because that-NEG not one-NOM found item-NOM
pidhä *sijtä Kihlacunnasta, cusa se löytty on,*
must that-ELAT county-ELAT where-INESS it found is
ennen ulwos ***wietämän***
before bring away-PASS INF
'Because not one found item may be brought away from the county where it is found, before...'

(83) Courthouse Chapter, 10:11
RWL: *Ei* ***pidä*** *yxikän asia, mualla cuin*
NEG must not one-NOM case-NOM elsewhere than
oikiasa Tuomio-istuimesa ylösotettaman
right-INESS court-INESS treat-PASS INF
'Not a single case may be heard elsewhere than in the correct court of law'.

Compare the more regular partitive case-marking in negated clauses:

(84) Punishment 5:4
RWL: *Ei* ***pidä*** *ketään tuomittaman*
NEG must no-one-PART sentence-PASS INF
wangiuteen wedelle ja leiwälle enämmäxi
prisonhood-ILL water-ALL and bread-ALL more-TRANSL t
aicaa, cuin yhdexi cuucaudexi
time-PART than one-TRANSL month-TRANSL
'No-one may be sentenced to be incarcerated with water and bread for more than one month.'

(85) Courthouse Chapter 11:7
RWL: *Kircosa ei* ***pidä*** *ketään haastettaman,*
church-INESS NEG must no-one-PART summon-PASS INF
mutta kyllä kirckomäellä
but yes church hill-ADESS

'No one may be summoned to court while in the Church, but on the Church hill, he may.'

On the other hand, sporadic vacillations in object-marking occur throughout the history of Old Finnish (Häkkinen 1994: 361) and one might also regard the high frequency of nominative-marked modifiers of passive infinitival complements as a function of the general division between nominative and genitive case-marking in dialectal Finnish: the nominative is used when the subject of *pitää* bears no agency with regards to the action described in the infinitival complement and can hence not be regarded as subject to deontic pressure: deontic pressure is directed to another, unmentioned, actor. This is obviously so with passive infinitival complements, and explains the occurrence of nominative/zero accusative marking with personal pronouns as patients of passive infinitival complements as well.

Thus, with Kollanius and RWL, the differences between the grammatical subject of *pitää* with an active infinitival complement (generally *-n* with Kollanius and RWL, more frequently so than with Ljungo and Martti) and the grammatical subject of *pitää* with a passive infinitival complement (generally *-ø* with Kollanius and RWL, more frequently so than with Ljungo and Martti) may best be explained as stemming from the dialectal basis of the variation between genitive- and nominative case-marking, which also would explain the low occurrence of nominative subjects combined with direct objects, as mentioned above. Case-marking, with Kollanius and RWL, has a clear semantic basis: the genitive *-n* is a "marker of manipulability" which occurs only with referents capable of agency. Hence, the near-absence of *-n* with patients of a passive infinitive in Kollanius' translations and RWL. As an aside, it should be noted that Kollanius, as common in Old Finnish and similar to the other writers as well, uses a marked accusative for the object of *pitää* and an active infinitival complement. With a passive infinitival complement, the patient/object remains unmarked, and the occasional absence of partitive case-marking with Kollanius may be seen as signifying a reanalysis of grammatical object to grammatical subject – while remaining semantically, however, a clear patient which hence receives no genitive marking (*-n*).

In other words, the variation in case-marking with Kollanius (and RWL) can be explained without supposing a redistribution of case-markers, as opposed to that of Martti and Ljungo. What happens with Martti and Ljungo is a "merger" of case-marking paradigms. Aside from the usage of the genitive in the plural (*-n*), which remains, albeit marginally, with *pitää* and active infinitival complements, the two systems are quite alike in assigning case-markers on the basis of lexical categories: plural nouns and pronouns appear with nominative/zero accusative *-t*, singular nouns as well as personal pronouns with genitive/marked accusative *-n*, etc. As the agent of *pitää* and an active infinitival complement, and the patient of *pitää* and a passive infinitival complement, are clearly distinct in that the former can be a manipulable agent of the action designated in the infinitival complement, whereas the latter never can, we would suppose that this semantical distinction, which remains in force and explains the assignment of case-markers with Kollanius and RWL, is lost with Martti and Ljungo. Instead, case-markers are reassigned on the basis of structural criteria, and the result is a composite system of case-marking which does not distinguish between agent and patient, subject and object.

Of great interest in this regard are coordinate clauses, occuring in all four texts, where the infinitival complement is active in one, but passive in the other. Some of those cases are listed below, in four of them (86, 87, 88, 91), the Swedish source text has a passive infinitive marked with *-s* in one clause, an active infinitive in the other; in the other two cases, the Swedish source text combines a passive infinitive with a conjunctive main verb in the other clause. Example 90 is, on the face of it, ambiguous: *oleman* could perhaps be a 3rd inf. illative modifier of *duomittaman* as well as a 3rd inf. instructive modifier of necessitive *pitää*. From a structural perspective, cases of ellipsis of the verbal modifier in coordinative clauses like the ones above would be an indication of the identity of their syntactic roles in both clauses.

(86) King's Chapter, 4
M: *Eli kuningan* ***pitä krunattaman,*** *eli Eirikin retke*
or king-GEN/ACC must crown-PASS INF or Erik's journey-ACC
aia
ride-INF
L1: *eli Kuningan* ***pitä crunattaman,*** *Erickin retkiä* ***aiaman***
K1: *Taicka Kuningaxi* ***pitä Crunattaman,*** *elickä Kuningaxi tulemistansa näywyttämäsä läpi maan* ***ajaman***
KrL: *eller konunger* ***scall kronas*** *eller erics gathu sina* ***ridha***
'Or the King must be crowned, or must ride his Erik's journey'

(87) Building, 12
M: *ios* ***ne*** ***pitä*** *sijtä* *pois* ***otettaman,***
if those-NOM/ACC must there-ELAT away take-PASS INF
taicka sijnä ***oleman***
or there-INESS be-INF
L1: *ios* ***ne pitä*** *sijtä pois* ***åtettaman*** *eli sijnä* ***pysymän***
K1: *joco* ***ne pitä*** *kijnni* ***pidettämän*** *elickä pois* ***otettaman***
KrL: *hwat* ***the sculu*** *helder qwar* ***gaa*** *eller bort* ***takas***
'Whether they should be taken away or remain there'

(88) Capital crimes, 14
M: *nijn* ***pitä hänen*** *raudhoin* ***lyötämän***
thus must he-GEN/ACC iron-ILL PL strike-PASS INF

ia pijspalda ripin ***ottaman****, ia* ***pitämän*** *hengens*
and Bishop-ABL confession take-INF and retain-INF life-ACC
L1: *nin* ***hänen pitä*** *rautohin* ***lyötämän*** *ia pispalta ripin* ***åttaman*** *ia ei hengens* ***mistamann***
K1: *Nijn pitä* ***hän*** *rautoihin* ***lyötämän****, sekä Pispalda ripin* ***ottaman****, ja hengensä* ***pitämän***
KrL: *tha* ***scal han iernslas*** *oc aff biscope script* ***taka****, oc liiff* ***behalda***
'Thus he must be shackled, take confession from the bishop, and keep his life'

(89) Purposeful murder, 29
M: *nijn* ***pitä hänen*** *miehen tappohon* ***sidhottaman***
so must he-GEN/ACC man-GEN murder-ILL bind-PASS INF
käreiäs, ninquin mwngin tappaian, ia
court-INESS just like another-ACC murderer-ACC and
maxaman *Syynsanoian 40. marka*
pay accuser-GEN forty marks
L1: *niin* ***pitä hänen*** *tappon* ***sidottaman****, nin quin mungin tappaian, ia* ***maxaman*** *Jutun isännälle 40 marca*
K1: *nijn* ***pitä se*** *Käräjäsä, cuin muutkin Miehen tappajat, Miehen tappajaxi* ***tehtämän****: Sekä* ***maxacaan****, Syynsanojalle, neljäkymmendä marca*
KrL: *tha* ***scal hona*** *til draaps* ***binda*** *a tinge som annan drapara, oc* ***böte*** *malsegendenom XL mark*
'So he must be found guilty of murder in court, just like any murderer, and pay the accuser 40 marks'

(90) Theft, 2
M: *Nijn* ***pitä hänen duomittaman*** *hirsi puhun,*
So must he-GEN/ACC sentence-PASS INF gallow-ILL
ia ***oleman*** *maxamat tekonsa tähden*
and be-INF without paying deed-GEN for
L1: *Nin* ***hänen pitä domittaman*** *åxan eli hirsipuhunn, ia* ***oleman*** *keluotoinna töidhens edestä*
K1: ***pitä se*** *nuorahan ja hirsipuhun* ***duomittaman****, ja* ***oleman*** *maxamatoinna työnsä tähdhen*
KrL: *tha* ***scal han dömas*** *til green oc galga, oc* ***ligge*** *ogilder fore sina gerning*
'This he must be sentenced to the gallows, and not pay for his crime'

(91) Theft, 11
M: *nijn* ***pitä hänen sidhåttaman*** *aitaan eli,*
thus must he-GEN/ACC bind-PASS INF fence-ILL or
Stuckijn ia ***mistaman*** *Selkänahkans*
pole-ILL and miss-INF back skin-ACC
L1: *nin* ***hänen pitä sidottaman*** *aithan eli hirthen ia nahkans* ***mistaman***
K1: *Nijn* ***pitä hänen*** *aitahan eli puuhun* ***sidhottaman****, ja selkä nahkansa* ***mistaman***

KrL: *tha* ***scal han bindas*** *widh gaard eller stok oc hwdh* ***mista***
'so he must be bound to a fence or a pole and miss the skin on his back'

Though Martti and Ljungo have ellipsis of a coreferential subject/object with active and passive infinitival complements in all examples above (or, perhaps in the case of 90), Kollanius only has so in 88, 90 and 91. In example 86, the clause is subjectless, in 87, Kollanius has a passive infinitival complement in both cases, and in 89, Kollanius has a main verb in the imperative in the second clause. Though in four of the six cases, the Old Swedish source text has a similar pattern with an active infinitival complement in one clause and a passive in the other, I would have reservations with assigning a direct role to the Swedish source pattern in facilitating coreferential subject ellipsis: though the Old Finnish passive infinitive appears as a translation equivalent of the Swedish *-s* passive quite often, it is also used as a translation equivalent of many other constructions (e.g., those with *man* as a subject, those with *haua* as a main verb, etc.). This notwithstanding, the Swedish source text provided the three translators with ample context in which coreferential subject/object ellipsis occurred, and thereby doubtlessly stimulated the identification between the agent of the active infinitival complement and the patient of the passive infinitival complement which led Martti and Ljungo to come up with a system of composite case-marking in which the distinction was lost.

I found the following two examples from RWL:

(92) Building, 26:1
Ennen cuin sencaldaisisa jotan eteen otetan,
before such-PL INESS something-PART raise-PASS
pitä *pitäjän miehet cocoon cutzuttaman,*
must community-GEN men gather-PASS INF
sijtä keskusteleman ja yhdistymän .
that-ELAT talk-INF and unite-INF
'Before anything is raised in such issues, the men of the community must be gathered, talk and reach consensus.'

(93) Courthouse Chapter, 10:24, 24
cuinga se rangaistaman ja wahingo maxaman ***pitä***
how he(?) punish-PASS INF and damage-? pay-INF must
'How he should be punished, and pay damages.'

The latter example is hard to interpret, as the subject/object of the second sentence, the demonstrative pronoun *se*, would normally refer to an inanimate referent. In that case, however, the second clause seems to be subjectless, in which case one would expect a passive infinitive *maksettaman*. Context seems to clearly favour the other interpretation: the one to be punished here is someone who falsely accused someone else.

Table 5:4. *The case-marking of the argument of pitää with active and passive infinitival complements with Ljungo and Martti.*

pitää	Active infinitival complement	Passive infinitival complement
singular nouns, dem. pronouns	-n (marginally -ø)	-n (marginally, -ø)
plural nouns, dem. pronouns	-t (marginally, -n)	-t
quanti-fiers, numersals	-n, -ø	-n, -ø
personal pronouns	-n	-n

Table 5:5. *The variation in case-marking with Kollanius and RWL in clauses with active and passive infinitival complements.*

pitää	Active infinitival complement	Passive infinitival complement
singular nouns, dem. pronouns	-n (marginally -ø)	-ø, more rarely -n
plural nouns, dem. pronouns	-n, more rarely –t	-t
quantifiers, numerals	-n, -ø	-n, -ø
personal pronouns	-n	-n, -ø

What we see with Ljungo and Martti is that, as mentioned before, the case-marking of the argument of *pitää* is by and large the same both as the deontic subject of an active infinitival complement and the patient of a passive infinitival complement, with the exception that the plural genitive does not seem to occur with passive infinitival complements (with the exception of a single case in Martti). With Kollanius and RWL, however, there is a clear difference in case-marking with active and passive infinitival complements: *-n* is common, much more so than with Ljungo and Martti, and also with plural nouns, when the infinitival complement is active, while sing. *-ø* and plural *-t*, nominative case-marking, is common with passive infinitival complements, including personal pronouns.

As mentioned earlier, there seems to be no correlation between transitivity, presence of a direct object and (by proxy) agentivity with Ljungo, and only a weak correlation with Martti. With Kollanius and RWL, however, the distribution of case-markers both with active and passive infinitival complements can be explained on the basis of these semantic distinctions: genitive *-n* is a marker of agentivity/manipulability and therefore prefers transitive clauses with direct objects, and is absent with passive infinitival complements.

With Martti and Ljungo, we must assume that this underlying semantic distinction was somehow lost, which created great pressure to identify the arguments of *pitää* with active and passive infinitival complements. In the previous chapter, we have seen how the presence of an auxiliary was a factor stimulating object promotion with the passive. It may well be that the presence of *pitää* provided a similar stimulus. Also, the presence of Swedish source constructions, where the patient of a passive infinitive is a subject, must have been a factor in Martti and Ljungo's identifying active subject and passive objects.

What this means is that the redistribution of case-markers in a manner similar to the marked accusative in Finnish is not quite a consequence of a reanalysis from subject to object. Rather, we have something that comes half way: the distinction between subject and object appears to be lost with *pitää*, and the resulting argument has partially subject-like, partially object-like features, which is reflected in its case-marking. As mentioned, the term "ject" has been proposed in Finnish by Karlsson (1982: 108-109) to account for the object-like features, in terms of case-marking, of the existential subject. The same term seems to be quite apt for the argument of *pitää* with Ljungo and Martti.

It should be noted that the similarities in terms of case-marking between the agent of *pitää* and an active infinitival complement and the patient of *pitää* and a passive infinitival complement means, in my opinion, that their case-marking cannot be explained on the same basis as the case-marking of the subject of *pitää* in dialectal Finnish is explained by Laitinen (1992). However, the subtle hierarchy proposed by Laitinen, with particularly personal pronouns being marked with the genitive, inanimate referents with the nominative, and everything in between with nominative or genitive in accordance with animacy, (potential) agentivity, etc., does propose a starting position for Martti and Ljungo to end up with their composite case-marking system: as Laitinen and Vilkuna (1993: 44) remark, the nominative "is preferred by plural or collective NPs as opposed to singular ones; generic or otherwise non-specific NPs as opposed to specific, individuated ones." The numbers involved with Kollanius (Appendix B) may be too small to provide a clear picture, but the presence of, for instance, 13 plural nouns marked with the nominative against 37 with the genitive in K1, where the ratio with singular nouns is 5: 79, at least speaks not against such a supposition (however, with K2, albeit a smaller text, the relationship is much less clear). An alternative way of looking at things would be to regard the composite case-marking paradigm of Martti and Ljungo as crystallizing tendencies for lexical categories and case-marking to correlate, already inherent in the dialectal base. In as far as Martti and Ljungo's case-marking paradigm is superimposed on an underlying division of case-markers according to transitivity, agentivity, etc. (which could be supposed with Martti, but would be much more difficult with Ljungo), we might designate the resulting system as one of split ergativity (Dixon 1979: 71) as opposed to the "ideal ergative" or active/stative base: splits in ergative systems based on lexical category or number do seem to occur to some extent (Dixon 1979: 78, 89). The distinction between the "ergative" (*-n*) and the "absolutive" (zero or *-t*) is lost in the category of the plural, with the exception of plural pronouns. Note that there is no distinction, as far as case-marking is concerned, between plural noun or demonstrative pronoun subjects and objects in Finnish in general: it is only with personal pronouns where such a distinction occurs. The resulting split ergativity could thus be seen as an instance of analogical extension within Finnish, and as another move towards a nominative/accusative alignment with *pitää* – one which has been taken, as mentioned, in some Finnish dialects close to Swedish.

The problem with this seems to me that whereas some correlation between agentivity, transitivity and the like can be discerned with Martti, none appears with Ljungo. In fact, the "composite" case-marking paradigm does not seem to distinguish between subject and object at all: the patient of passive infinitives, and the objects of active infinitives, are marked in almost exactly the same fashion as the agent of *pitää* and active infinitives. This circumstance – which is one in which Swedish influence clearly enters the picture – would be crucially lost if we were to regard Ljungo and Martti's composite paradigm as a crystallization of an earlier active/stative system on the basis of lexical categories, or as introducing split ergativity.

5.9. Evaluation: contact-induced change and internally driven change in case of *pitää*

As Laitinen (1992: 42, 50, 58) points out, some Finnish dialects in close proximity to Swedish-speaking areas show 1) nominative subject-marking (and accusative object-marking) in combination with an uninflecting necessitive *pitää* or 2) nominative subject-marking and accusative object-marking in combination with a necessitive *pitää* that agrees in person and number with the subject (see also Saukkonen 1965: 123, Kangassalo,

Nemvalts and Wande 2003: 157). Both are based on a well-established interlingual identification between Finnish *pitää* and Swedish *skal* and subsequent restructuring of the case-marking of the arguments of *pitää* after the model provided by Swedish *skal*. The Swedish auxiliary *skal* does not inflect for number (or person) in Modern Swedish, however, *skal* continued to agree with number with the subject in written language until well into the 20th century (Wessén 1970a: 284-285). The restructuring of the necessitive *pitää* and its arguments can be sketched in the following way:

Table 5:6. *Convergence of Finnish necessitive pitää and Swedish necessitive ska.*

NOM	*scal/sculu*	INF
GEN	*pitää*	INF

↓

NOM	*scal/sculu*	INF
NOM	*pitää*	INF

↓ ↓

NOM	*scal/sculu*	INF		NOM	*scal/sculu*	INF
NOM	*pitää*	INF		NOM	*pitää/pitävät*	INF

↓

NOM	*ska*	INF
NOM	*pitää / pitää/pitävät*	INF

The emergence of person/number marking on necessitive *pitää* – note that only a few cases of agreement of *pitää* in number with the subject was found, namely one in L2 and one in RWL, may be part of a further restructuring of the necessitive construction after the model provided by the Swedish source pattern, but it does not necessarily have to be. Agreement in person and number between the verb and its subject is the unmarked alternative in Finnish, just as absence of agreement in person and number is unmarked in Swedish. Confronted with the Swedish model pattern, both the persistence of an uninflecting necessitive verb with nominative-marked subject and a shift towards an inflecting verb in line with the unmarked

Finnish pattern just as the absence of inflection of *ska* in Swedish is in line with the general lack of person/number marking in Swedish could be expected on the basis of an interlingual identification between *pitää* and *ska.*

What we find in the corpus, particularly with Martti and Ljungo, however, is a complex interplay of internal and external factors. The change of the subject of necessitive verbs itself can be regarded as an analogical extension of the general nominative/accusative case-marking in Finnish to a marginal active/stative subsystem, both in Finnish dialects and in the corpus examined here – and it is indeed mentioned as such by Harris and Campbell (1995: 103-104). And at the same time, it can be regarded as a borrowing from Swedish. In fact, the two should not be regarded as mutually exclusive "causes" but as mutually reinforcing "factors".

With Martti and Ljungo, however, the primary role of the Swedish source text, and model language, seems to have been a different one. Erosion of the dialectal distinction between agentive and non-agentive arguments as a basis to assign case-markers led Martti and Ljungo to assign case-markers on the basis of lexical/structural criteria only (this, again, could be both due to internal factors – it is a distinction usually irrelevant for case-marking in Finnish, as opposed to the "existential vs. other" distinction; or as external, as the distinction plays no role in assigning case-markers with the subject of the Swedish model *skal*). Identification between the patient of the passive infinitive in Finnish and Swedish, as well as contributing "internal" factors such as the presence of an auxiliary *pitää* almost inviting a reanalysis of object to subject in case of passive infinitives, then caused Martti and Ljungo to come up with a composite system sharing some features of the original ergative (*-n*), others of the absolutive or the case-marking of the Finnish object (plural *-t*), ending up with a system in which objects and subjects are not distinguished with regards to case-marking.

This convergence is absent in K1, K2 and RWL. All of this notwithstanding, the distribution of case-markers in M and L1, and in L2 even more so, would also be in line with a much broader shift to nominative case-marking influenced directly by the presence of a Finnish/Swedish diaform *scal – pitää*, as what the change outlined above results in is the generalization of the nominative in certain lexical categories:

Table 5:7. *The "accusative analysis" as a waypoint in a long-term convergence process.*

	1 (K1, K2, RWL)	2 (L1, M)	3 (L2)	4
ACTIVE subs sg.	*-n*, (*-ø*)	*-n* (*-ø*)	*-ø*, *-n*	*-ø*
pron. sg.	*-n*	*-n*	*-n*, *-ø*	*-ø*, *-n*

subst. pl.	-*n*, (-*t*)	-*t*	-*t*	-*t*
pron. pl.	-*n*	-*n*	-*n*, - *ø*	-*ø*, -*n*
PASSIVE subst. sg.	-*ø*	-*n*	-*n*, -*ø*	
pron. sg.	-*n*	-*n*	-*n*	
subst. pl.	-*t*	-*t*	-*t*	
pron pl.	-*n*	-*n*	-*n*	

If 4 is taken to be the state represented by the NOM-*pitää* dialects in the vicinity of Swedish dialects, we see that both M and L1 favour case-markers identical to the nominative in the case of plural nouns (namely, the nom./acc. pl. -*t*) and that L2 favours nominative case-marking in case of singular nouns as well. In other words, though the analysis with apparently led Martti and Ljungo to redistribute case-markers seems not have resulted from a complex interplay of external and internal factors, the effect of that analysis was a case-marking more similar to that of the Swedish source-pattern than the supposed previous stage (which I take to be represented by Kollanius' system). Very tentatively, I would suggest that the presence of a diaform *scal-pitää* created a constant pressure on Martti and Ljungo to shift towards nominative case-marking, and this shift began at the point of least resistance: with plural nouns and pronouns, allowing Martti and Ljungo to frame nascent nominative case-marking within a general distribution of case-markers consistent with one of the grammatical cases of Finnish, i.e. the accusative. In other words, the shift GEN – *pitää* – INF ---> NOM – *pitää* – INF on the basis of NOM – *scal/sculu* – INF can be regarded as establishing a one meaning/one form relationship within a bilingual system. However, the smaller shift GEN/NOM – *pitää* – INF ---> ACC – *pitää* – INF may be regarded as an innovation to establish a one meaning/one form relationship within the confines of one language. If the latter constitutes one step within the former process, we are seeing internal and external factors of change in action: an internal linguistic innovation taking place to resolve a situation where one meaning is represented by various forms within a larger contact-induced process of change.

Concludingly, factors noted in the previous contributing to the assigment of case-markers in the texts examined are:

1) The dialectal distinction on the basis of agentivity, transitivity, personhood, etc. (K1, K2, RWL, to a lesser extent, M)

2) Word-order (M)

3) Composite case-marking on the basis of a merger of the arguments of active and passive infinitives, likely stimulated by Swedish source models (M, L1, to a lesser extent, L2)
4) Direct Swedish influence leading to a generalization of nominative subject-marking (possibly, L2)
5) In case of *tulla*: background of constructions as involving a beneficiary, as well as absence of passive infinitives stimulating a merger as in 3), leading to general retention of genitive case-marking (all texts)

Factors stimulating the above are:
1) Diaform between *pitää* and *skal* as well as between *tulla* and *aegher*, stimulating the retention of "beneficiary" connotations with the subject of the latter, and merger of passive patients and active agents with the former.
2) Word-order patterns of the Swedish source texts, with M.
3) Analogical pressure to conform with the general case-marking patterns of Finnish.

It is interesting to see that comparatively many of these factors apply to Martti's translation. With Martti, both word order, redistribution of case-markers, and to a smaller extent also presence/absence of a direct object seem to be factors guiding case-marking of the subject. Ljungo's and Kollanius' translations are comparatively simpler. With Kollanius and RWL, case-markers seem to be clearly assigned on the basis of agentivity/transitivity/personhood, whereas that factor is absent in L1. In M, L1 and also L2, on the other hand, case-markers seem redistributed following a merger of the case-marking paradigms of active agents and passive patients, which is not the case in K1, K2 and RWL, where these are kept distinct.

If the comparatively greater frequency of nominative case-marking in L2 is caused by an identification between *pitää* and *scal/sculu*, and its nominative subject, we see that this contact-induced restructuring does not take place without taking heed of the other factors influencing case-marking. Rather, it seems to take the road of least resistance, by first manifesting itself in context where a redistribution to composite case-marking seems possible, and in contexts where the absence of a direct object would seem to favour nominative case-marking. Thus it seems that contact-induced change, in this case, plays by the rules set by the internal structure of a language, and vice versa, internal factors play their part in reanalyzing linguistic variety created, partially, by contact-induced change. This may be another reason to regard contact-induced change and internal factors of change as opposing ends of a continuum rather than two sides of a strict dichotomy: not only may they be understood in partially the same terms, but they may also interact in the same process of linguistic change, as contributing factors, rather than as mutually exclusive causes.

6. RELATIVE PRONOUNS

6.1. Introduction

The relative pronouns in use in Modern Finnish are *joka, kuka* and *mikä*. The pronoun *kuka,* derived from the identical interrogative pronoun meaning 'who' (as well as inflected forms such as the inessive *kussa* which does not refer to a person), appears mostly in spoken language (Hakulinen et al 2004: 722) as well as in some independent relative clauses, where the referent is not mentioned (Hakulinen et al. 2004: 724). Hakulinen et al. mention that variation between *joka* and *mikä* appears to occur mostly along an axis of individualization: the more individualized and concrete the referent, the more common the usage of *joka,* which thus occurs with prototypical human, animate, singular, countable referents, whereas *mikä* seems to be concentrated on the opposite pole (Hakulinen et al 2004: 722). Pääkkönen (1988: 216-217) mentions, for instance, that *mikä* occurs more often as an object than *joka,* similarly, noun referents seem to strongly favour *joka* than *mikä,* with *mikä* occurring mainly with abstract referents (Pääkkönen 1988: 233-234), and in Standard Finnish, proper name referents take almost exclusively the relative pronoun *joka* (Pääkkönen 1988: 251). The usage of *mikä* with human referents appears to be highly marked, and seems to be actually popular in spoken Finnish as a marker of casualness (Pääkkönen 1988: 253). In general, *joka* is far more frequently used than either *mikä* or *kuka,* which seem to be relegated to specific, marked functions.

Etymologically, *mikä* is derived from the identical interrogative pronoun, meaning 'What?', whereas *joka* might have been, according to Pääkkönen[10] (1988: 16), derived from the indefinite pronoun *joka, jokainen* 'every'. In Finnish dialects, the situation is a bit more complex. In Southeastern dialects, *joka* appears not to occur whereas *kuka* is common, which may well be connected to a relatively higher frequency of sentence-initial indefinite relative constructions in East Finnic languages (Pääkkönen 1988: 29-31). In the Southwestern dialects, however, the relative pronouns that occur in Standard Finnish have been replaced with an uninflecting *ku(n)* (Hakulinen et al 2004: 723, Pääkkönen 1988: 28). Hakulinen (2004: 724) et al provide the following example:

10 Referring to a hypothesis by M.K. Suojanen in his Licenciate Thesis.

onk	*se*	*veli*	***ku***	*on*
is	it	brother	REL	is
siel	*se*	*pappi*		
there	that	priest		

'Is it the brother which is a priest there?'

Reports about the occurrence of *ku(n)* as a relative pronoun in Finnish dialects appear to be slightly ambiguous: Ikola, Palomäki and Koitto (1989: 207), as well as E.A. Tunkelo (1936: 150) report that *ku(n)* occurs mainly in West Finnish and more specifically Southwestern dialects, whereas Pääkkönen (1988: 28-29) reports only sporadic occurrences of uninflecting *ku(n)* as a relative pronoun, outside of its Southwestern core area and the surrounding areas (Pori, upper Satakunta, Häme, Western Nyland) where it competes with *joka* and *mikä*[11].

In remaining uninflected, *ku(n)* is a bit of an anomaly in Finnish. It has been noted that dialectally, *ku(n)* appears to occur mainly in the functions of subject and object (Pääkkönen 1988: 61), which share part of their case-markers in Finnish. In Old Finnish, based, of course, heavily on Southwestern dialects, *kuin* occurs as uninflecting relative pronoun, again, apparently mainly in subject and object functions (Ojansuu 1909: 166).

The polysemy of *ku(n)* in Finnish dialects, *kuin* in Old Finnish as well as *kuin* and *kun* in modern Standard Finnish should be made clear here. In Standard Finnish, *kuin* functions as a comparative conjunction as well as an adverb, meaning 'almost, as if' or 'just like', as the following examples from NS make clear:

Vamma	*on*	*vaarottavampi*	***kuin***	*se*
wound	is	less dangerous	**than**	it
alussa	*näyttikään*			
initially	appeared			

'The wound is less dangerous than it initially appeared.'

Sehän	*on*	*aivan*	***kuin***	*satua*
That	is	just	**like**	fairytale

'That's just like a fairytale.'

Additionally, Standard Finnish knows a temporal/causal conjunction *kun:*

Kun	*olin*	*matkoilla,*	*isäni*	*kuoli.*
When	I was	on travel	my father	died

11 It should be noted here that there seems to be a dearth of research on the area of relative pronouns in Finnish. Notably, Pääkkönen (1988), in what may be the only large published monograph on the subject, is forced to rely mainly on Masters and Licenciate Theses for her dialectal data.

"When I was travelling, my father died."

Old Finnish, however, uses *kuin* both as comparative conjunction/adverb and temporal/causal conjunction. The temporal conjunction *kun* started appearing halfway during the 18th century, but was used side by side with *kuin* until well into the 19th century (Häkkinen 1994: 384). Some examples from RWL::

(94) Marriage 15:11:
Cuin mies ja waimo tulewat laillisesti
When man and woman become legally
eroitetuxi wuotehesta ja leiwästä, ja miehesä sijhen wica on ; nijn
divorced from bed and bread and in man to that fault is, thus
istucon waimo paicallans omaisuden canssa .
may sit woman at her place possession with
'If a man and a woman are legally divorced, and the man is to blame for that, than the woman may remain at her homestead with her possessions.'

(95) Marriage 16:2:
Jos taloncappale on hucattu, eli sitä ei taita
if house-piece is disappeared or it NEG can
*tacaisin tuoda nijn hywänä, **cuin** se annettijn...*
back bring as good **as** it was given
'If something belonging to the home has disappeared, or it cannot be given back in as good a state as it was given in the first place...'

In addition, *kuin* occurred as a relative pronoun in Old Finnish, and NS mentions some examples dating from the late 19th, early 20th century of both *kuin* and *kun* in the functions of relative pronouns:

*Kiittäkäämme ja ylistäkäämme sitä aikaa **kuin** ollut on*
Let's thank and praise that time **which** was
*Täällä on yksi herra, **kun** haluaisi tavata rovastia.*
Here is one gentleman **who** would like to meet dean
'A gentleman is here who would like to see the dean.'

In dialects, *kuin* only occurs as a comparative adverb, with *ku(n)* occurring as both a temporal and a comparative conjunction, as well as a relative pronoun (Ikola, Palomäki and Koitto 1989: 89, Häkkinen 1994: 384).

The obvious explanation for dialectal *ku(n)* and Old Finnish *kuin* as a relative pronoun is a syntactic borrowing from Swedish (Häkkinen 1994: 475). Early Old Swedish *sum*, Modern Swedish *som* has developed similarly as a relative pronoun from a comparative conjunction, a development as early as the Viking Age (Wessén 1970b: 282). One would assume that a interlingual identification between the comparative conjunctions in Swedish and Finnish took hold, after which the additional function of Swedish *som*, namely, that of relative pronoun, was transferred to the Finnish conjunction as well. Pääkkönen (1988: 33) mentions that older prescriptive grammarians regarded the relative pronoun *ku(n)/kuin* as a sveticism.

One problem with this hypothesis is the uncertainty about the dialectal spread of *ku(n)*. As mentioned, Tunkelo (1936: 150) and Ikola, Palomäki and Koitto (1989: 207) report that *ku(n)* occurs to some extent in all Finnish dialects, including those that have not seen much direct Swedish influence. If this usage is sporadic, one might, perhaps, suppose some influence from written Old Finnish on these dialects. On the other hand, it might also be possible that the roots of the usage of *ku(n)* as a relative pronoun lie in factors other than Swedish influence, and that the much greater frequency of *ku(n)* in Southwestern dialects (as well as particularly its lack of inflection, which is anomalous in Finnish syntax) and Old Finnish might be due to a secondary interlingual identification between *ku(n)* and *som*.

Such a hypothesis has been proposed by Pääkkönen (1988: 201-202), who argues that the dialectal relative pronoun *ku(n)* might have developed from the temporal conjunction, or that, on the other hand, *ku(n)* may be an inflected form of the pronoun stem *ku-*, evident in the interrogative/relative pronoun *kuka*, as well as mentioned by NS and Lönnrot (SRS). NS mentions that the hypothetical genitive form of *ku* does not appear, and that plural forms are rare. The pronoun appears to be mainly confined to poetic language, and the examples listed stem from the *Kalevala* and Eino Leino's poetry. Additionally, *ku* occurs as a relative pronoun in Karelian (KKS). SRS lists more examples, some of which, notably, contain a relative pronoun *kun*. Pääkkönen (1988: 201-202) believes that a closer examination of Finnish dialects might confirm this hypothesis: if, dialectally, *ku(n)* would appear more frequently as an object than in other functions, one might suppose that it stemmed from an inflected, object form of the pronoun *ku-* rather than from a syntactic borrowing from Swedish affecting the comparative conjunction *kuin*. According to Pääkkönen, the usage of *ku(n)* in other functions than the object would nevertheless be the result of Swedish influence.

Another possible argument for the independent development of relative *ku(n)* should be mentioned. In English, *as* shows a similar polysemy as comparative conjunction (*as good as gold*) but also as a relative pronoun, although the latter usage is considered obsolescent (OED).

In the following, I intend to shed light on the variation between *joka* and *kuin* as relative pronouns in Old Finnish. My data consist of subject and object forms of both in the six texts examined. As mentioned, the occurrence of *kuin* as a relative pronoun in other functions appears to be rare. I only included relative clauses with an explicit antecedent (including a pronominal dummy antecedent), preceding the relative clause. The number of clauses thus excluded is, I believe, not very large, and it seems to me that the writers under scrutiny often prefer a pronominal antecedent such as *se* instead of a relative clause preceding the main clause. The clauses thus excluded also would feature *joka* rather than *kuin* – according to Ojansuu (1909: 126), *kuin* does not occur sentence-initially at least in Agricola's writings. I counted 26 cases in M of relative constructions either preceding the main clause, or not featuring an explicit referent, and all which preceded the main clause used *joka* rather than *kuin*.

I also, however, excluded clauses which were ambiguous as to whether *kuin* was used as a relative pronoun or as a comparative conjunction. At first sight, sentences such as the following example from RWL could be interpreted in both ways:

(96) Land 4:5 5
ja olcon heillä walda sen maan
and be to them power that land
lunastaa, ja laillisesti andaa käyttää, ***cuin*** *sanottu on*
redeem and legally give to use **as** said is
'And they shall have the power to redeem that land, and allow it to be used, as has been said'
or: 'And they shall have the power to redeem that land, and allow it to be used, which has been mentioned'.

The first interpretation, however, seems much more natural to me. However, instances such as the following from L1, where, on the basis of the plural verb in the relative clause, *kuin* seems to be in the place of a plural subject relative pronoun, have been taken into account:

(97) King's Chapter, 7
ia ne walat wannoman ***quin*** *ennen sanotut*
and those oaths swear **which** earlier mentioned
ouat
were
'And to swear those oaths which have been mentioned earlier'.

This might cause a slight bias in favour of non-singular referents with *kuin*. The fuzzy border between *kuin* as a relative pronoun and *kuin* as a comparative conjunction might, by itself, be taken for a possible argument in favour of the former's origin with the latter. Wessén (1970b: 282) mentions that the border between the relative pronoun *som* and the comparative conjunction *som* is similarly hazy.

The frequencies of *joka* and *kuin* with various variables is presented, in raw numbers, in Appendix D.

6.2. Relative pronouns as subject and object

In all six texts examined, *joka* is more frequent than *kuin*, thus, nowhere is the overwhelming frequency of *ku(n)* in the Southwestern dialects directly reflected in the corpus under examination. As Table 6:1 shows, *kuin* is most frequent in M, and much less so in the translations by Ljungo and Kollanius, whereas RWL seems to hold the middle ground.

Table 6:1. *Frequencies of joka and kuin in percentage points.*

	joka	*kuin*	n
M	52.7	47.3	594
L1	68.8	31.2	625
K1	71	29	534
L2	73.5	26.5	437
K2	72.3	27.7	436
RWL	61.4	38.6	1147

The difference in frequencies between M and the other authors might reflect dialectal differences, in as far as M reflects Southwest Finnish, and Kollanius (who hailed from Satakunta) and Ljungo (who had his origins in Ostrobothnia) less so. Nonetheless, the differences, particularly between L1 (which can be regarded to be partially based on M, the text of which was known to Ljungo) and L2 (a genuinely independent work) are small. The larger frequency of relative pronouns in Ljungo's translations in general is striking: it should be noted that K2 includes a translation of the Church Chapter of the *Upplandslagen* and is therefore quite a bit longer than L2.

Table 6:2 presents the percentages of objects and subjects with each relative pronoun. The second number is a division of the division of subjects and objects (or objects and subjects) within that pronoun category divided by the division between subjects and objects (or objects and subjects) in general. It thus reflects how much more, or less, frequently a form appears than would be expected, if subjecthood were totally neutral to the choice between *joka* and *kuin*.

Table 6:2. *Frequencies of joka and kuin as subjects and objects.*

	joka - subject	*joka* - object	*kuin* - subject	*kuin* - object	chi square	p less or equal than
M	82.7 **1.5**	17.3 **0.67**	69 **0.69**	31 **1.4**	15.37	0.001
L1	80.2 **1.29**	19.8 **0.78**	66.2 **0.62**	33.8 **1.6**	14.51	0.001
K1	79.2 **1.12**	20.8 **0.88**	72.3 **0.77**	27.7 **1.28**	2.97	0.10
L2	82.2 **1.48**	17.8 **0.67**	57.8 **0.44**	42.2 **2.29**	27.8	0.001
K2	80.9 **1.15**	19.1 **0.88**	72 **0.7**	18 **1.44**	3.8	0.10
RWL	78.7 **1.56**	21.3 **0.64**	56.9 **0.56**	43.1 **1.8**	61.9	0.001

This seems at least not to disconfirm Pääkkönen's hypothesis. Throughout the corpus, there seems to be a tendency for *joka* to occur with subjects, and *kuin* to occur with objects. This correlation appears to be strongest with L2 and with RWL. However, in either of Kollanius' translations, the correlation did not pass a Chi Square test of statistical significance. Nonetheless, it should be noted that in all six texts, *kuin* remains more frequent as subject than as object. In real numbers, *kuin* appears as subject in M 194 times, and as object 87 times. A few examples follow.

Subject pronouns:

(98) (Marriage, 4)
M: *ia duomari nimitettäkän 4. miestä käreiästä,*
and judge name-IMPER four men-PART court-ELAT
***iotca** händä seuraman pitä,*
which-PL him-PART follow must
L1: *ia domari nimittäkän 4 miestä käräiästä, **iotca** händä seuraman pitä*
K1: *ia duomari nimittäckään, neljä miestä Käräjäsä, **jotca** händä seuraman pitä*
'And let the judge name four men, which must follow him'

(99) Land, 7
L2: *Åsta iocu cartanon eli tontin toiselda,*
Buy-3SG someone garden-ACC or lot-ACC another-ABL
*warielkan se tontin **ioca** möij, ia*
defend-IMPER that lot-ACC who sold-3SG and
*omaisuttakan se hinnan **ioca** åsti*
own-IMPER that price-ACC who bought-3SG
K2: *Warjelcaan se codhixamen, joca myi ja tietkään se hinnan andaneensa, **joca** osti*

‘Let him that sold the lot vouch for it, and let him that bought it know the price.’

(100) Court, 17:35
RWL: *Sama oikeus olcon sillä, **joca** tulipalon cautta*
The same right be-IMPER he-ADESS who fire-GEN through
on wahingota kärsinyt
is-3P SING damage-PART suffered
‘Let him that has suffered damage in the fire have the same right’

Object pronouns:

(101) Purposeful murder, 26
M: *ia iocaitzen tule murha sakonn maxa, **quin** sijnä nimitetän*
and everyone must murder fine-ACC pay who there name-PASS
L1: *ia idze kungin tule murha sackon tehdä **quin** sijnä nimitethän*
K1: *Ja jocaihdhen pitä Murha sakon tekemän, **cuin** siehen nimitetään*
‘And everyone who is named there must pay the murder fine’

(102) Peace Oath, 5
L2: *Caicki se **quin** he sauat Cartanossa eli tomtisa,*
All that what they get-3PL garden-INESS or lot-INESS
on caicki keluotoin
is all void
K2: *Caicki se **cuin** he pihasa eli codhixemella sawat, on maxamatoinna*
‘All that may be inflicted upon them in the garden or on the lot will be void.’

(103) Court, 17:24
RWL: *Todistajain pitä todistaman sijtä,*
witness-GEN PL must testify that-ELAT
***cuin** he itze nähnet, eli asiasa cuullet owat,*
what they self seen or case-INESS heard be-3PL
*ja ei sijtä **cuin** he muiden puhen jälken tietäwät*
and not that-ELAT what they other-GEN speech-GEN after know
‘Witnesses must testify about what they have seen or heard themselves, and not about what they know through hearsay’.

Nevertheless variation between *joka* and *kuin* seems to be, to a large extent, determined by free variation as well, as the following example from L2 shows. Note that *kuin* seems to be interpreted as a plural relative pronoun, as judged by the succeeding plural verb, while the referent, *ioca radimies* ‘each councilman’, is strictly spoken singular (though it sports an indefinite pronoun, implying a multiplicity of councilmen):

(104) King’s Chapter, 13

Nin maxakan bårgmestarit ***iotca*** *sillä wodella*
Thus pay-IMPER mayors which that year-ADESS
istuat ia duomitzeuat idze cukin 40 marca. Ja ioca radimies
sit and judge each 40 mark. And each councilman
quin *heidhen cansans istuat ia duomitzeuat 20 marca*
which they-GEN with sit and judge 20 mark.
'Thus let the majors who sit and judge that year pay forty marks each. And let each councilman who sits and judges with them pay twenty marks.'

6.3. Relative pronouns and other variables

Subjecthood/objecthood appear to be not the only variables which govern the variation between *joka* and *kuin*. The following table shows the relative frequencies of the two pronouns and human/non-human referents.

Table 6:3. *Frequencies of joka and kuin with human and non-human referents*

	joka - human	*joka* - non-human	*kuin* - human	*kuin* - non-human	chi square	p less or equal than
M	81.1 **1.8**	18.9 **0.56**	58.7 **0.6**	41.3 **1.67**	35.9	0.001
L1	75.6 **1.33**	14.4 **0.75**	57.4 **0.58**	42.6 **1.72**	21	0.001
K1	81.5 **1.51**	18.5 **0.67**	57.4 **0.46**	42.6 **2.18**	33.69	0.001
L2	74.5 **1.67**	25.5 **0.6**	33.6 **0.29**	66.4 **3.46**	61.38	0.001
K2	84.5 **1.89**	16.8 **0.54**	43.9 **0.28**	56.1 **3.65**	68.59	0.001
RWL	73 **2.16**	27 **0.46**	27.8 **0.31**	72.2 **3.25**	225.42	0.001

The correlation between the pronoun and human/non-human reference seems to be much stronger than that between subjecthood and objecthood throughout, particularly in the two translations of Magnus Eriksson's City Law and RWL. In these three texts, *kuin* has a non-human referent in an absolute majority of cases. Notably, the correlation is significant with Kollanius' translations as well. A few typical examples follow.

Human reference:

(105) King's Chapter, 2
M: *nijn ombi sille kuningalle walda* ***ioca***
thus be-3SG that-ALL king-ALL power **which**
iälkin tule sitä oikeudella iällens otta
after come-3SG that-PART right-ADESS back take
L1: *nin on sillä Kuningalla walta* ***ioca*** *iälkin tule, sitä oikeudella iällens åtta*
K1: *nijn ombi sillä Kuningalla walda,* ***ioca*** *jälken tule sitä tacaperin omista*
'Thus let that King who comes after have the power to take it back'

(106) Punishment, 5:6 6
RWL: *Jos wangin-wartia salli jongun,* ***joca***
if warden allow-3SG someone-ACC who
wangiuteen wedellä ja leiwällä tuomittu on,
imprisonment-ILL water-ADESS and bread-ADESS sentenced is-3SG
nautita muuta juomaa ja ruoca
enjoy-3SG other-PART drink-PART and food-PART
'If a warden allows someone, who has been sentenced to imprisonment on water and bread, to enjoy other drink and food'

Non-human reference:

(107) Trade, 14
L2: *Karia sekä nuori että wanha, eli mingä caltainen*
cattle both young and old or whatever like
se on, ia mw cauppa calu ***quin*** *caupungin tule*
it is and other merchandise **which** city-ILL come-3SG
K2: *Nuorta ja wanha carja, mingäcaldaista se oliscan, ja muuta cauppa,* ***cuin*** *Caupungihin wiedhän*
'Young cattle or old, or whatever it is like, and other merchandise which is being brought to town'

(108) Crimes, 4:6
RWL: *olcon rickonut hengens, ja sen*
be-IMPER forfeited his life and that-ACC
cuin *hän nautinnut on*
which he enjoyed has
'Let his life be forfeit, and that [the bribes] which he enjoyed'

Additionally, there seems to be a correlation between the choice of the relative pronoun and number/countability, as the following table, plotting singular and countable referents against others, shows. It should be noted that the analysis of a referent as countable or non-countable must often be done with the help of context: whereas such referents as 'land' may be used in a non-countable sense in some contexts, in others (e.g. a piece of land as opposed to other pieces of land), they seem to be countable.

Table 6:4. *Frequencies of joka and kuin with singular countable and other referents.*

	joka - s.c.	*joka* - non-s.c.	*kuin* - s.c.	*kuin* - non-s.c.	chi square	p less or equal than
M	65.8 **1.58**	34.2 **0.63**	42.9 **0.61**	57.1 **1.64**	31.94	0.001
L1	61.4 **1.28**	38.6 **0.51**	42.1 **0.59**	57.9 **1.7**	20.31	0.001
K1	60.9 **1.23**	39.1 **0.81**	43.2 **0.6**	56.8 **1.66**	14.01	0.001
L2	57.9 **1.31**	42.1 **0.76**	32.7 **0.46**	67.3 **2.41**	21.63	0.001
K2	58.4 **1.19**	41.6 **0.84**	41.1 **0.82**	58.9 **1.68**	9.67	0.010
RWL	65.8 **1.7**	34.2 **0.58**	32.7 **0.43**	67.3 **2.31**	119.13	0.001

Some examples:

Singular/countable

(109) Capital Crimes, 9
M: *mwtoin ios hän seurapi sitä, **ioca** oikein on*
unless he follow-3SG that-PART who rightly be-3SG
waldakundan tullutt
realm-ILL come
K1: *Jolleica waiwoin hän nijtä seora, **jotca** oikein waldacundahan tulleet owat*
'Unless he follows those, who have rightfully entered the realm'

(110) Crimes, 54:4 4
RWL: *Jos kihlattu mies macaa sen naisen,*
if engaged man lie-3SG that-ACC woman-3SG
***joca** toiselda kihlattu on*
who someone else-ABL engaged is
'If an engaged man fornicates with a woman, who has been engaged with someone else'

Non singular/countable:

(111) Theft, 6

M: *Varastapi mies kulda, hopia,*
Steal-3SG man gold-PART silver-PART
walmit penningit eli watteit, heuoisen eli odhat,
ready money-ACC or clothes-PART horse-ACC or arms-ACC
eli mingäkaltainen warkaus se oliskan, ***ioca*** *Enämbi 1/2 ma~rka*
or whatever theft it be-COND **which** more mark
maxa
cost-3SG
L1: *Warasta iocun kulta, håpiata, walmihita penningitä heuoisen, wathe, asehen, eli mingä caltainen warkahus se olla taidais* ***ioca*** *enämbi on quin 1/2 marcan hinda*
K1: *Warasta mies culda, hopiata, walmista raha, hewoisen, waatteet, odhat, eli mikä warcaus se oliscan,* ***joca*** *on enämbi puolda marca*
'If a man steals gold, silver, money. a horse, clothes, weapons, or whatever theft, which is worth more than half a mark'

(112) Trade, 31
L2: *Sola ia mw raskas tauara* ***quin*** *Kestit tuouat*
salt and other heavy stuff which foreign merchants bring-3PL
pitä saatettaman Julkisin Catu puodin ia siellä
must be brought public-ILL street shops-ILL and there-ADESS
mytämän
be sold
K2: *Suolat ja muut cappalet,* ***cuin*** *Ihdheolewaiset culjettawat, pitä julkisesti raitibuodhihin pandaman, ja siellä myytämän*
'Salt and other wares, which are imported by foreign merchants, must be placed in public street stores and be sold there.'

The correlation appears to be weaker than that between pronoun choice and human reference, especially so with Kollanius' translations. Notably, as with the correlation between pronoun choice and human reference, the difference between the expected and actual values with *kuin* is larger than that with *joka*, which could mean that particularly the relative pronoun *kuin* appears to prefer non-human and non-singular/countable reference, with *joka* pushed to the other pole by default, as it were.

The following table reports occurrences of *joka* and *kuin* with the quantifier *kaikki* 'all', namely, those where the quantifier is followed by a plural noun or pronoun (*kaikki miehet*, 'all the men', *kaikki ne* 'all of them'), with a singular noun or pronoun (*kaikki vahinko* 'all the damage', *kaikki se* 'all of it'), or alone.

Table 6:5. *The quantifier kaikki and pronoun choice*

		kaikki + plural n.	*kaikki* + sing. n.	*kaikki*	tot.

M	*joka*	7	0	1	8
	kuin	22	13	11	46
L1	*joka*	11	5	5	21
	kuin	16	14	10	40
K1	*joka*	10	2	5	17
	kuin	11	18	2	31
L2	*joka*	9	9	8	26
	kuin	6	16	5	27
K2	*joka*	16	4	6	26
	kuin	9	28	3	40
RWL	*joka*	13	1	4	18
	kuin	7	14	3	24

What we see in the table above is that *kaikki* seems to strongly prefer *kuin* with M, but this relationship is much less clear with the other texts. However, what is striking is that *kaikki* in combination with a singular noun/pronoun is associated with *kuin* in all texts, whereas *kaikki* in combination with a plural noun/pronoun takes *joka* in a majority of cases with K2, L2 and RWL, *kuin* with L1 and K1. This seems to support countability/divisibility as a factor in pronoun choice: whereas, for a noun to appear in the plural with *kaikki*, it has to be countable and is often not divisible, nouns which appear in the singular with *kaikki* are mostly divisible, and not countable.

We must, of course, assume that the factors that have been mentioned here interact: that singular and countable nouns tend to have human reference more often than average, and that these tend to appear in subject positions more often than average. The following table plots the occurrences, in percentage points, of different combinations of the factors that have been mentioned here. The raw numbers, of course, are listed in Appendix D.

Table 6:6. *Combination of subjecthood, human reference, and singular countability*

subj.		1	1	1	0	1	0	0	0
hum.		1	1	0	1	0	1	0	0
s.c.		1	0	1	1	0	0	1	0
M	***joka***	**50.1**	**23.7**	**5.8**	**5.4**	**3.2**	**1.9**	**4.5**	**5.4**
	kuin	33.5	21.7	3.2	0.7	10.7	2.8	5.3	22.1
L1	***joka***	**45.6**	**24**	**6.3**	**5.1**	**4.4**	**0.9**	**4.4**	**9.3**
	kuin	31.8	21.5	2.6	2.1	10.3	2.1	5.6	24.1
K1	***joka***	**47.8**	**24.5**	**3.7**	**5.5**	**3.2**	**3.7**	**4**	**7.7**
	kuin	34.8	20	3.2	1.3	14.2	1.3	3.9	21.3
L2	***joka***	**48.3**	**22.4**	**4.4**	**2.5**	**7.2**	**1.2**	**2.8**	**11.2**
	kuin	20.7	11.2	3.4	1.7	22.4	0	6.9	33.6
K2	***joka***	**49.5**	**26.7**	**0.9**	**4.9**	**3.6**	**3**	**3**	**8.2**
	kuin	26.6	13.1	8.4	1.9	23.4	1.9	3.7	20.6
RWL	***joka***	**47.4**	**16.1**	**6**	**8**	**9.2**	**1.6**	**4.4**	**7.4**
	kuin	20.8	4.7	4.5	1.8	26.9	0.5	5.6	35.2

It is striking to see how similar the percentages listed are, across the six texts examined. Almost three-quarters of the occurrences of the pronoun *joka* are subjects and sport human referents, singular/countable or not. A small 'spike' of occurrences of subjects without human reference or singular/countability seems to occur with L2, but appears to be absent in other texts. A similar spike occurs at the tail, with objects, non-human reference, not singular/countable – except in M. With *kuin*, a fair percentage of occurrences are concentrated at the head, but far less so than with *joka*, especially with L2, K2 and RWL. A significant spike of occurrences of *kuin* occurs with subjects which have neither human reference or singular/countability, far greater in L2, K2 and RWL than in the three older texts, and at the tail of the diagram – with objects that have neither human reference nor sport singularity and countability.

There are some reasons to assume that semantic factors such as human reference and countability play a greater role in the choice of the relative pronoun than subjecthood/objecthood. For one, *kuin* is highly infrequent as an object, if the referent is both human and singular and countable – 0.7 percent in M, 2.1 percent in L1 and similar percentages in the other texts. Conversely, we see a spike in the usage of *kuin* in all six texts when the pronoun functions as a subject, yet has a non-human and non singular countable referent. This is consistent with the tables presented earlier, which showed stronger correlations between pronoun choice and the two semantic categories than between pronoun choice and subjecthood/objecthood. Disentangling the factors of human reference and singularity/countability may well be impossible.

If this state of affairs is representative of dialectal Finnish, as the uniformity across the six texts examined would suggest, Pääkkönen's hypothesis of the relative pronoun *kuin* as originally an accusative form of *ku-*, later extended to other syntactic functions through identification with Swedish *som*, becomes problematic, though not impossible. One might imagine, first of all, that after an original **ku-n* began to be used in the syntactic functions of subject as well, its semantic load of being an object relative pronoun of course disappeared, yet the typical roles in which objects might be expected to occur – non-human, non-countable – might remain. Second, it is, perhaps, not necessary to interpret the *-n* ending of the dialectal relative pronoun as an object marker. Pronominal nominative endings on *-n* are, after all, hardly unknown in Finnish (e.g. the personal pronoun *hän* 'he, she', as well as the interrogative pronoun *ken*, an archaic variant of *kuka* 'who'). It is important here to remember that the object case of divisible, non-countable nouns is the partitive (which happens to occur for *ku-* as mentioned in NS as well as the Karelian cognate mentioned in KKS), rather than the accusative.

6.4. Relative pronouns in the Swedish source text

Relative clauses in Old Swedish often appear without any relative pronoun or particle, occasionally with a demonstrative *thän* in the main clause (Wessén 1970b: 273). An example from MEL:

(113): *ok the rymen stadhen eig wilia thiaena*
and they flee-CONJ city not want serve
"And those who do not wish to serve should flee the city"

The frequency of relative clauses without any relative pronoun or particle seems to differ from text to text, thus they are quite frequent in the *Upplandslagen*, but far less so in the *Östgötalagen* (Wessén 1970b: 282,

Noreen 1904: 409-412). Lindblad (1943: 90) mentions that pronounless relative constructions seem to be especially common in central Old Swedish dialects, but less frequent in peripherical Old Swedish dialects.

There are a few clauses in which Ljungo seems to translate such source constructions isomorphically, without a relative pronoun. I found three such cases in L2, all close together:

(114) Land, 6
L2: *Ja ne cartanot ia tontit mies åsta*
and those gardens and lots man buys
MEL: *Ok the garddha ella tomptir man köpir*
'And those gardens and lots someone buys'

(115) Land, 13
L2: *Caicki se maa mies åsta eli waihetta maalta nin*
all the land man buys or exchanges land-ABL thus
Caupungin käykän maan lakia myödhen
city-ILL go land-GEN law-PART according
MEL: *Alla the iordh man skipter i stadhin eller sael, gange epter lanz laghum*
'But all the land a man exchanges from the countryside to the city will be treated according to the Land Law'

(116) Land, 13
L2: *Ja caicki ne tontit ia cartanoth mies waihetta eli caupungisa,*
and all the lots and gardens man exchanges
käykän caupungin lain iälkin
MEL: *ok alla the tompter eller gardha man skipter a landit, gange epter stadzins laghum*
'And all the lots or garden a man exchanges from the city to the countryside will be treated according to the City Law'

The oldest relative pronoun which seems to appear in Old Swedish is *är*, which is mainly confined to Runic Swedish (Noreen 1904: 409). Though it appears in the older County Laws, it does not occur in later Old Swedish (Wessén 1970b: 288). The relative pronoun *thän* appears to have had its start as a demonstrative correlate in the main clause, with the relative clause itself being pronoun-less (Wessén 1970b: 273). If it is placed on the border of a main clause and a relative clause, however, it may appear inflected according to the valence of the main verb of the relative clause (Wessén 1970b: 278). A few examples of *thän* from MEL:

(117)
(King's Chapter 16) *Swa böte ok then androm*
thus pay-CONJ also that to another

thet wither
that accuses
'Thus also he, who accuses another of that, will pay'

(118)
(Inheritance, 20) *gange ater gozit til then thet vtgaff*
go-CONJ back goods to that it gave
'Let the goods to back to he, who gave them'

(119)
(Purposeful wounding, 4) *Hogger man then naest aer tumulfingre*
cuts man that closest is thumb
'If someone cuts off the finger closest to the thumb'

Additionally, the uninflecting relative pronoun *thär* appears in Old Swedish, having possibly developed partially from a purely local adverb, partially from a combination of a demonstrative pronoun and the older relative pronoun *är* (Wessén 1970b: 283, 285). Noreen (1904: 409-412) mentions that *thär* is relatively infrequent as a relative pronoun, yet common in some older texts, such as the *Södermanlag* and the *Dalalag*. Lindblad (1946: 115) mentions *thär* occurs quite rarely in MEL. An example of the relative use of *thär* in MEL seems to be the following:

(120)
(Purposeful wounding, 20) *All affhog ther qwinno görs*
all wounds that to woman do-PASS
mædh wilia ok wredz hænde
willingly and in anger
'all wounds that are inflicted, willingly or in anger, on a woman'

Finally, of course, *sum*, Modern Swedish *som,* cognates of which occur in all Scandinavian languages (Stroh-Wollin 2002: 11) already occurs in Runic Swedish (Noreen 1904: 409-412, Stroh-Wollin 2002: 15), and grows more common in later texts, occurring "almost exclusively" (Noreen 1904: 409-412, see also Lindblad 1946: 114-115) in MEL. The occurrence of *som* and other relative pronouns such as *är* seems to be partially dialectally determined (Wessén 1970b: 289).

The following table shows the frequencies of source constructions of *joka* and *kuin*, namely, *som* or various other constructions (not necessarily relative clauses) in percentage points. This is based on a sampling of the translations of KrL, namely, the King's Chapter, the Building Chapter, and the Peace Oath Chapter. For the two translations of MEL, I sampled the whole text, excluding Kollanius' translation of the Church Chapter of the *Upplandslagen*. Examination of a sample of RWL (namely, the Court

Chapter) found other constructions than *som* to be marginal (132 of 148 source constructions of *joka* had *som*, as well as 125 of 148 source constructions of *kuin*).

Table 6:7. *Frequencies of source constructions (som and other) of joka and kuin in percentage points*

	M	L1	K1	L2	K2
joka < *som*	75.2	67.9	70.1	51.9	55.5
joka < other	24.8	32.1	29.9	48.1	45.5
kuin < *som*	64.6	60	68.3	41	35.5
kuin < other	35.4	40	31.7	59	64.5

What this table seems to show, interestingly, is that *som* occurs relatively more often as a source construction of *joka* than as of *kuin*, particularly in the translations of MEL, where constructions other than *som* appear to be vastly more frequent than in KrL, and which also have been sampled more. Superficially, the result is the opposite of what we would expect if an interlingual identification between *som* and *kuin* held in Old Finnish.

Things get more confusing if we examine the following table, which depicts the frequencies of *som* and other source constructions with subject and object versions of *joka* and *kuin*.

Table 6:8. *The source constructions of joka and kuin as subject and object. The number in brackets depict the raw numbers, the other are percentages*

	subj.	*som*	M	L1	K1	L2	K2
J	1	1	75 (75)	66.7 (76)	74.6 (88)	54.7 (133)	57.1 (133)
	1	0	25 (25)	33.3 (38)	25.4 (30)	45.3 (110)	42.9 (100)
	0	1	76.9 (10)	62.5 (15)	50 (13)	38.9 (21)	35 (14)
	0	0	23.1 (3)	37.5 (9)	50 (13)	61.1 (33)	65 (26)
K	1	1	70.6 (48)	69.6 (39)	68.3 (28)	45.5 (30)	30.1 (22)
	1	0	29.4 (20)	31.4 (17)	31.7 (13)	54.5 (36)	69.9 (51)
	0	1	51.6 (16)	37.5 (9)	68.4 (13)	33.3 (18)	47.1 (16)
	0	0	48.4 (15)	62.5 (15)	31.6 (6)	66.7 (33)	52.9 (18)

What this table indicates is that source constructions with *som* are relatively more frequent in subject positions, and that the translation choice – *kuin* or *joka*, seems irrelevant in this regard. Source constructions other than *som* occur relatively frequently as objects. This pattern is especially clear in the translations of MEL, less so – doubtlessly obscured by the low frequencies, in real numbers, of other source constructions than *som* – in the three translations of KrL. In other words, it is possible that the preference for *kuin* to occur in object positions seems to be related to the source text, but not in the way one would expect: *kuin* seems to be preferred as a translation equivalent of source constructions other than *som*, such as relative clauses without pronouns, with demonstrative *thän*, etc.

As the following two tables indicate, the same pattern re-occurs if we plot human/non-human reference, or singular and countable vs. either non-singular or singular non-countable:

Table 6:9. *The source constructions of joka and kuin with human and with non-human reference. The number in brackets depict the raw numbers, the other are percentages.*

	h	*som*	M	L1	K1	L2	K2
J	1	1	79.8 (71)	72.8 (67)	72 (85)	57.4 (128)	54.5 (121)
	1	0	21.2 (18)	27.2 (25)	18 (33)	42.6 (95)	45.5 (101)
	0	1	58.3 (14)	57.1 (24)	61.5 (16)	35.1 (26)	37.2 (16)
	0	0	41.7 (10)	42.9 (18)	38.5 (10)	64.9 (48)	62.8 (27)

K	1	1	67.3 (37)	64.2 (34)	71.9 (23)	56.4 (22)	39.5 (17)
	1	0	32.7 (18)	35.8 (19)	28.1 (9)	43.6 (17)	60.5 (26)
	0	1	64.3 (27)	51.9 (14)	64.3 (18)	33.3 (26)	32.8 (21)
	0	0	35.7 (15)	48.1 (13)	35.7 (10)	66.7 (52)	67.2 (43)

Table 6:10. *The source constructions of joka and kuin with singular countable and non-singular countable reference. The number in brackets depict the raw numbers, the other are percentages.*

	s.c.	*som*	M	L1	K1	L2	K2
J	1	1	73.6 (53)	70 (56)	71.9 (64)	60.7 (105)	59.5 (91)
	1	0	26.4 (19)	30 (24)	28.1 (25)	39.3 (68)	40.5 (62)
	0	1	78 (32)	63.6 (35)	66.1 (37)	37 (44)	41.8 (46)
	0	0	22 (9)	36.4 (20)	33.9 (19)	63 (75)	38.2 (64)
K	1	1	68.3 (28)	71.4 (25)	81.3 (13)	67.6 (25)	48.6 (18)
	1	0	31.7 (13)	28.6 (10)	18.7 (3)	32.4 (12)	51.4 (19)
	0	1	62.1 (36)	51.1 (23)	60 (24)	28.8 (23)	30.6 (22)
	0	0	37.9 (22)	48.8 (22)	40 (16)	71.2 (57)	69.4 (50)

This situation is probably related to the Swedish source text. Whereas originally, in Old Swedish, the choice of the relative pronoun seems to have been unrelated to its syntactical function or the semantics of its referent (Lindblad 1946: 100), during the course of Old Swedish *som* slowly grew to be obligatory in the subject position, with particularly pronounless constructions relegated to relative clauses where the referent is the object of the verb in the subordinate clause (Lindblad 1946: 101, Wessén 1970b: 290). In Modern Swedish, the use of *som* is obligatory in the subject position, with *den* only functioning as a relative pronoun in object positions (Wessén 1970b: 290, 293). It seems to me that *kuin,* then, was chosen as a translation equivalent of constructions where *som* may be absent and the referent is the object of the subordinate clause because of the semantic roles *kuin* already had in Finnish, rather than *kuin* gaining these roles (non-human, non-countable, etc.) through influence from the Swedish source text. For as mentioned, the preference for *kuin* for non-human, non-subject, non-singular or countable referents seems remarkably consistent across all the texts examined here, and especially strong in RWL. However, constructions not using *som* are rarer in KrL than in MEL, and quite marginal in the source text of RWL, so that positing influence from Swedish relative constructions not using *som* in RWL seems difficult.

6.5. The origins of relative *kuin*

Let us recapitulate the available hypotheses to explain relative *kuin* in Old Finnish, and relative *ku(n)* in dialectal Finnish. First of all, it is possible that the construction as a whole is borrowed from Swedish. We would need to assume an interlingual identification between Old Swedish comparative *sum*/*som* and Finnish *kuin*, after which an extension, modeled on the Swedish source construction, took place, adding a function as relative pronoun to *kuin*. The alternative hypothesis, raised by Pääkkönen (1988: 201-202), is that relative *kuin* had its origins in the relative pronoun *ku*, which occurs in other Finnic languages as well. We would then assume that an identification between comparative *kuin*, dialectal *ku(n)* and the hypothetical object form of the relative pronoun, *ku(n)* took place, itself modeled on the Swedish synonymy between relative and comparative *som*. Based on the model posed by Swedish, the original accusative form *ku(n)* began to appear in other functions than the object, displacing earlier inflected forms of *ku*. A third possibility, of course, is that *ku(n)* and Old Finnish *kuin* arose wholly independently from Swedish.

There are, however, good reasons to posit some influence of Swedish on the origin of relative *kuin*. First of all, while the dialectal spread of uninflecting relative *ku(n)* is not entirely clear, with both Tunkelo (1936: 150) and Ikola, Palomäki and Koitto (1989: 207) mentioning that it occurs, to some extent, outside of its Southwestern core area as well, it seems clear enough that it is most common in the Southwestern dialects, one of the main loci of direct contact between Swedish and Finnish. Additionally, the occurrence of an uninflecting relative pronoun in subject and object positions (though *kuin*, in Old Finnish at least, is not confined to these) is anomalous enough on the face of it to posit some extraneous influence on its development. Whereas it is quite typical for Finnish to use the same case endings, notably nominative and accusative *Ø* and partitive *-tA* as well as genitive *-n* and accusative *-n,* in both subject and object functions (see 3.1.), a total lack of case inflection seems decidedly foreign to Finnish structure. Finally, the similarities between Finnish *kuin* and Swedish *som*, both sharing functions as comparative conjunction and uninflecting relative pronoun, appear overwhelming.

It seems to me that the occurrence of a dialectal relative *ku* seems *a priori* supportive of Pääkkönen's thesis. Problematic, however, is that the inflectional paradigm of *ku* is incomplete, and a genitive/accusative *-n* seems to be unattested. Additionally, it is not at all certain that a hypothetical object form of *ku* would indeed take the ending *-n*, rather than *-t*, as the doubtlessly related interrogative pronoun *kuka, kene-* does. However, as mentioned earlier, the accusative *-t* for pronominal endings seems to be of East Finnish origin, with *-n* commonly occurring in West Finnish.

As I mentioned earlier, I am not sure whether it is necessary for Pääkkönen's hypothesis to posit an object form *ku(n)*, rather than *ku(n)* as a subject form, as nominative endings on *-n* are not entirely unknown for Finnish pronouns, as attested by the archaic literary interrogative pronoun *ken*.

The usage of *joka* and *kuin* in Old Finnish could be reconciled with Pääkkönen's hypothesis. As said, I believe the tendency for *kuin* to prefer object positions is a secondary effect of its preference for non-human, non-singular or countable referents, particularly as the latter tendency appears much more strongly in the examined texts than the former one, especially in Kollanius' translations. However, it may be possible to interpret this tendency as a remnant of a *kuin*'s origins as an object pronoun.

However, the examined texts strongly speak against positing an ongoing interlingual identification between *kuin* and *som*. If anything, something counterposed is taking place: *kuin* appears especially as a translation equivalent of constructions other than *som*, in as far as these constructions occur (they mainly do so in MEL, but much more rarely in the later source texts). As I posited, I believe this is an effect of the fact that, in later Old Swedish, *som* gradually crystallizes into a subject pronoun with other constructions, particularly absence of any relative pronoun or particle, being relegated to object functions. The pre-existing semantical and functional preferences of *kuin* would have made it a more fitting translation equivalent of the latter constructions. However, if we suppose that relative *kuin* arose, in some way, through an interlingual identification with *som*, we find little trace of such in the examined translations.

In addition to the tendency of *kuin* to prefer certain semantic and functional roles, there may be other factors contributing to what seems to be an interlingual disassociation between *kuin* and *som*. First of all, *som* is the more frequent source construction in all the source texts, overwhelmingly so in the later ones. In the translated texts, however, *joka* is more frequent, with *kuin* being somewhat more frequent in Martti's translations than in the other texts. Now, as Pääkkönen (1988: 28) mentions, *ku(n)* appears to be the most frequent relative pronoun by far in Southwestern dialects. It seems to me that this current situation is not represented in the translated texts: *kuin* is a more marginal alternative of *joka*. If this is to be taken as representative of the dialects that the translators spoke, it may be that an association arose between the most salient pronoun in the source texts (*som*) and the most salient one in the Finnish of their time and place (*joka*).

Saliency comes into question in other ways as well. There is a variety of more marginal constructions slowly displaced by *som* during the course of Old and Early Modern Swedish, but the most frequent appears to be absence of any relative pronoun. This construction could not and cannot be translated isomorphically in Finnish, though sporadic examples of such occur in L2. Now, dialectal *ku(n)* and Old Finnish *kuin* is, as a monosyllabic form, phonologically less salient than bisyllabic *joka*, and may therefore have come into play more frequently as a translation equivalent of a "zero pronoun".

Strong reasons to assume Swedish influence on the development of *kuin* remain, even if little evidence of an ongoing interlingual identification appears in the examined texts. However, it seems that the development of *kuin* as a relative pronoun must have taken place considerably earlier than the time-period examined here. As mentioned, the association between *som* and subject functions is a phenomenon of later Old Swedish and modern Swedish, whereas in earlier Old Swedish, *som* appears to be neutral to subjecthood.

It seems to me that the semantic and functional properties of *kuin* in the examined texts, and quite possibly in the Finnish dialects of that time as well, are a result of the consolidation of *kuin* within the paradigm of relative pronouns, rather than any influence from Swedish – I assume *kuin* arose at a time when Old Swedish *som* was neutral to subject/objecthood and the like. Primarily, I believe that the lack of case inflection of *kuin*, which as mentioned is anomalous in Finnish, made it especially apt for referring to non-singular and non-countable, and, by extension, non-human referents, as *kuin* was inherently unable to express number. Interestingly, it is only in the singular that case distinctions between nominative and accusative are consistently made in Finnish: the plural ending *-t* doubles as a nominative and an accusative ending, and a host of quantifiers (*paljon* 'a lot', *kaikki* 'all') have no specific accusative case-ending. The same goes for numerals other than *yksi* 'one'. I would suggest that *kuin* was pushed in a default role of non-singular reference, where ambiguity between object and subject marking already existed within Finnish.

There appears to be some vacillation in number marking with relative *joka* in the translations of MEL. The mentioned cases involve mainly irregular singulars with numeral correlates, and one case of plural with a non-countable noun correlate:

(121) Inheritance, 17

K2: *Ei pidhä myöskään yhdhelläkään oleman tahto*

NEG must neither anyone-ADESS be-INF desire-NOM
jotacun *perindöta* *ennen* *jaca* *cuin*
some-PART inheritance-PART before distribute as
welcaa *maxettu ombi,* ***jotca*** *hänen* *maxaxensa*
debt-PART paid is that-PL he-GEN pay-INF TRANS
tule
must
'Let no one have the desire to distribute the inheritance before the debts are paid, which he must pay.'

Some other examples from the translations of MEL:

(122) King's Chapter, 13
K2: *Ja* ***jocahinen Neuwomies*** *caxikymmendä marca,* ***jotca*** *nijdhen cansa owat*
'And every Councilman, who is with him, twenty marks'

(123) King's Chapter, 16
L2: ***Caxi*** *hyuä miestä heidhen pitä walitzeman* ***ioca*** *caicki Caupungin merkit pitämän pitä*
'They must choose two good man, who must preserve all the signs of the city'

(124) Marriage, 13
K2: *Ja* ***caicken muun jotca*** *Huomenlahjoinna seisatettu on*
'And everything else that is confirmed as dowry'

(125) Building, 21
L2: *Ja* ***se cansa ioca*** *sinä neliennes åsasa caupungisa asuuat*
'And the people that live in that quarter of town'

(126) Trade, 32
L2: *Edespäin on merkittäuä, Etei* ***yxikän kesti ioca*** *Vlkoa sisellä tuleuat Flanderista eli kusta he tuleuat*
'It should be noted that no guest, who come from abroad, from Flanders or wherever they may be from'

In examples 120 and 124, we have the correlates preceded by indefinite pronouns *(jokainen* 'every' and *ei yksikään* 'no, not one'). Example 121 shows a singular *joka* referring to the numeral *kaksi* 'two', whereas 123 shows a singular *joka* referring to the noun *kansa* 'people', only formally singular. In 123, as well as 124, the verb in the subordinate clause (the subject of which is the relative pronoun) nevertheless shows plural endings. In example 122, finally, we see a plural *jotka* referring to a formally singular (though non-countable) *kaiken muun* 'everything else'.

The following sentence from L1 shows a plural *jotka*, governing a verb which shows plural number marking, referring to a formally singular *palkaperhe* 'servant family':

(127) Courthouse Chapter, 26
L1: *Sama laki olkan palka perehestä* ***iotca*** *ennen märä päiuänsä pois juoxeuat*
'The same law holds for a servant family which runs away before their time is due'

What all these examples have in common is that in some way, either semantically or formally, through the presence of a numeral, quantifier or the presence of an indefinite pronoun, the number of the referent is somewhat ambiguous: if a correlate is preceded by the indefinite pronoun *jokainen*, for instance, it is formally singular, but refers to a whole group of people. As I argued, this would all be cases where relative *kuin,* with its lack of case and number marking, would avoid the need to come up with a singular/plural marker referring to a numerically ambiguous referent, and this may be why *kuin* was pressed in service first of all for cases like these. The tendency for *kuin* to occur with non-human referents may be a secondary consequence of this: non-countability and non-humanness are features which, as mentioned, often co-occur. Notably, of the examples above, only 122 seems to have a non-human referent.

There appear to be some cases where *kuin* occurs with a formally singular correlate in similar circumstances, but governs a plural verb:

(128) King's Chapter, 5
L1: *Sijttä mahta hän länit lainata, waldakundans hallita, ia* ***caicki*** *tehdä,* ***quin*** *ennen sanottut ouat*
'Thus may he hand out provinces, govern the realm, and do everything which has been mentioned before.'

(129) King's Chapter, 13
L1: *kilpein cadzelmus pitä oleman Kuningan puolesta* ***iocahitzes paikas quin*** *nimitetty ouat, ia sillä aialla.*
'Inspection of shields must take place, on behalf of the King, in every place that has been mentioned, and on that time'.

(130) King's Chapter, 13
L2: *Ja* ***ioca radimies quin*** *heidhen cansans istuat*
'And every councilman who sits with them'

(131) King's Chapter, 15
L2: ***Jocahainen quin*** *Caupungisa palueleuat ia on*
Everyone who city-INESS serve-3P and is-3SG
heidhen omaans ia hänen woitto cauppans 20 markan

their own-PART and his profit twenty marks
heidhen pitä Caupungin omaisudhen woittaman .
they must city-GEN possession-GEN win
'Everyone who serves in the city, who is his own man and owns 20 marks in merchandise, will receive citizenship.'

(132) King's Chapter, 19
K2: *nijn pitä* ***jocaihdhen, cuin*** *caupungisa rakendawat*
'Thus must everyone, who builds in the city'

Again, we see here mainly referents whose formal number marking does not quite square with their semantic reference, such as *kaikki* 'all' and the indefinite pronouns *joka* and *jokainen/jokaitsen* 'every'. Particularly example 129 shows a jumble of occasionally plural, occasionally singular pronouns and verbs. Though the need to specify number marking on the relative pronoun has been avoided by the usage of uninflecting *kuin*, it re-occurs with the main verb in the subordinate clause, in as far as *kuin* occurs as a subject pronoun. Agreement in number between relative *kuin* as subject and the main verb is normal, and relative *kuin* governs a plural verb if the referent is plural:

(133) Trade, 11
K2: *Ja ehdhikään oikeudhensa nijldä,* ***cuin*** *sen*
and search his right those-ABL who it-ACC
hänelle pandixi panit
him-ALL pawn-TRANS give-3P
'And let him claim his rights from those, who gave it to him as pawn'.

(134) Ships, 9
L2: *nijn pitä ne hahdet* **quin** *edellä makauat ia*
then must those ships that in front lie-3P and
tyhietyt ouat, sia sietämän
emptied-PL are-3PL give way
'Then those ships that are anchored in front of it, and that have been emptied, must give way'

It seems to me that the usual occurrence of *kuin* with non-countable and non-singular referents may have been a factor in causing these irregularities, through making the occurrence of such ambiguous referents more marginal, and hence more prone to irregularities, with *joka*.

I would thus suggest that *kuin* was positioned within the paradigm of Finnish relative pronouns in a way which put it at odds with the later development of its source construction, Old Swedish *sum/som*. The origin of *kuin* would then exemplify the points raised by Aikhenvald (2003) on the mechanisms of language contact. Though the usage of *kuin* itself as a relative pronoun is modeled on Swedish, it did not simply replace the pre-existing relative pronouns: its positioning with the paradigm of relative pronouns must involve a reanalysis of the whole system, wherein *joka* gets assigned a slightly more narrow role, referring to typical subject, human, singular and countable referents, and *kuin*, by virtue of its lack of case-markers, gets assigned the opposite role.

This was of course not virgin territory, but one occupied especially by relative pronouns formed on the basis of the originally interrogative *mikä*. Relative *mikä* does occur to an extent in the texts examined, usually in object situations, invariably with non-human reference, and almost invariably non-singular or non-countable. Relative *mikä* particularly seems to prefer the quantifier *kaikki* 'all'. These are exactly the roles which relative *kuin* seems to prefer, and indeed, it seems to have partially displaced *mikä*, which occurs, I believe, quite rarely in the examined texts. Interestingly, *mikä*, while having a full case paradigm, has only rudimentary number inflection: only the nominative appears in the plural.

Table 6:11. *The occurrence of relative mikä in the translations of KrL*

		M	L1	K1
subj.	sing., count.	1	0	0
	non-s.c.	6	5	0
	kaikki	5	4	2
obj.	sing., count.	0	0	0
	non-s.c.	7	2	10
	kaikki	15	10	6

It should be noted that the division between *joka* and *kuin* is nowhere near as clean as we would expect a division between *joka* and *mikä* to be. Relative *kuin* may occur much more often in object positions or with non-human reference than we would expect if it were neutral to these features, yet, in raw numbers, most occurrences of *kuin* refer to human, singular or countable referents, and *kuin* occurs in a subject position in a majority of cases. One might suggest it is through an identification with *som* that *kuin* expands on territory formerly the fiefdom of *joka* as well, yet on the basis of the discussion before, I am hesitant to posit such an identification.

As mentioned, the lack of inflection of *kuin* made it, in my opinion, especially apt for referents whose semantic number conflicts in various ways with the formal number marking of the correlate, and these are the positions which *mikä*, which like *kuin*, (mostly) lacks number inflection, formerly occupied. Additionally, *mikä* has always been the more marginal partner of *joka* in the paradigm of Finnish relative pronouns, the one assigned to non-prototypical semantic road. Recall that in the previous chapter, I posited that the subject-marking of the necessitive verb *pitää* in Old Finnish may be seen as a waypoint in a restructuring of the necessitive construction employing *pitää* on a Swedish model. Basically, the already fragile distinction between subjects of *pitää* and an active infinitival complements, and objects of *pitää* and a passive infinitival complements collapsed, leading to a situation where both were marked by, roughly, a genitive *-n* in the singular and a nominative *-t* in the plural. However, variation between genitive and nominative case-marking occurred within all lexical categories: the merger between active subject and passive objects in this particular case led to the generalization of the nominative, and marginalization of the genitive, within one particular lexical category – that of plural nouns and demonstrative pronouns. This change, while mainly internal in nature, moved the system as a whole closer to the Swedish, by exploiting the weakest points of the structural distinctions between the two languages. It may well be that language contact takes the road of least resistance here as well: the more marginal alternative, *mikä*, gets displaced by the Swedish-based newcomer, *kuin*, which just happens to have borrowed from Swedish the feature it shares with *mikä* – lack of number inflection – which makes it a viable replacement.

6.6. Evaluation

The relative pronoun *kuin* has generally been taken to be a borrowing from Swedish *som*, as both share the functions of comparative conjunction and relative pronoun. Swedish *som* has cognates in all other Scandinavian languages, making an inverse borrowing direction exceedingly unlikely; additionally, the usage of dialectal *ku(n)* seems to be concentrated in the Southwestern dialects, though there appears to be some uncertainty on the word's presence in other dialects. Pääkkönen (1988: 201-202) that the relative usage of *ku(n)* and Old Finnish *kuin* may be based on a dialectal *ku*, rather than a direct extension of comparative *kuin* on a Swedish model, though its lack of inflection is likely borrowed from Swedish. According to Pääkkönen, *ku(n)* may be originally an object form.

Though *kuin* appears to occur in object positions more often than expected in the examined texts, I believe this may be a secondary effect of its typical non-human, non-singular or non-countable reference. This tendency appears remarkably constantly in all six texts, and hence may be a feature of dialectal Finnish rather than something unique to the translators involved. However, I do not believe this necessarily invalidates Pääkkönen's hypothesis, and indeed am not sure whether it is necessary to posit *ku(n)* as an original object form for dialectal *ku* to have some role in the origins of relative *kuin*.

Unexpectedly, however, there appears to be no interlingual association between *kuin* and Swedish *som* in the six texts. To the contrary: the semantic and functional roles which *kuin* seems to prefer, to some extent, are those which are usually filled in by other constructions than *som* in the Swedish source text. This is connected to a tendency during late Old Swedish for *som* to crystallize as a subject form, and for other constructions, notably one without any pronoun, to be used when the referent is the object of the subordinate clause. In order to posit contact influence from Swedish *som* to Finnish *kuin* – and it seems exceedingly likely to me that the lack of inflection for *kuin* is based on a Swedish model, both on the basis of its dialectal spread and the, for Finnish structure, anomalous lack of inflection – we would have to posit that this contact happened quite early, at a point when *som* had not yet been assigned a typical subject position.

The reason why *kuin* was used primarily for non-human referents, etc., may lie mainly in that its lack of number inflection made it a viable choice for cases where ambiguity with regards to number exists on the part of the referent and correlate. Vaccillations in number marking with *joka*, when its correlate is preceded by an indefinite pronoun or when the formal number of the correlate is in other ways at odds with the semantics of the referent, attest to the difficulties faced by the writers in assigning number marking. In this way, *kuin* entered the system at its weakest point, by displacing the more marginal relative pronoun *mikä* and primarily referring to semantically less prototypical correlates.

7. LANGUAGE CONTACT AND STRUCTURAL CHANGE IN OLD FINNISH

7.1. Language contact and alignment change

The Finnish 'inverted ergative' system as proposed by Terho Itkonen (1992 [1979]) can be sketched as follows:

	Subject Case 1	Subject Case 2	Object Case
Transitive	ERG 1	ERG 2	ABS, PART
Intransitive	ERG 1	ERG 2, ABS	-
Existential	ABS, PART	ABS, PART	-
ERG 1	-∅		
ERG 2	*-n*		
ABS			-∅ /(-*n*)
PART			*-tA*

The "ergative" would be either the nominative case, or the genitive in case of necessitive verbs such as *pitää* and *täytyä*. They are thus in complimentary distribution depending on lexical criteria. The same goes for the two endings of the "absolutive": either zero, or *-n*, with *-n* only occurring with singular nouns if a subject is marked with the nominative/ergative 1 (or an implicit but dropped pronominal subject is present). With plural nouns, the absolutive ending is always zero: the only marker is the plural *-t*. In Standard Finnish, personal pronouns as well as the interrogative pronoun *kene-* sports a marked accusative *-t*, regardless of the presence or absence of nominative/ergative 1 subjects. Dialectally, however, the pronominal *-t* is restricted, and it does not occur in Old Finnish. The distinction between absolutive and partitive case-marking is mainly based on aspect and species: partitive being used with mass nouns, irresultative verbs as well as negated sentences.

Usually, existential verbs take an absolutive case-ending, usually unmarked (-∅), but marked in case of personal pronouns (*-t*). The distinction between absolutive and partitive occurs with existential verbs as well. In dialectal Finnish, the necessitive sub-class of verbs may show absolutive case ending also with non-agentive subjects. Regarding Old Finnish, one may suggest that the sporadic occurrence of pronominal *-t* for non-agentive subjects of necessitive verbs is an instance of the absolutive similar to the occurrence of pronominal *-t* as the subject case-marker of existential, possessive clauses in Modern Finnish (see 3.5): however, the rarity of such cases, and the possibility of other explanations, make this hypothesis problematic.

It is easy to see in what sense the system sketched above is an "inverted" ergative system: the "ergative" subject is generally unmarked, and in the presence of an overt or implicit ergative subject, the "absolutive" subject receives case-marking. This inversion, however, does not occur with the small class of necessitive verbs such as *pitää*, *täytyä*, *tulla*: here, the ergative is marked (*-n*) with the absolutive, in Modern Finnish at least, being unmarked.

The previous sections on the passive and on necessitive constructions have detailed a number of ways in which this system is under reconstruction. The zero accusative, or "unmarked absolutive", is on the way out, with the exception of plural nouns: the zero accusative object of the passive is reanalyzed as a subject with nominative case-marking, and the zero accusative object of necessitive verbs occurs only marginally in the texts, with marked accusatives being normal as they are generally in Old Finnish and West Finnish dialects (Häkkinen 1994: 362). In other words, these two changes may be seen as reconstituting an object case-marking system in which an underlying case is unmarked, with a marked alternative occurring in specific contexts, as an object case-marking system in which a singular case-ending *-n* and a plural case-ending *-t* alternate on the basis of number: in other words, the zero accusative is eliminated in these two contexts. This constitutes a step towards a nominative/accusative system of case-marking in that loss of the zero accusative as an object case opens the door for a reanalysis of the existential subject (with zero case-marking) as being marked with the nominative.

The corpus used here is uninformative as to the third context where the zero accusative is used, namely, imperative verbs. The texts are written virtually wholly in the third person, and 3rd person imperative verbs function as optatives which may receive, in Modern Finnish, a nominative subject and marked accusative case-marking (Hakulinen et al. 2004: 892). A trawl through M and L1 provided no examples of 2nd person imperative forms, and only sporadic and somewhat dubious cases of zero accusative marking with 3rd person imperative forms.

In Finnish spoken in Sweden, a number of phenomena similarly leading to a generalization of *-n/-t* as an object case have been described in the literature, as well as counterposed tendencies, leading to a generalization of -∅ at the expense of *-n/-t*. With regards to Meänkieli, Wande mentions that the zero accusative is generally replaced by a marked accusative with necessitive (Wande 1978: 83-84) and imperative clauses (Wande 1978: 85), and, to a lesser extent, the same phenomenon occurs with passive clauses as well (Wande 1978: 85-86), leading to a system in which the marked accusative is all but eliminated (Wande 1982: 62).

In essays written by Finnish-speaking children in Sweden, Nesser's (1982: 24) findings are much more equivocal: on the one hand marked accusatives replaced by unmarked ones – according to Nesser (1982: 25), lack of acquaintance with the words in question and with its case-marking paradigm may be a strong factor here. The usage of marked accusatives instead of unmarked ones is rare in Nesser's corpus, despite the frequency of passives here (Nesser 1982: 28), however, the possibility of reanalysis of a noun object of a passive as a subject may preclude usage of the marked accusative to some extent. However, usage of a zero accusative in place of a partitive is frequent (Nesser 1982: 30). Kangassalo and Andersson (2003: 60) mention a similar tendency for zero accusatives or nominatives to replace marked accusatives. Interestingly, the same phenomenon has been observed in American Finnish (Campbell 1980: 348).

The latter phenomenon – substitution of marked accusatives with unmarked ones – may be due to direct influence from Swedish or English (neither of which sport marked accusative forms with common nouns). The phenomenon detailed by Wande in Meänkieli, as well as the process (partially) dealt with here in Old Finnish, can be regarded as a more indirect process of convergence, as the model language (Old and Modern Swedish) has a nominative/accusative system of alignment. The difference between passive objects in Meänkieli and Old Finnish is interesting: Old Finnish shows contact-induced object promotion or reanalysis of the passive object as a subject; and Meänkieli shows analogical extension of marked accusatives to passive objects. The result, however – that the system of object-marking as a whole moves closer to that of the model language – is the same.

The changes in subject-marking of necessitive *pitää* can be placed in the same framework as well. In Modern Finnish, necessitive verbs such as *täytyä* and *pitää* form an active/stative subsystem with orthodox marking – i.e., marking of the agentive subject, while the non-agentive subject and the object remain unmarked. This subsystem is eliminated in dialectal areas bordering Swedish-speaking areas, where unmarked/nominative case-marking is generalized to agentive subjects as well (and, as in the Western dialects, the object is usually marked). Whereas more or less direct influence from Swedish can be supposed in these dialectal areas, the changes in the corpus treated here are considerably more complex. In two texts (M and L1), we saw a merger between the object of *pitää* and a passive infinitival complement, and the subject of *pitää* and an active infinitival complement, which resulted in a case-marking paradigm showing features from both (notably, *-t* for plural nouns, *-n* for singular nouns). However, this shift nonetheless resulted in the generalization of nominative-like subject marking in certain lexical categories. With L2, this composite subject-marking seems to have been a basis for further generalization of nominative subject-marking in other lexical categories as well. The role of language contact is, however, very indirect here: primarily, it was a catalyst for identification between the active and the passive infinitive which was a condition for the 'merger' of the case-marking of their arguments.

Where the system as a whole seems to shift to greater analogy with that of the model language, the individual changes that bring about that shift result from a complex interplay of language contact and 'internal' factors, such as the readiness for a reanalysis inherent in the structure of periphrastic passives, the presence of very similar conditions with the auxiliary *pitää* and a passive infinitival complement, etc. The divergence of Old Finnish and Meänkieli in case of the passive shows that the same process of convergence can include counterposed tendencies within the individual changes bringing about convergence; and the extension of zero accusatives in Sweden Finnish and American Finnish show that language contact, as such, can lead to counterposed results: linguistic history remains intrinsically unpredictable.

7.2. Direct and indirect contact-induced structural change

As mentioned the first chapter, the existence of direct contact-induced structural change, i.e. structural change not resulting from previous lexical borrowing,, is controversial. A detailed case arguing the latter does not occur has been put forth by Ruth King (2000: 51), who argues that

> When language contact does bring about grammatical change in the target language, it is because the addition of foreign lexical material has led to internal morphological and/ or syntactic reanalysis of the sort one also finds in (uniquely) internally-motivated change

It should be noted, however, that King regards borrowing of grammatical words such as conjunctions, etc. as instances of lexical borrowing as well (King 2000: 81) – and that the borderline between unbound and bound grammatical morphemes seems somewhat arbitrary, as also bound grammatical morphemes can have a definite meaning, and be salient to some extent to a speaker/listener: if one regards the borrowing of conjunctions as lexical, rather than grammatical borrowing, what of the borrowing of person/number verbal affixes in Meglenite Rumanian as described by Thomason (2001: 77)?

More importantly, the non-existence of syntactic borrowing is, for King, a theoretical premiss rather than an empirical result, as in the Principles-and-Parameters approach adopted by King (2000: 53):

> (...) syntactic structure is thought to be largely determined by lexical information, more precisely, by the feature specifications associated with particular lexical items. Syntactic variation among languages is explicable in terms of differences in the syntactic properties of particular lexical items. (...)From the generative perspective it is difficult to see how such structure could be transferred from one language to another without the borrowing of lexical items (carrying particular syntactic properties).

Thus, King's research tests the applicability of a theoretical approach in which (direct) syntactic borrowing does not occur, rather than testing the occurrence or non-occurrence of syntactic borrowing in an empirical fashion.

This is not meant as a criticism. To the contrary. One cannot judge the empirical evidence with regards to language contact without either an implicit or an explicit theoretical framework, and an explicit one is preferable to an implicit one. Though the theoretical basis of this research differs from King's to some extent, in the introductory sections I criticized the concept of syntactic borrowing as a mechanism of structural change from a theoretical, not an empirical perspective. And to a large extent, I feel the controversies surrounding contact-induced structural change result from lack of clarity about the concepts we are working with, as well as from all too clear but unhelpful dichotomies (such as that between internal and external change), rather than from the empirical data itself.

From my own perspective, I would doubt the viability of a category of direct grammatical or syntactical borrowing, as contact-induced structural change always results from prior identifications between structures from two different languages, and these structures (especially within a Whiteheadian/Fortescuean perspective) are always identified in actual language use (of course, actual language use includes a big part of everyday thought as well as communication). Syntactic structures cannot be abstracted and perceived by a speaker outside of language use. And actual language use always involves words as well as patterns. If we regard semantic borrowing as instances of lexical borrowing, it would be difficult to regard the borrowing of structural patterns involving frequently-occurring sequences of specific words, and abstracted from those sequences by a speaker/listener, as totally independent from lexical borrowing. Putting it differently, it would seem to me that direct syntactic borrowing would require one to subscribe to the autonomy of syntax as a linguistic subsystem. The theoretical approach I adopted here would seem to deny such an autonomy.

What, then, of the empirical material treated previously? Object promotion with the Finnish passive may be largely considered independently from lexical contact – though not necessarily from a possible interlingual identification between the two passive morphemes involved (Finnish *-ttA*, Swedish *-s*). However, the presence of multiple model languages involved in object promotion during the Old Finnish period (Itkonen-Kaila 1997) would make supposing any definite interlingual identification as a factor problematic. This said, to regard object promotion as a grammatical or syntactic borrowing would not do the whole picture justice, as the main starting point would seem to have been an internal reanalysis involving a single phonological surface structure (that of the periphrastic perfect passive) and two possible syntactic structures. This reanalysis, itself, may be regarded as resulting from an analogical extension, in this corpus at least, from Swedish to Finnish (namely, the auxiliary/copular *be* involved in both the syntactic structures, and the assignment of the argument of the passive clause to grammatical subjecthood). This does involve the lexicon, namely, the presence of the verb 'to be' in both languages (*olla*, *vara*). With Swedish perfect passives, *vara* receives a grammatical subject, which differs with the Finnish construction where the nominal argument remains the object of the passive construction as a whole, and thereby creates a possibility for the analogical extension mentioned above.

The role of the lexicon is clearer even with the two other phenomena examined here. In the case of relative *kuin,* the advent of a lack of case and number marking with a relative pronoun (which creates the opportunity for *kuin* to be used in the position where, in the text, it is used – namely, with non-countable and indefinite referents) can be regarded as a secondary effect of lexical borrowing – namely, a semantic borrowing between two function words. Provided, of course, that language contact did indeed play a major role in the development of relative *kuin*, which is not entirely certain.

With *pitää*, the contact-induced changes detailed before may be regarded as well as the transfer of grammatical features (valency, case assignment) associated with a specific, particular lexical item. The interlingual identification here, of course, was one between *pitää* and *skola*, one which, in contrast to the assumed interlingual identification between *kuin* and *som*, is well-established in research literature and clearly shows in the corpus as well. The changes in question could be regarded as lexical borrowing with secondary syntactic effects in King's (2000) sense. However, the secondary syntactic effects are rather more deep-going than those associated with relative *kuin*, as *pitää*, together with a small number of other necessitive constructions, all of which less frequent, forms a closed class in terms of alignment – one which alone makes up the active/stative subsystem within the inverted ergative system of alignment in Finnish. As detailed before, the changes in subject and object-marking with *pitää* can be considered an important step within a process of change from an inverted ergative to a nominative/accusative system. It should also be noted that, in the corpus, *pitää* may well be as frequent, if not more so, than semantically similar deontic constructions involving morphosyntactic means alone, such as imperatives and optatives. These two circumstances would seem to suggest that, even if contact-induced syntactic change may always be secondary to lexical borrowing, syntax is very porous to these secondary effects indeed, if the right words are involved.

In any event, the preceding chapters provide no evidence as to the existence of direct syntactic borrowing as opposed to indirect borrowing, but I must immediately add that the theoretical perspective adopted here does not allow for the inference of such existence. Interlingual identifications are made, they do not exist outside of actual linguistic usage – and that usage always involved the lexicon. It should also be noted that an emergentist view on linguistic structure, at least Hopper's (1987) radical view, would mean that syntax itself is a secondary effect of the repeated usage and storage of linguistic chunks: actual utterances, words and short sequences of words. The question of the "directness" of syntactic borrowing is meaningless here as well, as syntactic structures must first be abstracted by speakers before they can be stored in memory and indeed transferred from language to language – and the linguistic events from which they are to be abstracted necessarily involve (real or imagined) phonological surface forms.

7.3. Language contact and structural change

Regardless whether analogy indeed exists outside of the eye of the beholder, as Esa Itkonen (2005: 20) and Michael Cabot Haley (1988: 47) hold, analogy-as-state between linguistic structures must be perceived by a bilingual speaker/hearer before having any effect in actuating analogy-as-process, and it seems to me the two cannot be strictly held apart in the perception of a speaker/hearer. And one of the main premisses of this research is that analogy can be perceived between structures of two different languages as well as of one language, and that it is therefore useful to widen the scope of the main two analogical mechanisms in linguistic change – reanalysis and extension – to cover both contact-induced change and internal change.

Let's illustrate this with the partially contact-induced structural changes involving alignment and necessitive *pitää*. In the supposed pristine system, still extant in dialectal Finnish, *pitää* sports an active/stative system of alignment, which would mean that the patient of *pitää* and a passive infinitival complement shows object-like case-marking:

hänen	*pitää*	*tehdä*
he-'ERGATIVE'	must	do
se		

it-'ABSOLUTIVE'

se	*pitää*	*tehtämän*
it-'ABSOLUTIVE'	must	be done-PASS

In texts such as the translations by Kollanius as well as RWL, this system only partially survives, as the object of an active infinitival complement shows normal accusative case-marking. Whether that circumstance is the result of a contact-induced change involving Swedish, as it may well be, is beside the point here. The subject, however, still shows traces of the earlier active/stative system in that patients of passive infinitival complements, just like inactive grammatical subjects of active infinitival complements, show zero case marking:

hänen	*pitää*	*tehdä*
he-'ERGATIVE'	must	do
sen		
it-ACC		
se	*pitää*	*tehtämän*
it-'ABSOLUTIVE	must	be done-PASS

The key change resulting in the case-marking system visible in Martti's and Ljungo's translations, however, I have analyzed as the result of an identification between the arguments of active and passive infinitival complements which itself resulted from an identification between the Finnish and the Swedish passive infinitival complement. Thus, an identification between:

se	*pitää*	*tehtämän*
det	*ska*	*göras*
it	must	be done-PASS

resulted in a reanalysis where the argument *se* of the passive infinitive complement above was assigned the same paradigm as the grammatical subjects of active infinitival complements, rather than retaining its zero case marker on the basis of its lack of agentivity. In other words, *se* was assigned subjecthood, in as far as subjecthood is a meaningful term when dealing with *pitää*. The active/stative distinction was already essentially lost: it only concerned differences in subject-marking, without regards to the marking of the object. The only remnants of the earlier "absolutive" object-marking case were the passive object, and inactive grammatical subjects, of *pitää*. The assignment of grammatical subjecthood to the patient of passive infinitival constructions caused the foundations of the active/stative distinction to be finally removed. The result of this was Martti and Ljungo's composite case-marking system, which redistributed the case-markers involved (*-n* and *-ø*) on the basis of morphological, rather than syntactic or semantic criteria.

In other words, an analogical extension of the Swedish passive subject to the Finnish passive object (one restricted to *pitää* and its infinitival complement), resulted in a reanalysis on the Finnish side, which itself resulted in a subsequent cycle of reanalysis and extension, one which reinterpreted the semantically-based variable case marking paradigm as morphologically-based.

It seems to me that regarding syntactic borrowing as a mechanism in and of itself, counterposed to reanalysis and extension as internal mechanisms of change, does no justice to the complexity of events involved here. Also, I feel that the notion of syntactic borrowing as a mechanism of change becomes unnecessary, once we allow analogical extensions to take place between languages as well. The latter would seem, to me, to be more accurately descriptive of the change involved, as syntactic borrowing, in this view, is based on the same perception of similarity – sameness and difference – as internal analogy is, the only difference being the identity of the languages involved.

This point differs slightly from that argued by Aikhenvald (2003), who regards that language contact should be regarded as a background condition stimulating reanalysis and extension. This would be applicable to the reanalysis of the patient of a passive infinitival complement: i.e., the assignment of subjecthood to *se* in the examples above. Language contact here can indeed be regarded as a background factor stimulating this reanalysis. However, regarding reanalysis and extension as neutral with regards to internality and externality allows us to place language contact in a more dynamic light: the reanalysis in question was the immediate result of the extension of parts of the Swedish system of active and passive infinitival complements, which both have grammatical subjects as arguments, to the Finnish system.

Aikhenvald's point in general, namely, that contact-induced change cannot be regarded as isolated from more internal mechanisms of change, but that language contact must be seen as interplaying with internal tendencies of change in various ways, is vindicated, however, in this research. The redistribution of case-markers by Martti and Ljungo was, in itself, a purely internal reanalysis, even if it was a consequence of an external analogical extension, and could thereby be regarded as being contact-induced in its own right. And indeed, in L2, this redistribution was a stepping stone to generalizing nominative subject case-marking throughout the system. This, in turn, cannot be regarded as isolated from language contact: indeed, it seems to be an analogical extension of the Swedish nominative subject-marking associated with *skola*. The changes detailed above, again, may be regarded in light of the fact that the active/stative subsystem was shared by *pitää* and a very small, closed set of other necessitive constructions, and that generalizing nominative subject-marking with *pitää* created greater analogy within Finnish verbal paradigms. Internal tendencies of change and language contact subtly interact here.

Particularly the latter brings to mind multicausality as proposed by Aitchison (2001: 134):

> Like a road accident, a language change may have multiple causes. A car crash is only rarely caused by one overriding factor, such as a sudden steering failure, or the driver falling asleep. More often there is a combination of factors, all of which contribute to the overall disaster. Similarly, language change is likely to be due to a combination of factors.

To expand upon this metaphor: it should be noted here that the multicausality here would be of a very different nature if the car crashed into a tree without a driver. Regardless of whether the behaviour of the car as a whole (a Whiteheadian society of events) can be described in purely causal terms, the behaviour of each individual elementary particle making up the car (each Whiteheadian event or actual occasion) surely can. Placing a driver in a car, who may be inebriated, fatigued, unskilled, or distracted and thereby contributes to the overall result of the event, changes the whole process: it no longer can be regarded as emergent from the rigidly causal behaviour of elementary particles, but must be regarded in teleological terms, or rather, the failing teleology of a driver trying to keep his car on the road. Circumstances such as the slipperiness of the road, the alcohol level of the driver's blood, the wear and tear decreasing the effectiveness of the car's brakes, and the like, are then relegated to background conditions influencing the actions of the driver, and the effect of those actions, but not determining their outcome. In other words, teleological processes such as language change are necessarily multicausal. The move towards a generalization of nominative case-marking in case of the subject of *pitää* can be regarded as a teleological process, motivated both by the establishment of greater analogy (and thereby, greater iconicity between meaning and form) both within Finnish structure and between Finnish and Swedish structure (both co-existing in the minds of many bilinguals). The composite system of case-marking based upon which Ljungo generalizes nominative case-marking in L2 can be regarded as a background condition, or as a Whiteheadian object: the frozen result of past events, which remain immanent in the present in as far as they are relevant for current and future events.

Esa Itkonen (1978: 61) distinguished the teleology associated with contact-induced changes as one based on speaker solidarity – the desire of a speaker/listener to speak like other speaker/listeners – from the teleology of striving towards iconicity between meaning and form in morphology. Speaker solidarity (see also Aitchison 2001: 76), of course, plays an important role in the spread of innovations regardless of their internal or contact-induced origins: language contact here is language contact in Anttila's (1989: 154) sense, in that "the spread of any feature is borrowing as long as it is happening.". Contact in this sense is thus irrelevant as to the mechanisms by which the spreading innovation came about. And the teleology of contact-induced structural changes as bilingual reanalysis and extension seems to be clearly subject to the same teleological motivations as internal morphological changes: mainly, the establishment of iconicity between meaning and form, which is a direct and necessary effect of the establishment of analogy between paradigmatic relations within subsystems of language. The contact-induced generalization of nominative case-marking with the subject of *pitää* established greater iconicity between meaning and form by virtually eliminating an active/stative subsystem found with a small subclass of verbs: subjects are now marked with the nominative regardless of which lexical verb they are associated with. The elimination of the zero accusative – through object promotion in case of the passive, and substitution by a marked accusative in case of the infinitival complement with necessitive verbs, resulted in a similar iconicity between meaning and form. And the redistribution of case-markers with the subject of *pitää* in Martti's and Ljungo's translations restored iconicity by eliminating a case-marking paradigm which had all but lost its semantical basis (partially due to the generalization of marked accusatives in object position) and substituting it with one which had clear morphological criteria. The process of alignment change from 'inverted ergativity' with an active/stative subsystem to a nominative/accusative system as sketched in section 7.1. can be regarded as one proceeding from iconicity between meaning and form in that case-markers are assigned on semantic criteria to one establishing iconicity between meaning and form in that case-markers are assigned on morphosyntactic criteria. Reanalyses, including interlingual identifications, disturb the assignment of underlying syntactic structures on which this iconicity is based, whereas analogical extensions, including those between different languages, reestablish iconicity by extending one particular underlying syntactic structure into unambiguous contexts and thereby "forcing" the issue – as shown in case of object promotion with the Finnish periphrastic passive.

One case in which, at first sight at least, contact-induced change seems to negate iconicity between meaning and form would be the introduction of relative *kuin*, supposing that the explanation involving Swedish *som* as a model does indeed hold. Relative *kuin* does not receive any case or number marking, as opposed to relative *joka*, and would thereby seem to be a portmanteau morpheme (one form, multiple meanings). However, the assignment of *kuin* to referents somewhat indeterminate with regards to number, such as abstract referents, uncountable referents, and the like, could be regarded as establishing iconicity on another level: *joka*, with its case and number marking, gets assigned to referents to which number can be meaningfully assigned, and *kuin* to referents with which either singular or plural number-marking would be somewhat odd.

Iconicity between meaning and form can be regarded as involving structures from multiple languages as well as a single language: object promotion with the Finnish passive resulted in the Finnish and Swedish passives becoming more isomorphic to each other, and thereby, they could be regarded as sharing (partially) the same syntactic and semantic underlying structures – at least in the mind of the bilingual. This is essentially what processes of convergence or metatypy (Ross 1999) entail. The teleology of linguistic convergence proposed by Ross (1999: 13) and McMahon (1994: 213-214) involve minimizing the cognitive burden of bilingualism, ease of learning and the like. However, one could regard this as an effect of the establishment of iconicity between meaning and form, and as such, it could be extended to internal change as well: the cognitive burden of linguistic processing, linguistic storage, and the like becomes lesser if there is iconicity between meaning and form and analogy between parts of the system. As Esa Itkonen (2005: 22) remarks, the whole concept of linguistic structure is based on analogy: without analogy holding, for example, between the paradigmatic structure of different nouns and verbs, or within the phonological system, or between the alignment of subject and object markers associated with different verbs, there would be not much left of linguistic structure. And the cognitive processing that usage and storage of such a language would involve would be likely to be enormous.

Regarding convergence as making languages more similar without reference to iconicity between meaning and form would also lose sight of the circumstance that, as argued before, establishment of iconicity does not make structures more similar as much as direct focus to the relevant and meaningfully distinctive contrasts between them, rather than irrelevant ones. Speculatively, one might entertain the notion that, in similar fashion, convergence and metatypy allows for greater manipulability of languages as a marker of ethnic and social identity as in the famous situation in Kupwar (Gumperz and Wilson 1971: 153-154).

This brings me to a final reason why the dichotomy between internal and external changes in the form of the concept of syntactic borrowing as a mechanism of change counterposed to reanalysis and extension should be abandoned. Regarding contact-induced structural changes as reanalysis and extension *sui generis* would allow us to do justice to their identical teleological motivations as well as to the similarities with regards to the processes by which they take place, as opposed to the teleology of linguistic solidarity associated with the spread of innovations.

All of this allows us to subtly redefine our terms. *Language contact* could be relegated to contacts between speakers and their idiolects: similar enough to be used in communication, different enough for language to take place. In this sense, any innovation spreads through linguistic contact. However, with regards to the mechanisms by which structural change takes place, we might abandon a dichotomy between contact-induced and "internal" innovations, i.e. abandon "language contact" as a background factor present in some processes of change, and absent in others. The only thing present or absent – or, rather, more present and prominent in some cases and less so in others – would be structures of different languages exerting their influence on the (analogical) structural changes in question. It should be noted that I am not proposing one strong dichotomy to supplant another: the spread of innovations would, it seems to me, necessarily involve reinterpretations of linguistic structure on the basis of the speaker/hearer incorporating elements of another idiolect into his own – the radical emergentist view alluded to earlier, perhaps, would allow for the independent storage of "chunks" of language first, and later, abstraction of structure from those chunks by a reflecting speaker/hearer. In other words, language contact would be contact between idiolects in communication, which are bound by social conventions similar enough at least to allow successful communication. Language contact is, in Whiteheadian terms, relevant to the linguistic actual occasion or event, in that the event (involving a speaker/hearer) incorporates input (the language used by an interlocutor) that is somehow novel with regards to past events. "Structural change" would be the reinterpretation of structure (Whitehead's eternal object) abstracted from linguistic input and from past linguistic events immanent in the present through the memory of a speaker/hearer. And here, the presence of absence of linguistic contact is not really relevant. Not to the mechanisms, neither to the motivations of the structural change in question, but only in that the prominence of foreign linguistic structures in effecting a given structural change may be greater or lesser, and may be more or less plausibly argued for by the historical linguist.

SUMMARY

This study examines the problem of contact-induced structural change by taking a number of putatively contact-induced innovations in Old Finnish as a case study. The examined corpus consists of six legal translations: Martti's 1580 translation (M) of King Christopher's Swedish Land Law (KrL), Ljungo's (L1) 1601 translation as well as Abraham Kollanius' (K1) 1648 translation of the same text; Ljungo's (L2) 1609 translation of Magnus Eriksson's City Law of the mid-14th century, as well as Kollanius' (K2) 1648 translation of this text, and finally the 1759 translation (RWL) of the reformed 1734 Swedish law.

In the theoretical introduction, I examine what I regard as a problematic dichotomy between "internal" and "external" changes, contact-induced ones being grouped among the latter. The dichotomy fails, in my opinion, to take account of the fact that linguistic changes are actuated by speakers and have cognitive, logical mechanisms – something clearly apparent from the usage of terms such as reanalysis, extension, and analogy for internal syntactic changes. The causes of such are not causes in the sense used in the natural sciences: they do not exclude each other, and are never both necessary and sufficient among their own terms. Rather, they form the background against which a linguistic innovation may or may not be actuated. On the basis of this, I criticize the canonical trichotomy proposed by Harris and Campbell (1995) which counterposes syntactic borrowing as an independent mechanism to reanalysis and extension. Following Anttila (1989: 170), I identify syntactic borrowing with reanalysis and extension as a mechanism, the difference being that syntactic borrowing involves two codes, not one. On the level of the individual speaker, though, where linguistic innovations are ultimately actuated, the basic mechanisms are the same: it is only on the level of different languages as basic, opposing entities that the dichotomy between internal innovations and external ones makes sense.

Taking Fortescue's (2001) lead, I then argue that linguistic history becomes more comprehensible as human history, with its own teleological motivations and holistic background rather than necessary and sufficient causes which can be isolated from one another, by casting it on the terms of the process philosophy developed by Alfred North Whitehead (1861-1947). Whitehead regarded events, rather than substances, as the basic entity of the universe; events endowed with both a "physical pole", accounting for causality, and a "mental pole", accounting for memory and perception. In

Whitehead's view, each event relates to the whole of its own past; events, once they have become concrete, perish to live on partially in the events that succeed them. By taking some kind of singular moment of linguistic cognition as the equivalent of a Whiteheadian event, Fortescue succeeds in bridging the gap between function and structure as counteropposing poles rather than mutually exclusive analyses, and proposes a view on language which is well suited for a view of grammar as emergent upon usage, and synchrony as emergent upon diachrony, as proposed by Coseriu (1974 [1958]). Furthermore, the teleology Whitehead regards as guiding the becoming of events is, in my opinion, very applicable to that proposed in structural linguistic change as, for example, the principle of "one meaning-one form" – namely, a maximization of relevant contrasts based on some kind of common ground, either as a contrast between meaning-form units, or, in the case of linguistic convergence and on a smaller scale in contact-induced structural change as well, between opposing linguistic codes based on a common semantic substructure.

In the empirical part of this study, three main problems are examined: 1) the Old Finnish passive, which changed from a prototypical non-promotional passive, involving subject demotion but not concomitant reanalysis of the object as subject, to a partially promotional passive involving reanalysis of the subject as object, under the influence of, among others, the Swedish language, 2) Necessitive constructions, which in Standard Finnish exhibit an active-stative alignment with a marked active subject and an unmarked object, but which in various varieties of Finnish, notably in dialects bordering Swedish, show nominative-accusative alignment with unmarked subjects and marked objects, 3) the relative pronoun *ku(n)/kuin*, occurring in Old Finnish and the southwestern dialects, which is a bit of an oddity in Finnish due to its lack of case-marking, and has been thought to be a calque from Swedish *som*, with which it shares the same dual function of comparative conjunction/adverb and relative pronoun. All of these problems involve subject/object case-marking to a degree. For this reason, a short overview of alignment in Finnish is presented, based on Terho Itkonen's analysis of Finnish being an "inverted ergative" language in which the subjects of one particular class of intransitive clauses, namely, existential clauses, show the same case-marking as transitive objects. Nonetheless, Finnish in general marks objects, not subjects, exceptions being aforementioned necessitive clauses as well as passive objects, etc.

In case of the Finnish passive, I argue that a piecemeal transition from object to subject can be traced in the corpus. These involve mainly perfect-tense passives, which are formed with a copular *olla* and are to an extent analyzable as constructions involving a copular subject and a nominal predicate as well. This reanalysis is extended to constructions where no such ambiguity exists, though a significant extent of free variation does exist: virtually identical constructions may exhibit both clear object and clear subject case-marking. I furthermore argue that it seems likely that the reanalysis was promoted by certain semantic and syntactic factors. Notably, human objects seem to be reanalyzed as subjects a bit more often. At the same time, it seems clear that the change was stimulated as well by Swedish source constructions. In other words, we are dealing with a holistic "causation" of change in which a number of factors work as stimuli towards the same innovation. Also, the case of the Finnish passive is a paradigm case of a linguistic change in which an internal reanalysis and extension cannot be seen apart from external contact-induced change.

Necessitive constructions involving unipersonal verbs such as *pitää* 'must' in Standard Finnish have a subject marked with the genitive case except for existential clauses, where subjects are unmarked; objects are unmarked throughout. However, in dialectal varieties of Finnish, a more subtle gradient of case-marking is in force in which prototypical human persons (notably, those denoted with personal pronouns) tend to be marked with the genitive most often. In the corpus, this state of affairs seems to be found in Kollanius' translations as well as RWL. This concerns the verb *pitää*, the most frequent necessitive verb, with the lesser frequent one, *tulla*, strongly preferring genitive case-marking throughout. In Martti's and Ljungo's texts, however, genitive and nominative case-marking with *pitää* seems to be distributed according to lexical sub-groups, with plural nouns and plural demonstrative pronouns showing nominative case-marking, and singular nouns as well as singular demonstrative pronouns and almost all personal pronouns showing genitive case-marking. I argue that the distribution of case-marking with Martti and Ljungo is an indirect result of a merger of the subject of *pitää* and an active infinitival complement, and the object of *pitää* with a passive infinitival complement, both of which are clearly kept apart with regards to case-marking in Kollanius' texts and RWL (in which the object of *pitää* and a passive infinitival complement shows the zero case-marking normally accorded to passive objects). The merger itself seems to be the result of both the inherent ambiguity of the construction, which, like the perfect-tense passives formed with a copula, involve an auxiliary inviting a grammatical subject, but also from Swedish model patterns. In L2, however, aforementioned merger seems to have been a stepping-stone for the gradual extension of nominative case-marking throughout other lexical categories as well.

Finally, the origins of relative *ku(n)/kuin* are examined. In the corpus, this relative pronoun competes with the somewhat more frequent *joka*, which unlike *ku(n)/kuin* is also found in Standard Finnish. As a point of departure, a hypothesis proposed by Irmeli Pääkkönen (1988) according to which *ku(n)/kuin* may be based on an object form of a pronominal *ku-*, rather than the comparative conjunction *kuin* 'as', and thus be an internal development rather than a Swedish calque, is examined. The semantic basis of their distribution is examined, resulting in a picture in which *kuin* prefers referents which are objects, non-human, and either non-singular countable nouns or uncountable nouns such as mass nouns and abstract nouns, with *joka* preferring referents which are much the opposite. Though this does seem to support Pääkkönen's hypothesis, it is argued that the syntactic opposition between object and subject is an indirect result of the more basic semantic opposition between prototypical human, singular, countable etc. referents and prototypical non-human referents, mass nouns, etc. However, the latter forces us to relate sceptically to a proposed borrowing/calqueing explanation for *ku(n)/kuin*, as the Swedish model pattern, *som*, behaves exactly the other way around, strongly preferring a subject role. This is reflected in the corpus where *joka* occurs as a translation equivalent of *som* more often than of other relative pronouns. This notwithstanding, the dialectal occurrence of relative *ku(n)* does seem to support at least some kind of role for Swedish *som*: despite the distributional differences, the model pattern may have stimulated the spread of the innovation, if not the innovation itself. The development of relative *ku(n)/kuin* may indeed be explained purely on 'internal' grounds: both the usage of an *-n* in both subject and object cases, as well as lack of case and number distinction, are not entirely unknown within the Finnish pronominal system. I argue that it is exactly this lack of case and number distinction which led to the usage of *ku(n)/kuin* with referents such as mass nouns, where the obligatory case/number marking of *joka* could be problematic. A number of examples of inconsistency in the number marking of *joka* with plural or mass noun referents seem to support this analysis.

In the concluding section, the problems raised in the empirical chapters are examined against the theoretical premises proposed in the introductory sections. I argue that instead of mutually exclusive analyses of innovations as external or internal, we are dealing with linguistic innovations in which foreign model patterns as well as internal syntactic ambiguity etc. seem to both form the background against which an innovation is played out. Ruth King's (2000) arguments against the existence of grammatical borrowing as distinct and separable from lexical borrowing are dealt with. Though the problems examined do not clearly support the existence of rule borrowing without lexical interference as well, I argue that the theoretical framework adopted doesn't allow for it either. If linguistic innovations are based on cognitive operations such as reanalysis and analogy performed by a speaker on linguistic material (which may involve more than one code) during a Whiteheadian event of linguistic cognition (which does not necessarily involve actual communication with another speaker), then clearly syntactic innovations are ultimately inseparable from lexical material: syntactic structures always involving words as well. I also compare my criticism of the trichotomy of reanalysis, extension, and borrowing as basic mechanisms of syntactic change with that of Aikhenvald (2003) who argued that syntactic borrowing should be seen as inseparable from reanalysis, grammaticalization and the like. Though my criticism is slightly different from Aikhenvald's, I believe that the research here vindicates her arguments as well.

Finally, I argue that the contact-induced syntactic changes examined are identical in terms of teleological motivation as well as mechanism: they are analyzable as striving towards iconicity between meaning and form, or, in Whitehead's terms, maximization of balanced contrasts. This said, another teleological motivation argued for with regards to contact-induced change, namely speaker solidarity, should be taken into account as well. On the basis of this, I argue that language contact as a concept should be perhaps primarily applied to the spread of innovations, and the gradual adoption of them within a speech-community, rather than to the actuation of innovations, which seems proceed through basic mechanisms such as reanalysis and analogy regardless of the presence of more languages and identifications made between their structures as background factors.

ACKNOWLEDGEMENTS

My thanks go to my supervisors, Erling Wande and Kaisa Häkkinen; to Cornelius Hasselblatt and Tette Hofstra for their feedback in planning the research project which this is the result of; to my fellow doctoral students Virpi Ala-Poikela, Paula Ehrnebo, Anu Muhonen and Sari Pesonen for feedback on draft sections at various points and for various help and advice; to Nobufumi Inaba for his thoughts on the problems concerning necessitive constructions; to Tapani Lehtinen who was the opponent of the Licenciate Thesis version of this project; Östen Dahl for his feedback during a course on scientific method and the Swedish linguistics days in April 2006; to Raija Kangassalo for various thoughts and advice; and to Raimo Anttila for his thoughts on analogy and language contact. Additionally, my thanks go to my father Frans de Smit for stimulating discussions on philosophy and theology, including Whitehead.

Furthermore, my thanks go to my parents, Frans and Marina, and my brother, Yon, for their support at various points during my research, as well as to many friends who put up with me during my crankier moods (you know who you are).

REFERENCES

Corpus

Airila, M., Harmas, H. 1930: Kristoffer Kuninkaan Maanlaki Herra Martin suomeksi kääntämä 2. Toisintotekstit verrattuna Tukholman codexiin B96. Helsinki.

K1 = Rapola, M. (ed.) 1926: Legisterium regni Sveciae Christophorianum ab Abraham Kollanio. Helsinki. Sähköinen aineisto. Koostaja: Kotimaisten kielten tutkimuskeskus. 11.10.2001. Saatavissa: http://www.kotus.fi/aineistot.

K2 = Rapola, M. (ed.) 1926: Legisterium Civitatum Magnaeanum Cum Appendicibus ab Abraham Kollanio. Helsinki. Sähköinen aineisto. Koostaja: Kotimaisten kielten tutkimuskeskus. 11.10.2001. Saatavissa: http://www.kotus.fi/aineistot.

KrL = Schlyter, D.C.J. (ed.) 1869: Samling af Sweriges Gamla Lagar 12. Konung Christoffers Landslag. Stockholm. Scanned by Dietmar Gohlisch and Bo Wendt. Institutionen för Nordiska Språk, University of Lund: http://www.nordlund.lu.se/Fornsvenska/Fsv%20Folder/01_Bitar/B.L1.A-KrL.html

L1 = Ulkuniemi, M. (ed.) 1975: Ljungo Tuomaanpojan lainsuomennokset. Maanlain ja kaupunginlain teksti. Helsinki. Sähköinen aineisto. Koostaja: Kotimaisten kielten tutkimuskeskus. 11.10.2001. Saatavissa: http://www.kotus.fi/aineistot.

L2 = Ulkuniemi, M. (ed.) 1975.

M = Setälä, E.N., Nyholm, M. (ed.): 1905. Legisterium Sveciae Christophorianum 1 Codex Holmiensis B 96. Helsinki. Sähköinen aineisto. Koostaja: Kotimaisten kielten tutkimuskeskus. 11.10.2001. Saatavissa: http://www.kotus.fi/aineistot.

MEL = Schlyter, D.C.J. (ed.) 1865: Samling af Sweriges Gamla Lagar 11.Konung Magnus Erikssons stadslag. Stockholm.

RWL = Ruotzin Waldacunnan Laki. Helsinki. Sähköinen aineisto. Koostaja: Kotimaisten kielten tutkimuskeskus. 11.10.2001. Saatavissa: http://www.kotus.fi/aineistot.

SRL = Sveriges Rikes Lag: gillad och antagen på riksdagen år 1734. Faks.-utg. till 250-årsdagen av lagens tillkomst efter den första i antikva tryckta upplagan av år 1780. Stockholm 1984

UL = Schlyter, D.C.J. (ed.) 1834: Samling af Sweriges Gamla Lagar 3. Uplandslagen. Stockholm. Inskriven av Lars-Olof Delsing. Institutionen för Nordiska Språk, University of Lund: http://www.nordlund.lu.se/Fornsvenska/Fsv%20Folder/navigationsgrejer/aldre_ram.html
Ups = Upsalan Evangeliumikirjan Katkelma. Sähköinen aineisto. Kootaja: Kotimaisten kielten tutkimuskeskus. 30.03.2000. Saatavissa: http://www.kotus.fi/aineistot.

Other references

Aikhenvald, A. 2000: Areal typology and grammaticalization: the emergence of new verbal morphology in an obsolescent language – Gildea, S. (ed.): Reconstructing grammar: comparative linguistics and grammaticalization. Amsterdam p. 1-37.
- 2003: Mechanisms of change in areal diffusion: new morphology and language contact. Journal of Linguistics 39 p. 1-29.
Aitchison, J. 1995: Tadpoles, cuckoos and multiple births: Language contact and models of change – Fisiak, J. (ed.): Linguistic change under contact conditions. Trends in linguistics Studies and monographs 81. Berlin p. 1-13.
- 2001: Language Change: Progress or Decay?. Cambridge.
Almqvist, I. 1987: Om objektsmarkeringen vid negation i Finskan. Stockholm.
Andersen, H. 1973: Abductive and deductive change. Language p. 765-793.
- 1974: Towards a typology of change: bifurcating changes and binary translations – Anderson, J.M., Jones, C. (red.): Historical Linguistics II. Theory and description in phonology. Amsterdam p. 17-60.
Andersson, P., Kangassalo, R. 2003: Suomi ja meänkieli Ruotsissa – Jönsson-Korhola, H., Lindgren, A-R. (ed.): Monena suomi maailmalla. Suomalaisperäisiä kielivähemmistöjä. Helsinki p. 30- 163.
Anttila, R. 1977: Analogy. Trends in linguistics State-of-the-art Reports 10. The Hague.
- 1989: Historical and Comparative Linguistics. Current issues in Linguistic Theory 6 Amsterdam.
Asher, R.E. 1989: Tamil. London.
Birnbaum, H. 1984: Notes on syntactic change: Cooccurrence vs. substitution, stability vs. permeability – Fisiak, J. (ed.): Historical Syntax. Trends in Linguistics Studies and Monographs 23. Amsterdam p. 25-46..
Bladh, G., Wedin, M. 2005: "Att pä willmarken torpestellen optaga" Skogfinsk migration och kolonisation i Sverige under 1500- och 1600-talen – Bladh, G., Kuvaja, C. (ed.): Dialog och särart. Människor,

samhällen och idéer från Gustav Vasa till nutid. Svenskt i Finland, Finskt i Sverige 1. Helsinki p. 42-84.
Briscoe, T. 2002a: Introduction – Briscoe, T. (ed.) Linguistic evolution through language acquisition. Cambridge p. 1-21
- 2002b: Grammatical acquisition and linguistic selection – Briscoe, T. (ed.) Linguistic evolution through language acquisition. Cambridge p. 255-300.
Bybee, J., Hopper, P. 2001: Introduction to frequency and the emergence of linguistic structure – Bybee, J., Hopper, P. (ed.): Frequency and the emergence of linguistic structure. Amsterdam p. 1-24.
Campbell, L. 1980: Towards new perspectives on American Finnish – Congressus Quintus Internationalis Fenno-Ugristarum Turku 20.-27.VIII.1980 Pars III. Turku
- 1987: Syntactic change in Pipil. Journal of American Linguistics 53 p. 253-280.
- 2002: Areal linguistics: a closer scrutiny. Paper for the 5th NCWL International Conference. Linguistic Areas, Convergence and Language Change. Manchester November 2002.
Cannelin, K. 1926: Ruotsinkielen vaikutus nykyiseen yleiskieleemme. Virittäjä p. 76-80.
Carlsson, S. 1985: Suomi Ruotsin valtakunnan osana – Nemlander-Sjöberg, C. (ed.): Suomen asema Ruotsin valtakunnassa. Helsinki p. 7-17.
Carpelan, C., Parpola, A., Koskikallio, P. 1999: Early Contacts between Uralic and Indo-European: Linguistic and Archaeological Considerations. Papers presented at an international symposium held at the Tvärminne Research Station of the University of Helsinki, 8–10 January 1999. Suomalais-Ugrilaisen Seuran Toimituksia 242. Helsinki.
Chaudenson, R, Mougeon, R, Beniak, É. 1993: Vers une approche panlectale de la variation du francais. Montmagny.
Collingwood, R.G. 1993 [1946]: The Idea of History. Revised Edition. Oxford.
Comrie, B. 1975: The antiergative: Finland's answer to Basque. Chicago Linguistics Society 11 p. 112-121.
- 1977: In defense of spontaneous demotion: the impersonal passive – Cole, P., Sadock, J.M. (ed.): Grammatical Relations. Syntax and Semantics 8. New York p. 47-58.
Coseriu, E. 1974 [1958]: Synchronie, Diachronie und Geschichte. Das Problem des Sprachwandels. München.
De Geer, E. 1985: Suomalaisa ja ruotsalaisia kieliryhmiä ja vähemmistöjä Ruotsissa ja Suomessa – Nemlander-Sjöberg, C. (ed.): Suomen asema Ruotsin valtakunnassa. Helsinki p. 43-65.
De Smit, M. 2004: Negation in Old Finnish Legal Texts. Wiener Elektronische Beiträge des Institutions für Finno-Ugristik 3/2004. http://webfu.univie.ac.at

- 2005: Nesessiivirakenteiden subjektimerkinnästä vanhimpien lainsuomennosten kielessä. Sananjalka p. 64-90.
Dixon, R.M.W. 1979: Ergativity. Language 55 p. 59-138.
Elsayed, K. 1997: Infinitiivin subjekti manipuloinnin kohteena. Sananjalka 39 p. 99-117.
- 2000: Modaliteettien ilmaiseminen vanhassa lakisuomessa – Punttila, M. Jussila, R., Suni, H. (ed.): Pipliakielestä kirjakieleksi. Kotimaisten kielten tutkimuskeskuksen julkaisuja 105. Helsinki p. 108-114.
Fehling, D. 1979: The origins of european syntax. Folia Linguistica Historica I:2 p. 353-387.
Field, F. W. 2002: Linguistic borrowing in bilingual contexts. Amsterdam.
Filppula, M. 1991: New models and typologies of language contact – Ojanen, M., Palander, M. (ed.) Language Contacts East and West. Studies in Language 22. Joensuu. p. 5-31.
Forsman-Svensson, P. 1983: Satsmotsvarigheter i finsk prosa under 1600-talet: participialkonstruktionen och därmed synonyma icke-finita uttryck i jämförelse med språkbruket före och efter 1600-talet. Helsinki.
- 1990: 1600-luvun saarnakirjallisuuden partisiippiattribuutteja: "Hyvinoppinut mies ja hyvillä tavoilla kaunistettu matroona." Virittäjä p. 307-327.
- 1992a: Karl IX:s minnesskrift – kanslisvenska i finsk översättning. Fenno -Ugrica Suecana 11 p. 1-23.
- 1992b: Vanhan kirjasuomen nominaalirakenteista. Stockholm.
- 1994: 1600-luvun tekstien liitepartikkelit. Virittäjä p. 377-403.
- 1998: Kolmannen infinitiivin illatiivi Petter Schäfferin päiväkirjassa. Virittäjä p. 56-73.
- 2000: Petter Schäfferin päiväkirja – ruotsinkielisen suomeako? – Punttila, M., Jussila, R., Suni, H. (ed.): Pipliakielestä kirjakieleksi. Kotimaisten kielten tutkimuskeskuksen julkaisuja 105. Helsinki p.134-151.
Fortescue, M. 2001: Patterns and Process. A Whiteheadian perspective on linguistics. Amsterdam.
Fougstedt, G. 1984: Finlandssvenskarna under 100 år – Engman, M., Stenius, H. (ed.): Svenskt i Finland 2. Demografiska och socialhistoriska studier. Helsingfors p. 19-35.
Givón, T. 2001a: Syntax. An Introduction. Volume 1. Amsterdam
- 2001b: Syntax. An Introduction. Volume 2. Amsterdam
Gläser, C. 1973: Die Verbalkomposita im Gebetbuch Mikael Agricolas. Sovietskoye Finno-Ugrovidenye 9 p. 15-24.
Grönholm, M. 1988: Ruotsalaiset lainasanat Turun murteessa. Åbo.
Gumperz, J.J., Wilson, R. 1971: Convergence and creolization. A Case from the Indo-Aryan/Dravidian border in India – Hymes, D. (ed.): Pidginization and creolization of languages. Proceedings of a conference

held at the University of the West Indies Mona, Jamaica, April 1968. Cambridge p. 151-167.
Guy, G.R. 1990: The sociolinguistic types of language change. Diachronica 7 p. 47-67.
Hakulinen, L. 1979: Suomen kielen rakenne ja kehitys. Neljäs, lisätty ja ajanmukaistettu painos. Keuruu.
Hakulinen, A. and Karlsson, F. 1988: Nykysuomen lauseoppia. Suomalaisen Kirjallisuuden Seuran Toimituksia 350. Helsinki.
Hakulinen, A., Vilkuna, M., Korhonen, R., Koivisto, V., Heinonen, T.R., Alho, I. 2004: Iso suomen kielioppi. Helsinki.
Haley, M.C. 1988: The semeiosis of poetic metaphor. Bloomington.
Hall, E.W. 1963 [1930]: Of what use are Whitehead's Eternal Objects? – Kline, G.L. (ed.): Alfred North Whitehead: Essays on his philosophy. Englewood Cliffs p. 102-116 [Journal of Philosophy 27 p. 29-44].
Harris, A., Campbell, L. 1995: Historical syntax in cross-linguistic perspective. Cambridge Studies in Linguistics 74. Cambridge.
Harris, M. 1982: On explaining language change – Ahlqvist, A. (ed.): Papers from the 5th International Conference on Historical Linguistics. Current Issues in Linguistic Theory 21. Amsterdam p. 1-14.
Hartig, M. 1983: Sprachwandel und Sprachkontakt – Nelde, P.H. (red.): Gegenwärtige Tendenzen der Kontaktlinguistik. Bonn p. 67-79.
Haugen, E. 1950: The Analysis of Linguistic Borrowing. Language p. 210 -231.
Heath, J. 1981: A case of intensive lexical diffusion: Arnhem Land, Australia.Language 57 p. 335-367.
- 1998: Hermit crabs: formal renewal of morphology by phonologically mediated affix substitution. Language 74 p. 728-759.
Hegel, G.W.F. 1975 [1830]: Hegel's Logic. Being part one of the Encyclopaedia of the Philosophical Sciences (1830) translated by William Wallace. With foreword by J.N. Findlay, F.B.A. Oxford.
Hidalgo, R. 1994: The pragmatics of de-transitive voice in Spanish: from passive to inverse? – Givón, T. (ed), Voice and Inversion. Amsterdam p.169-186.
Hofstra, T. 1985: Ostseefinnisch und Germanisch. Frühe Lehnbeziehungen im nördlichen Ostseeraum im Lichte der Forschung seit 1961. Groningen.
Hopper, P.J. 1987: Emergent Grammar. Berkeley Linguistics Society 13 p. 139-157. http://home.eserver.org/hopper/emergence.html
Hopper, P. J., Thompson, S.A. 1980: Transitivity in grammar and discourse. Language 56 p. 251-299.
Huovinen, S. 1985: Suomen kielen asema yhteisessä valtakunnassa – Nemlander-Sjöberg, C. (ed.): Suomen asema Ruotsin valtakunnassa. Helsinki p. 67-83.
Häkkinen, K. 1993: Verbiketjut 1500-luvun kirjasuomessa – Systeemi ja

poikkeama. Juhlakirja Alho Alhoniemen 60-vuotispäiväksi 14.5.1993. Turku p. 207-227.
1994: Agricolasta Nykykieleen. Suomen kirjakielen historia. Porvoo.
1997: Kuinka ruotsin kieli on vaikuttanut suomeen? Sananjalka p. 31-53.
2003: Suomen kielen ruotsalaiset lainat: tuloksia, ongelmia, mahdollisuuksia - Pörn, M., Åstrand, A. (ed.): Kieli tienhaarassa. Juhlakirja Maija Grönholmin 60-vuotispäivän kunniaksi 23.9.2003. Åbo p. 44-57.
Ikola, O. 1949: Tempusten ja modusten käyttö ensimmäisessä suomalaisessa raamatussa verrattuna vanhempaan ja nykyiseen kieleen I. Turku.
- 1950: Tempusten ja modusten käyttö ensimmäisessä suomalaisessa raamatussa verrattuna vanhempaan ja nykyiseen kieleen II. Turku.
- 1959: Eräistä suomen syntaktisista siirtymistä. Sananjalka p. 39-60.
- 1966: Eräistä murteellisista kieltolauseiden konjunktioista. Virittäjä p. 9-15.
- 1971: Lauseenvastikkeista ja upotetuista lauseista. Sananjalka p. 17-51.
- 1978: Lauseenvastikeoppia. Helsinki
- 1988: Agricolan äidinkieli – Koivusalo, E. (ed.): Mikael Agricolan kieli. Helsinki p. 25-68.
Ikola, O., Palomäki, U., Koitto, A.-K. 1989: Suomen murteiden lauseoppia ja tekstikielioppia. Helsinki.
Inaba, N. 2000a: Vanhan kirjasuomen datiivinen genetiivi I. Eräät nykysuomesta kadonneet lausetyypit Kuningas Kristoferin maanlain ensimmäisen suomennoksen valossa – Pajunen, A. (ed.): Näkökulmia kielitypologiaan. Suomi 186. Helsinki p. 109-152.
- 2000b: Genetiivin ja partitiivin datiivinen käyttö vanhassa kirjasuomessa: sijanmerkinnän ja sijajärjestelmän suhteesta. Sananjalka 42 p. 47-86.
Itkonen, E. 1978: Short-term and long-term teleology in linguistic change – Papers from the Conference of General Linguistics Seili 24.-25.8.1978. Publications of the Linguistic Association of Finland 2. Turku p. 35-68.
- 2002: Grammaticalization as an analogue of hypothetico-deductive thinking – Wischer, I. (ed.): New reflections on grammaticalization. Amsterdam p. 413-422.
- 2005: Analogy as structure and process: Approaches in Linguistics, Cognitive Psychology and Philosophy of Science. Amsterdam.
Itkonen, T. 1964a: Proto-Finnic final consonants. Their history in the Finnic languages with particular reference to the Finnish dialects. I:1. Helsinki.
- 1964b: Sananrajaisten äänneilmiöiden synkroniaa ja diakroniaa. Virittäjä p. 225-232.
- 1974: Ergatiivisuutta suomessa (1). Virittäjä p. 379-398.
- 1975: Ergatiivisuutta suomessa (2). Virittäjä p p. 31-65.
- 1993 [1979]: Subject and object marking in Finnish: An inverted ergative system and an "ideal" ergative sub-system – Aloja ja aiheita. Valikoimia kolmen kymmenluvun tutkielmia (1959-1979 Suomalais-Ugrilaisen

Seuran Toimituksia 216. Helsinki p. 307-329. [– Plank, F. (ed.): Ergativity. New York p. 79-101]
Itkonen-Kaila, M. 1974. Passiivilauseiden suomentamisesta. Virittäjä 210 -214.
- 1991: Agricolan Uuden Testamentin temporaalirakenteet. Suomi klassisten ja germaanisten kielten taustaa varten. Virittäjä p. 255-280.
- 1992: "Ja Jerusalem pite talattaman Pacanoilda."Ablatiiviagentti ja sen perilliset Agricolasta uuteen raamatunsuomennokseen. Virittäjä p. 137-164.
- 1997: Mikael Agricolan Uusi Testamentti ja sen erikieliset lähtötekstit. Suomi 184. Helsinki.
Jutikkala, E. and Pirinen, K. 1973: Suomen historia. Helsinki.
Juttikala, E. 1987: Finlands befolkning och befolkande. Historisk Tidskrift för Finland 3 p. 351-373.
Kallio, P. 2000: Posti's Superstrate Theory at the Threshhold of a New Millenium – Laakso, J. (ed.): Facing Finnic: Some challenges to historical and contact linguistics. Helsinki p. 80-99.
- 2006: Suomen kantakielten absoluuttista kronologiaa. Virittäjä p. 2-25.
Karlsson, F. 1982: Kieliteorian relevanssi suomen kielen opetukselle – Karlsson, F. (ed.): Suomi vieraana kielenä. Porvoo p. 89-114.
Kangasmaa-Minn, E. 1980. Suomen kielen persoonallisesta passiivista. Sananjalka p. 57-70.
Kangassalo, R., Nemvalts, P., Wande, E. 2003: Ruotsin itämerensuomalaisten kielten syntaksi – Muikku-Werner, P., Remes, H. (ed.): Viro ja suomi: kohdekielet kontrastissa. Lähivertailuja 13 p. 156
King, R. 2000: The Lexical Basis of Grammatical Borrowing. A Prince Edward Island French case study. Amsterdam.
Kiuru, S. 1993: Agricolan Uusi Testamentti ja ensimmäiset Raamattumme. Virittäjä p. 51-68.
KKS = Karjalan Kielen Sanakirja. Helsinki 1968-
Klövekorn, M. 1960: Die sprachliche Struktur Finnlands 1880-1950. Veränderungen im sprachlichen Charakter der finnlandschwedischen Gebiete und deren bevölkerungs-, wirtschafts- und sozialgeographischen Ursachen. Helsingfors.
Koivulehto, J. 1999 [1983]: Seit wann leben die Finnen im Ostseeraum? Verba Mutuata. Suomalais-Ugrilaisen Seuran Toimituksia 237. Helsinki p. 229-244.
Korhonen, M. 1981: Johdatus lapin kielen historiaan. Helsinki.
Krausch, S. 1926: Analogy as a factor in semantic change. Language 2 p. 35-45.
Krishnamurti, Bh., Gwynn, J.P.L. 1985: A grammar of modern Telugu. Delhi

Laakso, J. 1995: A spade is always a spade – comment in "The 'Pragmareal' challenge to genetic tree models" – Suhonen, S. (ed.): Itämerensuomalainen kulttuurialue. The Fenno-Baltic cultural area. Helsinki p. 70-75.
Laanest 1982: Einführung in die Ostseefinnischen Sprachen. Hamburg.
Laitinen, L. 1992: Välttämättömyys ja persoona. Suomen murteiden nesessiivisten rakenteiden semantiikka ja kielioppia. Helsinki.
Laitinen, L., Vilkuna, M. 1993: Case marking in necessive constructions and split intransitivity – Holmberg, A., Nikanne, U. (ed.): Case and other functional categories in Finnish syntax. Berlin p. 23-48.
Langacker, R. 1977: Syntactic Reanalysis – Li. N. (ed.) Mechanisms of syntactic change. Austin p. 57-139.
Lass, R. 1980: On explaining language change. Cambridge.
- 1997: Historical linguistics and language change. Cambridge.
Lauttamus, T. 1991: Borrowing, Code-Switching and Shift in Language Contact: Evidence from Finnish-English Bilingualism – Ojanen, M., Palander, M. (ed.) : Language Contacts East and West. Studies in Language 22. Joensuu. p. 32-53.
Lehtinen, T. 1984. Itämerensuomen passiivin alkuperästä. Helsinki.
- 1985: Vanhan persoonallisen passiivin jatkajiako? Virittäjä p. 270-289.
Lightfoot, D. 1988: Syntactic change – Newmeyer, F. (ed.): Linguistics. The Cambridge Survey. Volume I. Linguistic Theory: Foundations. Cambridge p. 303-323.
Lindblad, G. 1943: Relativ satsfogning i de nordiska fornspråken. Lund.
Lindén, E. 1963: Kieltolauseen sanajärjestyksestä suomen kirjakielessä. Virittäjä p. 214-226.
- 1964: Aiheetonta agenttirakenteen käyttöä suomen kirjakielessä. Virittäjä p. 344-353.
Mattsson, G. 1933: Konjunktiven i fornsvenskan. Lund.
McMahon, A. 1994: Understanding language change. Cambridge.
Nadkarni, M.V. 1975: Bilingualism and syntactic change in Konkani. Language 51 p. 672-683.
Nau, N. 1995: Möglichkeiten und Mechanismen kontaktbewegten Sprachwandels unter besonderer Berücksichtigung des Finnischen. München.
Nesser, A. 1982: Subjekt, Objekt och Predikativ i sverigefinska barns uppsatser. FUSKIS/FIDUS 5. Uppsala.
Nikkilä, O. 1985: Apokope und altes Schriftfinnisch. Zur Geschichte der i-Apokope des Finnischen. Groningen.
NS = Nykysuomen Sanakirja. Juva 1996.
Noreen, A. 1904: Altnordische Grammatik 2. Altschwedische Grammatik: mit Einschluss des Altgutnischen. Halle.
Nuolijärvi, P. 1988: Kielenulkoisten taustamuuttujien huomioon ottaminen 1800-luvun ja 1900-luvun alun murretutkimuksessa. Kieli 3 p. 117-160.

OED = The Oxford English Dictionary. Second Edition. Oxford 1989.
Ojansuu, H. 1906: Ruotsin kielen vaikutus suomen murteiden äänneasuun. Virittäjä p. 23-27.
- 1909: Mikael Agricolan kielestä. Suomi IV:7.
OSSGL = Schlyter, D.C.J. 1877: Ordbok til Samlingen af Sweriges Gamla Lagar. Lund.
Pajula, P. 1955: Ensimmäinen lainsuomennos. Lisiä suomen lakikielen varhaishistoriaan. Helsinki.
- 1960: Suomen lakikielen historia pääpiirteittäin. Porvoo.
Palmer, L.R. 1972: Descriptive and comparative linguistics. A critical introduction. London.
Penttilä, A. 1963: Suomen kielioppi. Helsinki.
Petander, F.L. 1893: Esitys Piispa Eerikki Sorolaisen kielestä. Suomi III:6.
Posti, L. 1953: From Pre-Finnic to late Proto-Finnic. Finnisch-Ugrische Forschungen 31 p. 1-91.
- 1980: The origin and development of the reflexive conjugation in the Finnic languages – Congressus Quintus Internationalis Fenno-Ugristarum Turku 20.-27.VIII.1980 Pars I. Turku p. 111-144.
Pyöli, R. 1996: Venäläistyvä Aunuksenkarjala. Kielenulkoiset ja –sisäiset indikaattorit kielenvaihtotilanteessa. Joensuu.
Pääkkönen, I. 1988: Relatiivisanan valinnasta. Helsinki.
Rapola, M. 1925: Äännehistoriallinen tutkimus Abraham Kollaniuksen lainsuomennosten kielestä. Suomi V:5. Helsinki.
- 1930: Piirteitä Ruotsin vallan aikaisen kirjasuomen kehityksestä. Virittäjä p. 81-91.
- 1960: Pajula, Paavo: Suomalaisen lakikielen historia pääpiirteittäin (review). Virittäjä p. 199-207.
- 1965: Suomen kirjakielen historia I. Helsinki.
- 1967: Suomenkielinen proosa ruotsin vallan aikana. Helsinki.
- 1969: Vanha kirjasuomi. Helsinki.
Romaine, S. 1995: Bilingualism. Second edition. Oxford
Ross, M. 1999: Exploring metatypy: how does contact-induced typological change come about? Keynote talk given at the Australian Linguistic Society's annual meeting. Perth.
Saarimaa, E.A. 1934: Ruotsin kielen vaikutus Aleksis Kiven kielenkäyttöön. Virittäjä p. 281-298.
- 1942: Käännössuomea. Virittäjä p. 102-107.
- 1971: Kielenopas. Porvoo.
Sadeniemi, M. 1942a: Nominatiivi-genetiivi? Virittäjä p. 197-201.
- 1942b: Käännössuomea. Virittäjä p. 333.
Sankoff, G. 2002: Linguistic outcomes of language contact – Chambers, J.K., Trudgill, P., Schilling-Estes, N. (ed.): The Handbook of Language Variation and Change. Oxford p. 638-668.
Saukkonen, P. 1965: Itämerensuomalaisten kielten

tulosijainfinitiivirakenteiden historiaa I. Helsinki.
Savijärvi, I. 1977: Itämerensuomalaisten kielten kieltoverbi I. Suomi. Helsinki.
- 1988: Agricolan kieltolause – Koivusalo, E. (ed.): Mikael Agricolan kieli. Helsinki p. 69-93.
Schelletter, C. 2002: The effects of form similarity on bilingual children's lexical developments. Bilingualism: Language and Cognition 5:2 p. 93-107.
Schlachter, W. 1986: Lehnsyntax im Finnischen – Gerstner, K., Hahmo, S. -L., Hofstra, T., Jastrzebska, J., Nikkilä, O. (ed.): Lyökämme käsi kätehen. Beiträge zur Sprachkontaktforschung im Bereich des Finnougrischen und Germanischen A.D. Kylstra zum 65. Geburtstag. Amsterdam p. 107-117.
Schmeidler, E. 1959: Über den Gebrauch von Verbalkomposita in Mikael Agricolas Neuem Testament. Ural-Altaische Jahrbücher p. 387-391.
Selinker, L. 1992: Rediscovering Interlanguage. London.
SEO = Hellquist, E. 1966: Svensk etymologisk ordbok. Lund.
Shibatani, M. 1985: Passives and related constructions. A prototype analysis. Language 61 p. 821-848.
Siewierska, A. 1984: The Passive. A comparative linguistic analysis. London.
Singh, R. 1999: A tale of two cities: A response to Treffers-Daller. Bilingualism: Language and Cognition 2 (2) p. 88-90.
Sridhar, S.N. 1990: Kannada. London.
SRS = Lönnrot, E. 1930 (1874-1880): Suomalais-Ruotsalainen Sanakirja. Finskt-Svenskt Lexikon. Porvoo.
SSA = Suomen sanojen alkuperä. Etymologinen Sanakirja. Helsinki 1992-
Stolz, C., Stolz, T. 1996: Funktionswortentlehnung in Mesoamerika. Spanisch-amerindischer Sprachkontakt (Hispanoindiana II). Sprachtypologie und Universalienforschung 49:1 p. 86-123.
Streng, H. 1915: Nuoremmat ruotsalaiset lainat varhemmassa suomen kirjakielessä. Helsinki.
Ståhle, C.I. 1958: Syntaktiska och stilistiska studier i fornnordiskt lagspråk. Lund.
Stroh-Wollin, U. 2002: Som-satser med och utan som. Uppsala.
Tarkiainen, K. 1990: Finnarnas historia i Sverige 1. Inflyttarna från Finland under det gemensamma rikets tid. Helsinki.
- 1993: Finnarnas historia i Sverige 2. Inflyttarna från Finland och de finska minoriteterna under tiden 1809-1944. Helsinki.
Thomason, S.G. 1997: On mechanisms of interference – Language and its ecology. Essays in memory of Einar Haugen. Berlin p. 181-207.
- 2000: On the unpredictability of contact effects. Estudios de Sociolinguistica 1.1 p. 173-182.
- 2001: Language contact: an introduction. Edinburgh.

- 2003. Contact as a source of language change – Joseph, B.D., Janda, R.D. (ed.): Handbook of historical linguistics. Oxford p. 687-712.
- forthcoming: Can rules be borrowed? – Festschrift for ... In press.
Thomason, S.G., Kaufman, T. 1988: Language Contact, Creolization and Genetic Linguistics. Los Angeles.
Thors, C.E. 1981: Finska påverkningar på de finlandssvenska folkmålen – Loman, B. (ed.): De finlandssvenska dialekterna i forskning och funktion. Åbo.
Timberlake, A. 1977: Reanalysis and Actualization in Syntactic Change – Li, N. (ed.) Mechanisms of syntactic change. Austin p. 141-177.
Treffers-Daller, J. 1999: Borrowing and shift-induced interference: Contrasting patterns in French-Germanic contact in Brussels and Strasbourg. Bilingualism: Language and Cognition 2 (1) p. 1-22.
Tunkelo, E.A. 1936: Havaintoja ku(n)-lauseiden merkitystehtävistä suomen murteissa. Virittäjä p. 143-
Virtaranta, P. 1982: Havaintoja Kurravaaran murteesta – Språkhistoria och språkkontakt i Finland och Nord-Skandinavien. Studier tillägnade Tryggve Sköld den 2 November 1982. Stockholm p. 287-306.
Wallén, H. 1932: Språkgränsen och minoriteterna i Finlands svenskbygder omkr. 1600-1865. Åbo.
Wande, E. 1978: Ackusativmarkering i högfinskan och tornedalsfinskan. Fenno-Ugrica Suecana 1.
- 1982: Ruotsin Tornionlaakson suomi ja sen ominaispiirteet – Suomen kieli ruotsissa. Stockholm p. 39-71.
- 1996: Tornedalen – Lainio, J. (ed.): Finnarnas historia i Sverige 3. Tiden efter 1945. Helsinki p. 229-254.
Weinreich, U., Labov, W. Herzog, M. 1968: Empirical Foundations for a Theory of Language Change – Lehmann, W.P., Malkiel, Y. (ed.) p. 97-195.
Weinreich, U. 1974 [1953]: Languages in Contact. Findings and Problems. The Hague.
Wendt, B. 1997: Landlagsspråk och stadslagspråk. Stilhistoriska undersökningar i Kristoffers landslag. Lund.
Wessén, E. 1970a: Schwedische Sprachgeschichte. Band I: Laut- und Flexionslehre. Berlin.
- 1970b: Schwedische Sprachgeschichte. Band III: Grundriss einer historischen Syntax. Berlin.
Whitehead, A.N. 1929: Process and reality. An Essay in Cosmology. Cambridge.
- 1933: Adventures of Ideas. Cambridge.
Wiik, K. 1989: Suomen kielen morfofonologian historia I. Turku.
Winford, D. 2003: An introduction to contact linguistics. Oxford.
Yang, C.D. 2000: Internal and external forces in language change. Language Variation and Change 12.

APPENDIX A

Frequency of subject case-marking is indicated on the vertical level, frequency of object case-marking on the horizontal level. A question mark indicates that the exact noun case could not be determined with confidence. With Ljungo and Kollanius, the first number indicates the number found in their translations of King Christopher's Land Law, the second in their translations of Magnus Eriksson's City Law (including, in Kollanius' case, a translation of the Church Law from the Uppland Country Law (*Upplandslagen*).

MARTTI

pitää active

343	nom.	acc.	part.	0	?	
nom.		29	9	47	7	92
gen.	1	101	12	60	16	190
part.				2		2
0	1	5	2	5		13
?		11	1	11	1	24
ellipsis	1	13	4	1	3	22
	3	159	28	126	27	

pitää passive

135	nom.	gen.	acc.	part.	0	?
0	5	1	101	11	8	9

tulla active

162	nom.	acc.	part.	0	?	
nom.		1	4	8	3	16
gen.	6	45	20	40	26	137
part.						
0		2	2	1		5
?				1		1
ellipsis		1	1		1	3
	6	49	27	50	30	

tulla passive

22	nom.	gen.	acc.	part.	0	?
0	10		7	5		

LJUNGO

pitää active

373 /275	nom.	acc.	part.	0	?	
nom.	1/0	45/37	13/5	50/64	7/20	116/126
gen.	2/0	81/58	19/8	76/36	23/13	201/115
part.				2/0		2/0
0		1/2	1/0	2/4		4/6
?		10/11	2/1	9/7	1/1	22/20
ellipsis	1/0	18/4	5/3	1/0	3/1	28/8
	4/0	155/112	40/17	140/111	34/35	

pitää passive

149/ 103	nom.	gen.	acc.	part.	0	?
0	19/33		96/45	10/3	10/7	14/13

tulla active

180/17	nom.	acc.	part.	0	?	
nom.		8/1	7/0	11/2	2/0	28/3
gen.	5/1	60/4	29/2	35/2	13/2	142/11
part.						
0		1/1	0/1	1/1		2/3
?				4/0		4/0
ellipsis		1/0		1/0	2/0	4/0
	5/1	70/6	36/3	52/5	17/2	

tulla passive

24/0	nom.	gen.	acc.	part.	0	?
0	10		8	5		1

KOLLANIUS

pitää active

393/311	nom.	acc.	part.	0	?	
nom.		12/18	7/3	53/64	2/1	74/86
gen.	7/0	124/88	40/23	89/85	19/16	279/212
part.				5/4	1/0	6/4
0	1/1	6/2		1/1	1/0	9/4
?		0/1		2/2		2/2
ellipsis		13/0	7/2	2/0	1/0	23/2
	8/1	155/109	54/28	152/156	24/17	

pitää passive

146/125	nom.	gen.	acc.	part.	0	?
0	71/54	0/1	47/37	8/9	10/7	10/17

tulla active

138/83	nom.	acc.	part.	0	?	
nom.				4/3		4/3
gen.	2/4	54/36	24/11	27/16	15/12	122/79
part.						
0	1/0	1/0	3/1	2/0		7/1
?						
ellipsis		1/0	3/0		1/0	5/0
	3/4	56/36	30/12	33/19	16/12	

tulla passive

15/4	nom.	gen.	acc.	part.	0	?
0	7/1		3/2	3/0		2/1

RWL

pitää active

338	nom.	acc.	part.	0	?	
nom.		11	4	80	3	98
gen.	1	74	26	79	21	201
part.				25		25
0	1					1
?		3		7		10
ellip sis		1			2	3
	2	89	30	192	26	

pitää passive

292	nom.	gen.	acc.	part.	0	?
0	142	0	59	44	31	16

tulla active

42	nom.	acc.	part.	0	?	
nom.						
gen.	1	19	2	12	4	37
part.						
0						
?		1			3	4
ellip sis						
	1	20	2	12	7	

tulla passive

0	nom.	gen.	acc.	part.	0	?
0						

APPENDIX B

Division of nominative- and genitive-marked subjects. With Ljungo and Kollanius, the first number indicates the number found in their translations of King Christopher's Land Law, the second in their translations of Magnus Eriksson's City Law (including, in Kollanius' case, a translation of the Church Law from the Uppland Country Law (*Upplandslagen*).

MARTTI

	pitää		*tulla*	
	N-	G-	N-	G-
ne/nämä	22	-	1	3
ne/nämä + noun/num.	4	-	-	3
plural noun	21	2	3	9
plur. rel. pron.	2	-	1	-
plur. possessee	2	-	-	-
he	-	20	-	13
me	-	1	-	-
numeral >1	1	-	2	-
numeral >1 + noun.	6	-	1	1
yksi	-	1	-	
yksi + noun	-	1	-	
kaikki	2	-	1	-
kaikki ne	1	-	1	-
kaikki + noun	3	1	1	1
kaikki (plur.)	-	2	-	2
sing. noun	23	81	3	61
sing. possessee	2	1	1	1
sing. rel./interr. pron.	1	5	-	2
se	2	19	-	8
hän	-	54	1	23
minä	-	-	-	-
neg./other pron.	-	2	-	10
sum	92	190	16	137

LJUNGO

	pitää N-	G-		*tulla* N-	G-
ne	18/2	2/-		1/-	4/-
ne + noun/num.	8/6	-/1		2/-	-/-
plural noun	44/21	3/2		10/-	12/-
plur. rel. pron.	4/9	-/-		1/-	-/-
plur. possessee	-/2	-/-		-/-	-/-
he	2/6	18/25		1/-	11/1
me	-/-	-/-		-/-	-/-
numeral >1	1/4	-/-		3/1	-/-
numeral >1 + noun.	2/7	-/-		-/-	-/-
yksi	-/1	1/-		-/-	-/-
yksi + noun	-/-	-/-		-/-	1/-
kaikki	1/1	-/-		-/-	-/-
kaikki ne	-/-	1/-		1/-	-/-
kaikki + noun	4/2	4/-		1/-	1/-
kaikki (plur.)	-/-	3/-		-/-	4/-
sing. noun	23/24	81/26		4/-	61/2
sing. possessee	3/6	-/2		2/-	1/-
sing. rel./interr. pron.	1/16	3/-		1/1	2/-
se	1/4	19/10		-/-	6/-
hän	2/10	61/46		1/-	29/7
minä	-/-	-/3		-/-	1/-
neg./other pron.	2/5	4/-		-/1	9/1
sum	116/126	201/115		28/3	142/11

KOLLANIUS

	pitää			*tulla*	
	N-	G-		N-	G-
ne/nämä	2/3	32/20		-/-	9/4
ne/nämä + noun/num.	7/4	4/4		-/-	1/-
plural noun	13/5	37/27		1/-	11/7
plur. rel. pron.	2/4	5/7		-/-	-/1
plur. possessee	2/4	-/-		-/-	-/-
he	2/-	9/9		-/-	2/-
me	-/-	3/-		-/-	-/-
numeral >1	12/9	-/-		-/1	1/-
numeral >1 + noun.	10/14	4/6		-/1	1/-
yksi	-/-	1/-		-/-	-/-
yksi + noun	-/2	-/-		-/-	1/-
kaikki	1/-	-/-		-/-	-/2
kaikki ne	-/1	-/-		-/-	1/1
kaikki + noun	3/3	3/3		-/-	-/-
kaikki (plur.)	-/-	4/4		-/-	4/-
sing. noun	5/14	79/46		2/-	56/37
sing. possessee	8/10	3/1		-/-	-/-
sing. rel./interr. pron.	2/5	6/3		-/-	5/-
se	4/6	23/20		1/1	5/3
hän	-/-	60/51		-/-	19/17
minä	-/-	-/-		-/-	1/1
neg./other pron.	1/2	6/11		-/-	5/6
sum	74/86	279/212		4/3	122/79

RWL

	pitää			*tulla*	
	N-	G-		N-	G-
ne/nämä	4	5		-	-
ne/nämä + noun/num.	-	-		-	-
plural noun	10	13		-	2
plur. rel. pron.	4	1		-	3
plur. possessee	-	-		-	-
he	1	11		-	1
me	-	-		-	-
numeral >1	1	-		-	-
numeral >1 + noun.	-	-		-	1
yksi	-	1		-	
yksi + noun	1	-		-	
kaikki	-	-		-	-
kaikki ne	-	-		-	-
kaikki + noun	4	-		-	-
kaikki (plur.)	-	7		-	1
sing. noun	34	84		-	11
sing. possessee	15	1		-	1
sing. rel./interr. pron.	13	15		-	11
se	10	14		-	1
hän	-	34		-	5
minä	-	2		-	-
neg./other pron.	1	13		-	1
sum	98	201		0	38

APPENDIX C

Case-marking and word order with *pitää*. S = Subject, V = Necessitive auxiliary, I = Infinitival complement, O = Object. GA = Genitive-Accusative, NA = Nominative-Accusative, etc.; G = Genitive, N = Nominative, P = Partitive, ? = Unknown, 0 = Absent. With Ljungo and Kollanius, the first number indicates the number found in their translations of King Christopher's Land Law, the second in their translations of Magnus Eriksson's City Law (including, in Kollanius' case, a translation of the Church Law from the Uppland Country Law (*Upplandslagen*).

MARTTI
pitää active

	SVOI	VSOI	SVIO	VSIO	SVI	VSI	SIV	VIS	SOIV	SOVI	OVSI	OSVI	VOSI
GA	18	43	5	11						2	15		3
NA	9	5	6	2							4	1	
GP	4	4	1	3									
NP	1	2		3					1				
G?	2	6	1	5							1	1	
N?	2	1		2								1	
GN		1											
NN													
G0					15	39	2	3					
N0					29	10		7					

pitää passive

	OVI	VOI	OIV	VIO
0N	1	3		1
0A	39	38	1	
0P	1	8		1
0?	1	4	1	2

LJUNGO

pitää active

	SVOI	VSOI	SVIO	VSIO	SVI	VSI	SIV	VIS	SOIV	SOVI	OVSI	OSVI	VOSI
GA	21/24	33/10	5/3	6/4					1/-	4/2	9/6	-/4	
NA	8/8	14/8	2/3	1/1					1/12	1/1	12/2	1/1	2/1
GP	3/4	5/2	3/-	3/-					-/1				
NP	4/1	3/-	1/1	2/-					1/3				
G?	4/2	10/7	1/1	6/1							-/1		
N?	2/-	1/3	1/1	2/-					-/2	-/1		-/1	
GN		1/-		1/-									
NN									1/-				
G0					22/14	43/17	6/1	-/1					
N0					26/24	14/22	3/12	4/1					

pitää passive

	OVI	VOI	OIV	VIO
0N	11/18	8/6	1/2	
0A	48/37	43/13	2/-	-/1
0P	1/-	6/2		
0?	-/6	7/3	2/2	1/2

KOLLANIUS

pitää active

	SVOI	VSOI	SVIO	VSIO	SVI	VSI	SIV	VIS	SOIV	SOVI	OVSI	OSVI	VOSI
GA	31/25	59/43	5/1	4/2					1/1	2/1	15/12	-/1	1/1
NA	-/5	4/2							-/1	1/4	5/4	1/-	1/-
GP	14/13	15/4	1/2	1/1					1/-	2/-	3/2	-/1	3/-
NP	2/1	1/-							2/-	2/1	-/1		
G?	6/3	11/10										-/1	
N?	2/-	-/1											
GN	2/-	5/-											
NN													
G0					38/30	42/41	2/6	1/-					
N0					10/23	26/28	3/3	9/7					

pitää passive

	OVI	VOI	OIV	VIO
0N	23/26	43/27	1/1	
0A	19/19	25/16	1/1	
0P	1/6	5/1	-/1	
0?	1/7	9/10		

APPENDIX D

Breakdown of the occurrences of the relative pronouns *joka* and *kuin* in the five texts examined, according to subjecthood, human referents (h, -h), and singular countable referents (sc).

	M	L1	K1	L2	K2	RWL
JOKA - subj, h, sc	157	196	181	155	163	334
- subj, h, -sc	74	103	93	72	88	113
- subj, -h, sc	18	27	14	14	3	42
- subj, -h, -sc	10	19	12	23	12	65
tot	*259*	*345*	*300*	*264*	*266*	*554*
JOKA - obj, h, sc	17	22	21	8	16	56
- obj, h, -sc	6	4	14	4	10	11
- obj, -h, sc	14	19	15	9	10	31
- obj, -h, -sc	17	40	29	36	27	52
tot	*54*	*85*	*79*	*57*	*63*	*150*
KUIN - subj, h, sc	94	62	54	24	29	92
- subj, h, -sc	61	42	31	13	14	21
- subj, -h, sc	9	5	5	4	9	20
- subj, -h, -sc	30	20	22	26	25	119
tot	*194*	*129*	*112*	*67*	*77*	*252*
KUIN - obj, h, sc	2	4	2	2	2	8
- obj, h, -sc	8	4	2	0	2	2
- obj, -h, sc	15	11	6	8	4	25
- obj, -h, -sc	62	47	33	39	22	156
tot	*87*	*66*	*43*	*49*	*30*	*191*
n	594	625	534	437	436	1147

Studia Fennica Stockholmiensia

Published by Stockholm University
Editor: Erling Wande

1. INGRID ALMQVIST. Om objektsmarkeringen vid negation i finskan. (On negation and object marking in Finnish.) Stockholm 1987. 201 s.

2. BIRGER WINSA. Östligt eller västligt? Det äldsta ordförrådet i gällivarefinskan och tornedalsfinskan. (East or west? The oldest vocabulary in Gällivare Finnish and Torne Finnish.) Stockholm 1991. 267 s.

3. ULLA LUNDGREN. Predikativadverbialet och dess numeruskongruens i finskan. (The predicative adverbial and its number agreement in Finnish.) Stockholm 1992. 194 s.

4. IRENE VIRTALA. Narkissos i inre exil. En studie i begärets paradoxer i L. Onervas roman *Mirdja*. (Narcissus in Inner Exile. A Study of the Paradoxes of Desire in L. Onerva's Novel *Mirdja*.) Stockholm 1994. 166 s.

5. MARJA WECKSTRÖM. Hur tvinnas Manillarepet? En fenomenologiskt strukturstudie av Veijo Meris roman. (How is the Manila Rope twined? A Phenomenological Structural Study of Veijo Meri's Novel.) Stockholm 1997. 240 s.

6.TUULA VOSTHENKO. Det tänkande landskapet. Landskapsskildringarna i Olavi Paavolainens Synkkä Yksinpuhelu (Finlandia i moll). /The Thinking Lanscape. The Landscape Portraits in Olavi Paavolainen's Synkkä Yksinpuhelu (Gloomy Soliloquy)/. Stockholm 1997. 333 s.

7. PIRJO JANULF. Kommer finskan i Sverige att fortleva? En studie av språkkunskaper och språkanvändning hos andra generationens sverigefinnar i Botkyrka och hos finlandssvenskar i Åbo. (Will Finnish survive in Sweden? A study of language skills and language use among second generation Sweden Finns in Botkyrka and Finland Swedes in Turku.) Stockholm 1998. 317 s.

8. EVA HERNER. Svenska recensenter läser finska böcker. En studie i receptionen av finsk prosa, översatt på 1960-talet. (Swedish critics Reviewing Finnish Books. A Study of the Reception in Sweden of Finnish Fiction translated in the 1960s.) Stockholm 1999. 284 s.

9. MERLIJN DE SMIT. Language contact and structural change. An Old Finnish case study. Stockholm 2006. 227 s.

Subscriptions to the series and orders for single volumes should be addressed to any international bookseller or to the publisher:

Almqvist & Wiksell International, P.O. Box 614 SE-151 27 Södertälje, Sweden.

Universities, libraries, learned societies and publishers of learned periodicals may obtain the volume of the series or other publications of Stockholm University in exchange for their own publications. Inquiries should be addressed to Stockholms universitetsbibliotek, SE-106 91 Stockholm, Sweden

ACTA UNIVERSITATIS STOCKHOLMIENSIS

Corpus Troporum
Romanica Stockholmiensia
Stockholm Cinema Studies
Stockholm Economic Studies. Pamphlet Series
Stockholm Oriental Studies
Stockholm Slavic Studies
Stockholm Studies in Baltic Languages
Stockholm Studies in Classical Archaeology
Stockholm Studies in Comparative Religion
Stockholm Studies in Economic History
Stockholm Studies in Educational Psychology
Stockholm Studies in English
Stockholm Studies in Ethnology
Stockholm Studies in History
Stockholm Studies in History of Art
Stockholm Studies in History of Literature
Stockholm Studies in Human Geography
Stockholm Studies in Linguistics
Stockholm Studies in Modern Philology. N.S.
Stockholm Studies in Musicology
Stockholm Studies in Philosophy
Stockholm Studies in Psychology
Stockholm Studies in Russian Literature
Stockholm Studies in Scandinavian Philology. N.S.
Stockholm Studies in Sociology
Stockholm Studies in Statistics
Stockholm Studies in the History of Ideas
Stockholm Theatre Studies
Stockholmer Germanistische Forschungen
Studia Baltica Stockholmiensia
Studia Fennica Stockholmiensia
Studia Graeca Stockholmiensia. Series Graeca
Studia Graeca Stockholmiensia. Series Neohellenica
Studia Juridica Stockholmiensia
Studia Latina Stockholmiensia
Studies in North-European Archaeology